Bishops and Power in Early
Modern England

SUI

Bishops and Power in Early Modern England

Marcus K. Harmes

Bloomsbury T&T Clark
An Imprint of Bloomsbury Publishing Plc

B L O O M S B U R Y
LONDON • NEW DELHI • NEW YORK • SYDNEY

Bloomsbury T&T Clark
An imprint of Bloomsbury Publishing Plc

Imprint previously known as T&T Clark

50 Bedford Square	1385 Broadway
London	New York
WC1B 3DP	NY 10018
UK	USA

www.bloomsbury.com

BLOOMSBURY, T&T CLARK and the Diana logo are trademarks of
Bloomsbury Publishing Plc

First published in 2013
Paperback edition 2015

Marcus ht, Designs and work.

SURREY LIBRARIES

All rights ced or transmitted
in any fo ing photocopying,
recording ut prior permission

Askews & Holts	01-May-2015
941.06 GRE	£24.99

No resp ation acting on or
refraining ion can be accepted

British Library Cataloguing-in-Publication Data
A catalogue record for this book is available from the British Library.

ISBN: HB: 978-1-472-50835-5
PB: 978-1-474-23296-8
ePDF: 978-1-4725-0975-8
ePUB: 978-1-4725-0918-5

Library of Congress Cataloging-in-Publication Data
A catalog record for this book is available from the Library of Congress.

Typeset by Deanta Global Publishing Services, Chennai, India

To my family

Contents

List of Illustrations	viii
Acknowledgments	ix
Bibliographic Note	x
Introduction	1
1 Bishops and the Reformation in England	7
2 A Bishop and Therefore No Puritan: Episcopal Authority and 'Conforming Puritans' in Jacobean England	21
3 Exorcising Demons and Defending Episcopacy	45
4 Reformed Episcopacy Under Pressure	59
5 The Uncertain Path to Restoration	79
6 The Restoration, Episcopal Self-representation and the Defence of Vestments	93
Conclusion: Identifying Reformed Authority	117
Notes	123
Bibliography	165
Index	217

List of Illustrations

Figure 1	Thomas Cranmer by Gerlach Flicke oil on panel, 1545, © National Portrait Gallery	102
Figure 2	William Warham after Hans Holbein the Younger oil on panel, early seventeenth century (1527), © National Portrait Gallery	103
Figure 3	Effigy of Matthew Hutton c.1606 South Choir Aisle, York Minster, © Dean and Chapter of York: Reproduced by kind permission	105
Figure 4	Effigy of Richard Sterne South Choir Aisle, York Minster, © Dean and Chapter of York: Reproduced by kind permission	106
Figure 5	Effigy of John Dolben South Choir Aisle, York Minster, © Dean and Chapter of York: Reproduced by kind permission	107
Figure 6	Effigy of Thomas Lamplugh By Grinling Gibbons, c.1691 South Choir Aisle, York Minster, © Dean and Chapter of York: Reproduced by kind permission	108

Acknowledgments

This book has developed from several years of research and a number of people deserve my most grateful thanks over this time for help of various kinds. Dr Marion Diamond of the University of Queensland has guided my research and my historical thinking since my undergraduate years and through to the supervision of my doctorate. Working with her has never been less than inspirational. Professor Emeritus Sybil M. Jack has been unstinting in her advice and good ideas. Dr Andrew Foster has offered the most generous and stimulating levels of advice, as well as immense encouragement and enthusiasm for the overall project. All three have read the manuscript of this book or substantial portions of it, freely giving their time and talent in doing so and I could not have done without this help. Librarians at a number of institutions have assisted with research, including at the Fryer Library of the University of Queensland, the Library of Ormond College at the University of Melbourne, the State Library of Victoria, the British Library, Lambeth Palace Library and Dr Elizabeth Hallam-Smith at the House of Lords Library. At the Bloomsbury Group, Frances Arnold, Emily Drewe, Emma Goode, Rhodri Mogford and their teams have been a constant source of advice. Most of all, my family in Queensland, Australia, has never ceased to offer their support and love during my research and writing.

Bibliographic Note

Unless otherwise stated dates are in the modern style. I have left the original italics and mostly the original spelling and punctuation of the primary documents intact, not least as they indicate the emphasis that authors wished to place on words or phrases for the benefit of their readers. An exception is the latin 'ſ', which I have changed to the standard 's' for the sake of clarity.

Introduction

In 1601 Richard Bancroft, the Bishop of London, raised and led a troop of pikemen against the Earl of Essex's rebellion.[1] Nearly a century later, in 1688 during the so-called 'Glorious Revolution', Henry Compton the Bishop of London, in 'a buff coat and jack boots, with a sword at his side, and pistols in his holsters', snatched Princess Anne from Whitehall Palace and led her out of London at the head of an armed troop of men, including the infamous rake the Earl of Dorset.[2] These may not be actions we typically associate with the bishops of the Church of England.[3] However, in the sixteenth and seventeenth centuries, they were not entirely atypical of the combative personalities who occupied England's bishoprics. Bishops wielding arms indicate to us the militancy of the episcopate, although in both these instances Bishops Bancroft and Compton marched in defence of the State as much as of the Church. This book particularly focuses on the Church; it addresses challenges to the episcopate as the third tier of the ordained ministry, above the priesthood and diaconate. It examines what was at stake for bishops in the numerous combats, mostly intellectual but sometimes physical, that contested their authority and decried the entire episcopate as a popish relic in post-Reformation England. From the mid-sixteenth century and into the seventeenth, heated debate in England questioned whether episcopacy should be the chief instrument of ecclesiastical authority. Arguments about bishops could take place in public forums, in printed pamphlets and in more subversive forms including scurrilous verse and mocking illustrations. Bishops could also be directly threatened. In the years between Bancroft and Compton taking up arms, we get another view of bishops, this time harried and in danger. During the 1641 debates on episcopacy in the House of Commons, the bishops arriving by carriage were intimidated by torch-wielding mobs.[4] The violence against bishops in 1641 reflected doctrinal challenges to their authority and to the very notion of bishops governing a reformed church that resounded in sermons, tracts, prints, proverbs and street-side talk.

The writer of an anonymous English tract, one polemically opposed to bishops, put his finger on the problem many critics in England, Scotland and even in Europe had with bishops; he argued that writers such as the pamphleteer William Prynne (1600–1669) had exposed English episcopacy as popish. The anonymous author also stressed that these criticisms 'send them [bishops] to seek their pedigree and original'.[5] Indeed bishops did seek. While this anonymous author was hostile to bishops in general, he points us to a characteristic of episcopal thought in which English bishops gradually but clearly re-oriented the rhetorical standing of the episcopate in response to the condemnation of bishops as a popish relic.

In the study that follows I examine those arguments challenging the authority of bishops and the counter arguments which stressed the necessity of bishops in England and their status as useful and godly ministers. In making their claims, apologists for episcopacy constructed a number of identities for reformed bishops, based on what they did and what other people did to them. Writers including Josias Nichols, John Harington, Richard Bancroft, Samuel Harsnet, Arthur Duck, John Gauden, William Laud and Edward Hooper advanced arguments that bishops could be identified through their agency in patronizing godly preachers, defending Protestantism from Catholic enemies, wielding authority which was deemed impeccably Protestant not only in Europe but also in England, and as the generals in an army fighting for the Reformation against popish Catholicism. Bishops and their defenders also attempted to explain why and how apparent signs of popishness, especially episcopal raiment, could actually be freshly interpreted as evidence of the godliness of reforming English bishops.

The chronological span covered in this book is close to 150 years. This period allows consideration of the emergence and consolidation of the episcopate, its participation in political events and significant challenges to the episcopacy over many decades, all of which fuelled polemical writings by and about bishops. This time span also welds the bishops to a political environment that shaped and changed the development of reformed episcopacy, taking in the duties of Thomas Cranmer under the 'boy king' Edward VI to the restoration of the bishops in the later seventeenth century. The full span of the seventeenth century separates some of these writers from each other, but their ideas on the episcopate developed across the century as bishops and clergy associated with them claimed episcopal identity as agents of Protestant authority. We should however be cautious in thinking about 'bishops' as a coherent body of clergymen. In fact they were often in violent disagreement with each other. Archbishop John Williams (d.1650) detested William Laud (d.1645), the Archbishop of

Canterbury under Charles I. Laud in turn had openly disparaged the authority of Archbishop George Abbot (d.1633).[6] Archbishop John Tillotson was left speechless with anger by the perceived effrontery of George Hooper, the future Bishop of Bath and Wells during an argument in Convocation, the Church's parliament.[7] Most shatteringly to episcopal unity, the 'Glorious Revolution' of 1688 split bishops into nonjurors loyal to the deposed James II (including the Archbishop of Canterbury William Sancroft) and those prepared to serve the usurping William and Mary.[8] Accordingly there are no definitive arguments in defence of bishops, nor any all-encompassing identity. What bishops and writers and clergy sympathetic to them said shifted according to the priorities and views of individual bishops, or to the changes in the body politic of Tudor and Stuart England. But this diversity is central to the ideas I shall explore. As is suggested by the fact that the Bishops of London, Bancroft and Compton, were engaged in armed conflict almost a century apart, the episcopate over this time was constantly on the defensive for different reasons. It might have been that they were perceived to be the repressive, inquisitorial enemies of godly preachers or godly exorcists. Some had artworks in their residences that were suspiciously popish. All bishops wore the rochet and chimere that many detractors regarded as outward signs of inner popery.[9] They were constantly on the defensive, so the emphasis that bishops and their defenders gave to different aspects and functions shifted, as did their conceptualizations of church authority and the signs which they believed showed bishops to be godly rather than popish.

I interpret the repertoire of arguments which bishops used to show how the Reformation functioned as a legitimating agent for episcopal authority. To do so, what follows is a series of case studies of both particular moments in time, such as the treason trial of Archbishop William Laud, and of longer lasting issues, including heated argument over what vestments bishops wore, to the calls for the reduction of episcopacy and the intervention of some bishops in witchcraft trials. What is the link from treason to witchcraft to vestments? The answer of course is bishops. The case studies that will follow illuminate different aspects of what bishops did, what they looked like and said as they performed their functions, and what their critics said about them. They are not intended to provide a comprehensive review of the history of the Church in the sixteenth and seventeenth centuries, nor even of the episcopate in the same time. Broader studies of both, such as Fincham's work, or studies by Heal, Manning, Kennedy, Chibi, Smith, Sheils and others,[10] have been supplemented by biographies of individual bishops.[11] There are also sustained if dated studies of the episcopate in particular epochs, such as Trevor-Roper's study of the Jacobean bishops and Simon's of the Restoration episcopate.[12] Between them, these shed much light on the episcopate and its intersection with Tudor and Stuart history at multiple levels. This book examines some focused issues involving bishops, but also in keeping an eye out for the broader pattern of events and developments, I aim to suggest what was at stake for bishops as they defended their order and constructed intellectual understandings of their authority and the terms upon which they were both attacked and defended.

The five case studies illuminate key aspects of the functions and identities of the episcopate. The writings of Josias Nichols and John Harington engage with different external perceptions of bishops and the nomenclature of puritanism and orthodoxy that surrounded them. The investigations into witchcraft and exorcism by Bishop Bancroft show a clash between bishops and not only devils but godly communities as well, clashes that generated extensive writings on demonism that modulated into anti-episcopal polemic. Putting Archbishop Laud on trial for treason ultimately condemned that prelate to death. Before that, however, the trial gave Laud a platform from which to articulate a defence not only against the treason charge, but also of the episcopate in general. Laud looked back to Archbishop Cranmer to argue for an identity of bishops as reformed. After Laud's execution we find episcopacy in the wilderness and to the extent that some bishops argued for the 'reduction' of episcopacy, meaning the reducing of its powers and the introduction of elders and presbyters. Against these views, John Gauden the future Bishop of Exeter wrote in defence of an episcopate that he insisted was already reformed. Finally, what bishops looked like, meaning the raiment they habitually wore, generated anti-episcopal polemic, but also provided a locus of discussion about the functions (sacramental and secular) of bishops.

It is timely to review what was said by and about bishops in the sixteenth and seventeenth centuries. The contours of many recent arguments about the English episcopate, its challenges and its functions, were shaped by Sykes's 1957 text *Old Priest and New Presbyter*. Sykes drew together a range of evidence explaining the importance of the retention of episcopacy in post-Reformation England; arguments which Sykes felt were shaped by the awareness of English churchmen of developing reformed church hierarchies in Europe.[13] He argued that churchmen (especially John Jewel, John Whitgift, Richard Hooker and William Laud) were alert to the solutions for church government reached in Sweden, Denmark, Germanic areas and in post-Tridentine Catholic areas, and sought to show the English pattern was one of several possible means of church government.[14] *Old Priest and New Presbyter* is in essence a collection of lengthy primary source quotations, bridged by Sykes's linking commentary. He concluded that English episcopal churchmen would not reject any form of polity that had grown up within a godly commonwealth. Advancing his analysis into the seventeenth century, Sykes used selected quotations from Laud, John Lightfoot (1601–75) and Joseph Hall (1574–1656) to develop this point, identifying that while William Laud made more exalted claims for *jure divino* episcopacy (or episcopacy that was divinely ordered[15]), he was still prepared to accept that other types of polity should not be rejected and that the hierarchies of European reformed churches were valid.[16]

Sykes suggests that the episcopate in England branded itself as reformed, yet he gives little attention to considering how the episcopate and supporters could substantiate this claim. I propose to show that the same or similar evidence which Sykes examined can reveal a more dynamic engagement with the implications of the Reformation for church government than he supposed, and that episcopal writers upheld the necessity episcopacy but also its identity as godly and reformed, rather than presenting it as simply one type of church government among several forms.

Some more recent scholarship including that of Felicity Heal, Ralph Houlbrooke and Barrett Beer, has argued that bishops were patrons of reform who publicly argued for an identity in which they could be *seen* as agents of reform.[17] In particular, in *Of Prelates and Princes*, Heal argues that processes of English evangelical reform significantly complicated how bishops expressed their own ideas on their duties and status. Bishops could be patrons of godly reform, lords of the manor, courtiers and protectors of the poor or could assume a range of other identities.[18] For example, John Foxe the Elizabethan martyrologist recounted the generous hospitality of Bishop John Hooper of Gloucester (d.1555), where 'As for the revenues of his bishopricks, he ... bestowed it in hospitality', providing 'a table spread with a good store of meat, and beset full of beggars and poor folk'.[19] Importantly, Heal's survey of economic evidence makes clear that from Edward VI's reign, both bishops and clergy and laypeople from beyond the ranks of the episcopate clashed over the identity of the episcopate as lordly or reformed.[20]

Surveys of the English Reformation have led scholars to suggest how the names or deeds of reformers could inspire religious dissent from the episcopal hierarchy.[21] Patrick Collinson suggested that many English reformers saw the significance or otherwise of the order of bishops as a 'matter indifferent' or as an issue without clear guidance from Scripture, but he also distilled these arguments down to two central issues, namely whether the Church of England could survive without bishops and whether further reform would extirpate episcopacy.[22]

The arguments in the following chapters are taken largely from print evidence and especially that emanating from the clergy closely associated with the episcopate: registrars, chancellors, chaplains and prebendaries. The print evidence, including printed sermons, tracts or scurrilous writings, entered the public domain, which was the same realm in which bishops operated. Above all, controversy about bishops was public controversy. Many detractors of bishops wrote anonymously, which suggests evidential problems with attribution or identity. Many others however, including John Milton, William Prynne, Henry Burton and others who issued enormous numbers of tracts against episcopacy put their names to their works, as did the bishops and their supporters. Debate about bishops engaged with the raiment they wore in public, with the artistic and physical traces of their office, with their intervention in public exorcisms, and in other realms of public activity in which bishops staked claims to particular identities. What we will see in the following studies is a focused assessment of the different ways bishops defended themselves and the diverse ways they putatively caused affront to their opponents. We begin with an overview of the ways that bishops during the reigns of Henry VIII, Edward VI and Elizabeth I became involved in reforming the Church, but also how particular bishops, including Archbishops Cranmer and Parker of Canterbury, publicly expressed their sense of the change wrought by religious reform on their office and how they understood the role of episcopacy in a Church that had undergone evangelical reform.

1

Bishops and the Reformation in England

Introduction

In 1621 the Bishops of Bangor and Coventry and Lichfield complained in the House of Lords about 'tauntes' received 'when the Bishops offer to instructe' their congregations.[1] This was not an isolated complaint and although bishops expected to be able to enforce discipline and to exercise authority, actually doing so was frequently a contested and complicated undertaking. What was the background to this plaintive comment from 1621? Polemical debate over the scope of episcopal powers and its status or otherwise as a godly agency can be charted from the reign of Edward VI (1547–1553), during which members of the episcopate began publicly to explain why bishops still existed and what their singular responsibilities were.

Overall, my intention in this chapter is to survey arguments offered by bishops and clergy who supported bishops for their responsibilities within a reformed Church in order to provide both a context and a framework for the specific case studies that follow. It takes the coronation of Edward VI as its starting point, an event presided over by Archbishop Thomas Cranmer (1489–1556) and who used the occasion to offer a sustained analysis of how the preceding years of religious reform had altered his office as Archbishop of Canterbury. Next, Matthew Parker's consecration as Archbishop of Canterbury in 1559, some years after Edward's coronation, highlighted a complex dialogue between the episcopate's past and present, which he felt the need to resolve. Both Cranmer and Parker suggested that the episcopate was dislocated from its unreformed medieval origins. For Parker, this disconnection between the episcopal line originating with St Augustine of Canterbury and the reformed episcopate was significant, as he wrote of his desire to harmonize apparently discordant church traditions. For Cranmer, it was clear that evangelical reform influenced and altered what he did as a bishop. The coronation and the consecration by necessity brought to light some of the tensions and peculiarities of post-Reformation episcopacy, and both events refracted questions about the source of episcopal authority and the scope of episcopal functions.

The coronation of Edward VI and its significance

The episcopate survived through processes of reform during the reigns of Henry VIII and Edward VI because the 1549 *Book of Common Prayer*, an important statement of reformed English doctrine, placed the episcopate within the threefold ministry of bishops, priests and deacons and provided an Ordinal for their consecration.[2] In creating this prayer book, Cranmer operated within a political system, notably the parliaments of Henry VIII, which had preserved episcopacy and indeed created more bishops and therefore more dioceses, even as episcopal revenues diminished.[3]

It is important not to lose sight of why, to many English laity and clergy, it was simply odd that by the reign of Elizabeth I, but even during the reign of Edward VI, there were still bishops in England. Reformers across Europe came to the conclusion that bishops had no place in reformed religion.[4] The picture is not absolute; there were bishops in the Scandinavian kingdoms but episcopacy rarely survived on the continent, reformed authority being embedded instead in presbytery, magistracy or consistory.[5] Closer to home for English bishops, the Scottish episcopate fluctuated in strength over the sixteenth and seventeenth centuries, and its institutional continuity faltered. The leaders of the Scottish Kirk declared that episcopacy was unscriptural.[6] The Lords of the Congregation thus gave voice to the view that episcopacy was a popish remnant and an embodiment of incomplete reform.

In England, as with the Scandinavian episcopate, episcopacy survived because bishops were retained by monarchy. Indeed, Henry VIII actually ended up with more bishops as a result of the Dissolution of the Monasteries. A Henrician Act of Parliament created new dioceses out of dissolved monasteries at Bristol, Chester, Gloucester, Oxford, Peterborough and Westminster.[7] The impression of monarchy working to preserve episcopacy is, however, inconsistent. The new dioceses began with limited resources, and the endowments of the older dioceses were much diminished by Tudor monarchs.[8] Polemicists and churchmen considered the six new dioceses and the new cathedrals to be products of reform, known in the seventeenth century as the 'new foundations'.[9]

Thomas Cranmer created the order for the consecration of bishops in the *Book of Common Prayer* of 1549; in doing so, he ensured the continuity of bishops as a distinctive level of the clergy throughout the reforms of liturgy and doctrine.[10] The order for consecration did more than ensure continuity of episcopal appointments during the Reformation: Cranmer's service attempted to spell out the necessity of bishops and their significance to the reformed Church. The dialogue he wrote between the bishop elect and the presiding metropolitan asked and then answered a series of questions on the significance, necessity and duties of bishops. Bishops were necessary to 'driue away all erronious and straunge doctrine' and to punish 'such as be unquiete, disobedyent, and criminous'.[11] While Cranmer's bishops would administer discipline, he stressed their pastoral responsibilities as well as the greater age and gravity which ideally characterized bishops.[12] Thinking of Cranmer's Ordinal is a useful moment to pause and consider what bishops actually did. They legislated, in that they sat in the House of Lords and sometimes on the Privy Council.[13] During the reign of James I, clergy started to become more heavily involved in government and secular administration.[14] In the religious realm they ordained and licensed clergy, consecrated churches and confirmed people. They conducted visitations of their dioceses and held conferences with their clergy.[15] Often they also lived in palaces or grand houses and maintained households of servants. In these actions they are not particularly different from the twenty-first-century bishops of the Church of England. More controversially in the sixteenth and seventeenth centuries, they also seemed to their detractors to be no different from their medieval and therefore popish predecessors, unlike the godly magistracies or consistories that governed reformed confessions in Europe.[16] In time one personal difference would become apparent between pre-Reformation bishops and reformed bishops: some of the latter had wives. Even this circumstance, however, was not a major distinction. Archbishops including Grindal, Whitgift, Bancroft and Laud were bachelors.[17] Other bishops did marry. While Cranmer was worse off than Warham in terms of the scale of revenues and manors of the archdiocese of Canterbury, because Henry VIII appropriated so much, unlike Warham he was able to share what was left with a wife.[18]

Thomas Cranmer's archiepiscopate (1533–1555), while much examined by modern scholars, merits greater analysis at this point for what it reveals of claims Cranmer made for the episcopate to have been reformed, beyond just being able to marry. The coronation of Edward VI in 1547 was the first coronation of the post-Reformation period and Cranmer, the presiding archbishop, was the last in

England (with the obvious exception of Cardinal Pole during the reign of Mary) to wear the papal pallium.[19] To observers, much must have seemed familiar. As ever, the coronation (on 20 February 1547) took place in Westminster Abbey, and afterwards, on Shrove Tuesday, there were the usual masques and revels to celebrate the event. Yet there were some breaks with tradition apparent. The Recognition and the oath had both been revised by the Council, and of course this was the first coronation in English history where the king was also proclaimed as the Head of the Church.[20] As Hunt points out, the act of this proclamation added additional drama to the event, and ensured that it intersected with the politics of supremacy.[21] Cranmer was sensitive to the implications of these changes. He had been made an archbishop by papal authority but now served royal authority that, as embodied in Edward VI, actively pursued evangelical religious reform.

He acknowledged in his sermon that religious reform had altered the office of archbishop.[22] During his sermon, he informed Edward VI and the congregation that, as Archbishop, he did not have the power to depose or reject a king. Although preaching after he had anointed Edward's body with oil, he also disputed that kingly authority was conferred by that sacramental action. He observed of sovereigns that 'their persons . . . are elected by God'. On the actual sacrament of anointing performed by an Archbishop of Canterbury, Cranmer dismissed it as 'but a ceremony'.[23] This sermon and the coronation ritual surrounding it attempted to clarify the authority of monarchs crowned without papal sanction; it also allowed Cranmer to expound the changes to his functions as a reformed primate and the intersection of his office with English kingly authority.[24]

At Edward's coronation, Cranmer stressed what he could no longer do as an archbishop; other works directly composed or commissioned by Cranmer, including his Register, often stress continuity rather than change. Some administrative changes are apparent though. During his time as archbishop, Cranmer founded the Faculty Office, intended to take over the power from Rome for dispensing faculties, or dispensations. In doing so, argues his modern biographer Diarmaid MacCulloch, Cranmer 'usurped powers' of the papacy in what was a 'radical break with the past'.[25] The Faculty Office did nonetheless operate closely in line civil sources of authority, notably Chancery, but did mean that the legal work of the archbishopric could be carried out without recourse to Rome or a legate.[26]

But Cranmer's Register reveals that other business, such as confirming bishops, granting licences and faculties, ordering and conducting visitations and offering instructions, continued unchanged during the processes of parliamentary legislation in the 1530s and 1540s that gave the English Church independence from Rome. Cranmer's Register and the activities it records are reminiscent of those of medieval prelates. In his study of Cranmer's Register, Paul Ayris notes that the documents contained within it, including Papal Bulls authorizing his consecration as primate, were customary and traditional.[27] The work of the Primate of All England, and more particularly the areas and extent of his authority, remained unchanged by the reform which separated the English Church from that of the Roman.

During his tenure, Cranmer expounded the circumstances which made him a reformed bishop. He used neither the term 'Protestant' nor the term 'reformed'. Instead, as an archbishop, he was a preacher and a pastor. In a letter to the Vicar General, Thomas Cromwell, he expressed the pious hope that 'I, and all my brethren the bishops, would leave all our styles', meaning that the dignity and wealth of episcopal office could be reduced.[28] His contemporary bishops offered similar definitions of the pastoral characteristics of reformed bishops. Hugh Latimer of Worcester urged that bishops should be 'faithful stewards', while John Hooper of Gloucester wished to see the administrative and sacramental aspects of the episcopate reduced and simplified.[29] During the reign of Edward VI, Bishop John Ponet of Winchester (1516–1556) lamented that 'the name of *bishop* hath been so abused, that when it was spoken the people understood nothing else but a great lord'.[30] At the time of his appointment, Ponet not only offered his commentary on the unreformed excesses of episcopacy, but also presided over the rationalization and reduction of his episcopal revenues, although this reduction was more to the benefit of the Edwardine exchequer, not a reduction in taxes from the people. It possibly also reinforced Ponet's conception of a reduced and more pastoral episcopacy.

In surveying early modern episcopal authority, modern scholars have argued that claims for the pastoral foundations of the episcopacy underpinned the powers of bishops and gave meaning to their functions and activities. Kenneth Fincham argues that the pastoral activities of bishops were intended to embody apostolic ideals. He notes that a bishop like Martin Heton of Ely (in office from 1599) assiduously presided over his diocesan visitations, became personally acquainted with his parochial clergy and preached often.[31] Other bishops fulfilled their obligations in a similar fashion. The diary of Heton's contemporary at Durham, Toby Matthew, shows that Matthew had frequent contact with parochial clergy and lay members of his flock and was an assiduous preacher.[32] Ralph Houlbrooke has also examined the pastoral responsibilities of sixteenth-century bishops, reconstructing the emphasis which they gave to these responsibilities and the influence of pastoral work in shaping the form and substance of reformed episcopacy.[33]

The godly episcopate that Cranmer's consecration service had made provision for had been an instrument of equally godly reform. A number of bishops, chiefly Cranmer, Nicholas Ridley of London and Latimer (who had held the bishopric of Worcester in Henry VIII's reign), superintended significant doctrinal reforms.[34] The frontispiece of Henry's Great Bible of 1539 gave visual form to the work of these reforming bishops and a sense of their place in a hierarchy, as Henry VIII handed the vernacular Bible down to Cranmer, the metropolitan, who then disseminated the text to his suffragans, who in turn distributed the text among lower clergy and thence to the laity, gathered in an excited crowd at the base of the frontispiece.[35] Significantly, however, disseminating the Word of God was not an exclusively episcopal task in the frontispiece, and this illustration considerably confuses what it was that bishops did. Henry VIII also handed the Bible to Thomas Cromwell, the Vicar General, and therefore Cromwell and other courtiers and lay gentlemen had their part alongside bishops in furthering reform; indeed, the laity in the image acclaimed the king and not his bishops, exclaiming '*Vivat Rex*'. While this title page shows the bishops at work reforming the Church, it considerably confuses and complicates their place, status and function in the reformed Church.

Edward's coronation occurred as the dynamic between episcopacy and reform was sharply changing. This coronation was conducted by an archbishop who had worn the papal pallium but who also belittled coronation anointment; it also featured a pastoral archbishop who resembled a medieval prelate in terms of his functions, status and revenues.[36] While Cranmer and some of his colleagues asserted their distinctions from the medieval episcopate, other Tudor bishops such as Stephen Gardiner and Cuthbert Tunstal were not reforming bishops. Under the more (for them) congenial rule of Archbishop William Warham (d.1532), Cranmer's predecessor, conservative bishops had been responsible for disciplining reform.[37] The biblical translator and exegete William Tyndale described his contemporary bishops (including Tunstal and Gardiner) as 'them that walk in darkness' and condemned the 'pomp of our prelates'.[38] Looking back from the Restoration, the martyrologist Samuel Clarke (1599–1682) reiterated Tyndale's point, stressing that because of Tyndale's efforts to publish the Scriptures in the vernacular, 'the *Popes* instruments raged exceedingly'.[39]

Later polemicists would see much less of the godly element of episcopacy than was suggested by Cranmer's actions and assert that the popish element dominated the episcopate in general. A doggerel epitaph written in the 1550s about Edmund Bonner, the Marian bishop of London, stressed that he could scarcely have been English because of his episcopal office:

> A man there was, a *quondam* great
> Of might, of pomp, and praise
> Of Englishe blood, though Englishe loue
> Were small in all his wayes.[40]

At least in this case, the attack was directed towards a Roman Catholic bishop, but detractors of post-Reformation bishops considered all of them to be crypto-papists, holding the office of bishop because of its consonances with popish religion and their sympathies with popery. Archbishop Whitgift was lampooned after his death in 1604 and in fact during his funeral procession for being 'the Jesuits' hope'. His successor, Richard Bancroft (d.1610), was a willing host of the 'Strumpet of Rome', according to contemporary polemic.[41] The complexity of Cranmer's archiepiscopate shows itself in these later episcopal reputations, in which the popish aspects of episcopal office seemed more obvious to polemicists than the reformed attributes.

Elizabeth's reign: Matthew Parker and his consecration

Late-sixteenth-century debates over the basis of episcopal authority necessarily draw attention to a complex dialogue between the episcopate's past and present. This dialogue can be seen during the later sixteenth century in two events in particular: the consecration of Archbishop Parker and the publication of the *Acts and Monuments* of John Foxe. Defenders of English bishops, as well as bishops themselves, stressed the reformed character of the episcopate and its authority. In doing so, bishops were claiming, ipso facto, an ancient lineage for themselves; many reformers in Tudor England as much as on the continent concurred in claiming that they intended their reforming actions to restore the ancient face of the Church.[42] It can be difficult to discern distinctions between assertions that bishops were reformed in character and claims for their divine and apostolic origin, since a core plank of Reformation polemic was an appeal to the standards and achievements of the early Church. Nevertheless, contemporaries were alert to some distinctions between ancient and reformed churches. Matthew Parker, Archbishop of Canterbury under Elizabeth (in office 1559–1575), caused consternation in clerical circles for disparaging the 'best reformed churches overseas', or those of 'Germanical natures'.[43] At this time, Parker defended holding high ecclesiastical office by looking to the Ancient Church and clearly demarcated between it and reformed sources of authority.[44] For Parker, the comparison between apostolic and reformed was negative, but during the sixteenth century episcopal churchmen made more positive appeals to reformed precedents in order to justify the episcopate's enduring presence in the English Church.

Two events from the Elizabethan period bring clarity to the intellectual and doctrinal steps which were taken to define and defend reformed episcopacy against a background of sustained and wide-ranging attack. The first was the consecration of Matthew Parker in 1559, the first consecration of an archbishop since Cardinal Pole's in 1556.[45] Parker was consecrated in the chapel of Lambeth Palace on 17 December 1559, and a major part of the ceremony went according to tradition. The archbishop-elect was consecrated by Miles Coverdale, the Bishop of Exeter, John Scory, the Bishop of Chichester, John Hodgkins, the Suffragan Bishop of Bedford, and William Barlow, the Bishop of Bath and Wells. As was often the case with consecrations in the Canterbury diocese, the Archdeacon of Canterbury (Edmund Guest, the future Bishop of Salisbury) also participated. But these bishops were among the few still free to participate in events of any kind since the accession of Elizabeth I and the rapid suspensions and in some cases house arrests of Marian bishops, such as Cuthbert Tunstal of Durham. There was more that was unusual about this consecration than the absences of particular bishops. The event uncomfortably reminded its participants that there were no precedents for an archiepiscopal consecration without papal bulls, as both Cranmer and Pole had proceeded to consecration under these. Many bishops refused to consecrate Parker; even the normally compliant Bishop Owen Ogelthorpe of Carlisle, who had agreed to crown Elizabeth, refused to participate in Parker's consecration. Parker was a noted antiquarian so it is ironic that his consecration was inevitably a novelty and carried the implication that, by becoming archbishop in this way, he was somehow breaking away from his unreformed predecessors. Parker cherished the foundation of the archbishopric of Canterbury by Augustine in the sixth century. His own history of the archiepiscopate was an inevitably personal document, as Parker charted the line of bishops from Augustine to himself, the seventieth Archbishop. But elsewhere, in correspondence with fellow divines, he also argued that Augustine's foundation was 'corrected' by Henry VIII. It is not necessary here to consider historical scholarship of the sixteenth century which asserted that an early British Church and episcopate predated the Gregorian Mission and the introduction of a papal episcopate. But like later episcopal scholars in this field such as Edward Stillingfleet, Parker followed a line of argument which stressed that an historic episcopate need not be a popish creation.[46] His attempt to align the Anglo-Saxon archbishop with Henry VIII reflects the tensions apparent at his consecration as a reformed bishop into an ancient office.[47]

The second event is the publication of Foxe's *Book of Martyrs* in 1563. Foxe included material which indicated the episcopal failings of Bishop Robert Farrar of St David's (d.1555), one of the Marian Martyrs and Cranmer's contemporary. While Foxe recorded the godly and edifying details of Farrar's death, he also ignored pleas from his contemporaries not to include the less flattering evidence of Farrar's episcopal mismanagement.[48] He included this material in order to highlight the appropriate conduct of reformed bishops.[49] Foxe's work became an early anti-papal benchmark; in it Farrar's ungodly preoccupations with worldly issues offered a contrast with the more suitable activities of godly, reformed bishops. As he listened to Cranmer preach at his coronation, Edward VI may have been nodding in agreement, while Parker may have squirmed uncomfortably through his consecration. For a moment, let us consider the major contours of the political and religious backdrops to both events.

Three points of significance immediately present themselves as relevant to the identities claimed by bishops in the wake of the reforms enacted under Edward VI and consolidated, albeit conservatively, by Elizabeth I. First, apart from the years 1646–1660, the status, duties and resources of the episcopate largely withstood assaults from different sources during reforms. Their exclusive functions (such as laying on of hands, consecrating churches and ordaining and licensing clergy) remained the province of bishops and an imparity of ministers prevailed in the English Church. Bishops enacted their powers through means such as visitations of the churches in their dioceses, demonstrating as they did so their superiority to the other layers of clergy.[50] As the Elizabethan Archbishop John Whitgift informed his Presbyterian disputant Thomas Cartwright (d.1603) during an exchange of polemical tracts on church government in 1570 known as the Admonition Controversy: 'To say that a bishop and a priest is equal, how can it be possible? For the order of bishops is the begetter of fathers'.[51] The wealth, revenues and status of bishops also largely withstood assault; in fact

Tudor monarchs were a greater threat to episcopal revenues than Protestant polemicists.[52] Second, therefore, challenges to episcopal functions derived from sources other than economic depredations and were inspired by the widely held and strongly expressed view that the Reformation was not a fixed point in time, but rather a process not yet completed. Polemicists viewed the abolition of episcopacy as a necessary step in completing the Reformation.

Third, the dioceses and the provinces of the Church of England were coincident with the borders of the English Kingdom.[53] Successive English monarchs viewed their bishops as organs of royal and conciliar authority, and as a source of money. Again apart from the years 1646–1660, the connection between monarchy and episcopacy remained an integral feature of the English Royal Supremacy and many bishops were animated by their desire to defend the Supremacy and the authority of godly princes to rule the Church. A reciprocal expectation also existed that monarchs would serve as protectors of the Church of England's bishops, and English bishops operated in circumstances where their functions and duties were shaped by the authority of princes. Clergy acclaimed both Henry VIII and Edward VI as 'godly princes' and reformers found appropriate precedents for their actions in King David and King Josiah respectively, while Elizabeth was, in the eyes of many of her clergy, a Deborah.[54]

These enthusiastic epithets reflected the status of English monarchs as the patrons of the English clergy. Monarchs such as Elizabeth and James VI and I saw their bishops as loyal and useful servants.[55] Indeed, attempts by individual bishops or their satellite clergy to define episcopacy as apostolic, divinely ordained or indebted to any other source of authority and origin, bar the Royal Supremacy, provoked suspicion from monarchs and their secular courtiers.

Episcopal understandings of their purpose and authority shifted with the wishes of different monarchs across the sixteenth and seventeenth centuries. Episcopal authority remained intricately bound up with the power of the Royal Supremacy and the powers peculiar to bishops can be difficult to disentangle from these other sources of authority. Indeed, it would be dangerously anachronistic to do so, as many bishops were content with the Erastian settlement which defined the post-Reformation episcopate. Edward VI headed a church which was reforming but episcopal, and from 1558 Elizabeth worked strenuously to fill vacant bishoprics. The Elizabethan correspondence collected in the *Zurich Letters* (correspondence to and from the evangelical communities who had gone into exile in Mary's reign) revealed the reluctance of many clergymen to be Elizabethan bishops and stressed the efforts by the Elizabethan Privy Council to preserve episcopal rule in England by filling vacant bishoprics.[56] The Privy Council also promulgated the 39 Articles which convocation revised from the original 42 Articles, of which the 35th endorsed episcopal rule.[57]

But as I noted above, claims by bishops during the sixteenth century to be anything more than royal servants alarmed the members of Elizabeth's council. Churchmen who enunciated alternative justifications for episcopacy diverged from the ecclesiastical and political mainstream. The courtier and politician Sir Francis Knollys protested against writings by Thomas Bilson and Richard Bancroft (both future bishops) that obliquely suggested the sacramental independence of bishops from the royal settlement.[58] Although a layman, Knollys's objections to these claims reflected those of churchmen like John Whitgift, who identified the source of episcopal authority as deriving from the Royal Supremacy.[59]

While monarchs, especially Elizabeth, worked to preserve the episcopate and viewed it as an organ of authority, it is also the case that the supreme governors were not always the champions that bishops wanted or needed. Whitgift acknowledged that princes could be both persecutors and patrons of Christianity; the capacity of princes to persecute stressed the benefit of living under a godly prince. His contemporary Richard Eedes (1555–1604), the Jacobean Dean of Worcester, identified the existence of persecuting princes as well as godly princes. Eedes acknowledged the persecution of the Church by lay rulers such as the Emperor Nero, at the time when the Church was 'so far from being entertained in the Courts of princes, as that she was banished from the borders of their kingdoms'.[60] Elizabethan divines knew themselves to be living under a godly prince; nonetheless Elizabeth's preservation of the episcopate was on her terms, including the financial depredations of diocesan revenues, prolonged delays in replacing deceased bishops and the almost total exclusion of bishops from office on the Privy Council. Elizabeth's successors experienced similar complexity in their dealings with the episcopate. In 1629 King Charles issued instructions to Archbishop William Laud which made clear the duties and the powers of bishops. The King insisted that 'Bishops shall engage in Tryennial Visitations' and thus stipulated the power of bishops to regulate their dioceses.[61] Charles ensured that vigorous and disciplinarian bishops were appointed to important sees such as London.[62] Yet both Charles and his father presided over a Church where the authority of the episcopate was critically weakened by the suspensions of Archbishop George Abbot, on one occasion because he fatally wounded a gamekeeper while hunting and on another because of his opposition to Charles I's forced loans.[63]

However, an emphasis on episcopal authority remained constant over these decades and so did the sense that bishops operated within the parameters of royal authority. Charles's instruction was no innovation and neither was the conducting of episcopal visitations.[64] One official who participated in visitations was Clement Corbet, Chancellor of Matthew Wren, the Caroline Bishop of Norwich. Corbet reminded Wren of the powers which bishops could exercise. Referring to the custom of clerics holding lectureships in East Anglian towns, Corbet told his bishop that it was Wren's responsibility to see 'the ratesbane of lecturing be abolished.' It lay in the bishop's power, urged Corbet, to establish 'such a uniform and orthodox church as the Christian world cannot show the like'.[65] Bishop Wren clearly concurred, regulating the lectureships and placing 'a straighter tie' on the clergy who held these positions.[66]

Neither the role of Archbishop Cranmer in Edward VI's coronation, nor the legal terms of Archbishop Parker's consecration, nor the actual functioning of the bishops of the reformed English Church under Elizabeth and her successors actually wholly clarified the source of reformed episcopal authority. Nor did it resolve arguments that bishops were in various ways popish; if anything, the sacramental and legal ambiguities of coronation and consecration simply made the ambiguity of a reformed episcopate more obvious. The idea that English bishops were popish runs powerfully through countless tracts and sermons, amplifying and expanding on points on the government of the Church raised from the 1570 Admonition Controversy and the 1572 *Admonition to Parliament*, which had protested against the 'tyrannous Lordship' of the bishops.[67] The points made in the 1570s continued to inform anti-episcopal polemic into the seventeenth century, and formed an extensive literature decrying episcopacy as unreformed and an impediment to the full reform of the Church.[68]

Arguments against bishops as being a popish remnant reached their fullest extent in the seventeenth century in the Root and Branch Petition offered to the Long Parliament in the 1640s, which called for (and then achieved) the extirpation of the episcopate.[69] As Lord Say and Seale pointed out through metaphor, parliament intended that bishops 'shall be taken away Roote and branch' as unproductive branches from the tree.[70] The Root and Branch petition submitted to the Long Parliament in the debates between 1642 and 1646 described episcopacy as 'ungodly' and papist.[71] These sentiments, most thunderous in the 1640s, emerged from the earlier decades of the public discussion of episcopacy, including Cranmer's thoughts delivered from the pulpit when he crowned Edward VI.

English bishops performed their duties in an environment which questioned their necessity to the Church and disputed the legitimacy of their authority. Attacks on the episcopate were components of highly charged polemical debate about the implications for church authority of the sixteenth-century Reformations. Proceeding by rhetorical exaggeration (such as the persistently repeated story that the Elizabethan Archbishop of Canterbury Matthew Parker was consecrated in a public house), polemical attacks on bishops say much about why the English episcopate was disliked in several quarters, but much less about the daily duties and functions of bishops. When English bishops themselves ventured into the pulpit, into the House of Lords or into print to explain, defend and justify their duties, they outlined their roles and responsibilities, but many episcopal writers hesitated to insist upon the apostolic significance or antiquity of the episcopate. Instead, it was enough to say that bishops could be considered useful to godly Protestantism. Bishop Robert Sanderson of Lincoln (1587–1663) was content that the only necessary parts of any church were the 'preaching of the Gospel and the administration of the Sacraments'; bishops could preach and administer the sacraments, but in Sanderson's view bishops were not intrinsic to this activity.[72] Writers Richard Field (1561–1616) and John Davenant (1572–1641, who became bishop of Salisbury) concurred in preferring episcopacy as the form of ecclesiastical authority but also acknowledged the possibility that bishops could be actively counter-productive to the propagation of godly religion.[73] Field stated that 'ordinarily the care of all churches is committed to bishops', but that at different times and places bishops had been unworthy ministers. Davenant perceived that in places where 'all the Bishops have fallen into heresy or idolatry', their duties had been taken over by more godly sources of authority.[74] But Field's preference was for bishops. While there could be defective bishops, there could also be godly and useful bishops.

It is now time to consider some specific ways in which these points could be made. To start we move on in time from Elizabeth's reign into that of her successor, James VI and I (on the English throne from 1603), and to writings by two men who were poles apart in outlook and position in society: Sir John Harington, a courtier and friend of the Prince of Wales; and Josias Nichols, a deprived vicar from Kent. Put together they contribute mutually contrasting and illuminating understandings of episcopacy at a moment when the Hampton Court Conference of 1604 brought arguments about episcopacy to a head.

2

A Bishop and Therefore No Puritan: Episcopal Authority and 'Conforming Puritans' in Jacobean England

Introduction

Using writings on the episcopate by the wit, courtier and historian Sir John Harington (1561–1612) and the dissenting minister Josias Nichols (1553–c.1640), in this chapter I will show how episcopal authority could be aligned with the dissent of the so-called 'conforming puritans'.[1] While rebellion *from* the authority of the established Church and its bishops is a familiar part of the modern scholarly landscape, I will survey the rebellion which some churchmen and writers identified as occurring *within* the established Church and which was expressed using the episcopal hierarchy and structures of the Church of England. These writings expound the idea that there were dissenting or puritan bishops.

The historical setting of this dissent is informed by the Hampton Court Conference of 1604, a major flashpoint of controversy and the scene for protracted arguments between bishops, Presbyterians and King James VI and I. Today the Conference is best remembered as the occasion which led to the commission of the translation of the Bible called the 'Authorized Version'.[2] But for contemporary observers, the Conference was not the beginning of a process of biblical translation but rather one stage of longstanding arguments about where authority was to lie in the reformed English Church. The records of the debates at the Hampton Court Conference also show the meaning of terms including 'dissenter' and 'puritan' to have been contested and shifting, rather than fixed. According to the 1662 legislation for uniformity in religion, a seventeenth-century non-conformist or dissenter was one who did not have an episcopal license. This clarity is not apparent earlier in the seventeenth century. The shifts in meaning occurred not only in definitions, but also in the status of clergy from conformist and orthodox to dissenting or puritanical. This transition in meaning is raised by the Hampton Court Conference where the processes of debate pitted bishops against Presbyterians and drew lines in the sand between episcopacy and the opponents of episcopacy.

The proceedings and outcomes of the conference are central to the points about church government advanced by both Harington and Nichols.[3] Both were on the scene. As we shall see, Harington was listening in horror to what some clergy and their auditors were saying against bishops in the pulpits and streets of London in the period immediately after the conference. Nichols was at a loose end around 1604; his bishop had deprived him of his living and he was effectively an unemployed vicar. According to both authors, the distinction between authority and dissent was nebulous. Harington privileged one meaning of dissenter which stressed dislocation from episcopal authority and, at the most fundamental level, suggested clergy pushing against the established structures of the Church. While asserting this definition, doing so in a catalogue of bishops he wrote for Henry Prince of Wales (d.1612), the eldest son of James VI and I, Harington was alarmed that the established structures of the Church were threatened not simply by external dissent, but by churchmen who remained within the Church of England and used the reputations of reforming bishops to justify their own views. These arguments occurred in the world encountered in the previous chapter of the testing and contesting of bishops' authority. Harington asserted a particular vision which clarified distinctions between authority and dissent which he felt were being dangerously blurred. Harington's contemporary, Josias Nichols, although a deprived clergyman, pledged his loyalty to the Church of England and argued that a godly episcopate was contiguous with his own actions and churchmanship. His polemical works *Abrahams Faith* and *The Plea of the Innocent*, written in self-defence when church authorities deposed him from holy orders and his living of Eastwell in Kent, argued that meanings of orthodoxy and dissent were not absolute but were contingent on the expectations and agency of individual bishops.[4]

It was precisely this uncertainty in meaning which Nichols exploited to show that according to episcopal precedents, the label of dissenter should not be attached to him. Harington's catalogue, the *Supplie or Addicion,* was circulating in manuscript form by the early seventeenth century.[5] *Abrahams Faith* and the *Plea of the Innocent* were published by 1602.[6] Nichols, like other deprived ministers, resorted to publications to plead his case and defend his reputation. Nonetheless he stressed his fidelity to the Church of England and its episcopal hierarchy. He did so by summoning up in writing a reformed episcopate.

The works examined in this chapter reveal that defining the meaning and function of reformed episcopacy could be as much 'bottom up' as 'top down'.[7] Both Christopher Hill and Patrick Collinson have substantially contributed to the more recent understandings of interactions between episcopacy and Puritanism, although they draw markedly different conclusions about the forces which motivated and inspired Puritanism. Hill stresses the possibility of puritans 'purifying the Church from the inside'.[8] Writing from a Marxist perspective, Hill's thoughts on the economic foundations of Puritanism diverge from Collinson's interpretation. In many books and articles, Collinson dismantled monolithic conceptions of Puritanism and instead offered more nuanced readings of the priorities and conduct of the 'Godly'.[9] Despite profound distinctions in their methodological approach and their theoretical foundations, both scholars reveal that puritans need not be viewed as extrinsic from the English Church. More recently, Peter Lake has argued for the existence of 'establishment Puritans', meaning Puritans who were part of the Church, not dissenters from it, and other scholars including Alastair Bellany point out that apparently Puritan ecclesiology existed within the Church of England.[10] He echoes the earlier assessment of E. T. Davies, whose study of the late-sixteenth-century episcopate stressed that churchmen such as Thomas Cartwright, Whitgift's opponent in the Admonition Controversy, were fighting for ecclesiastical dominance from 'within' the Church of England.[11]

At the turn of the seventeenth century, 'godly' churchmen, the self-consciously godly who did not have episcopal licences, demanded the extirpation of episcopacy; yet godly writers could also use the recent history of the episcopate to show that allegations against them of being Puritans were misplaced, and they attempted to place 'godly' characteristics within an episcopal framework. Conversely, it is increasingly apparent that political and religious personnel, including parliamentarians and courtiers, often assumed by scholars to have supported bishops, could also display anti-episcopal sentiments. Distinctions between the godly, meaning those pursuing reform at the expense of episcopal licensing, and those who existed within episcopal frameworks were by no means clear. Michael Graves argues that even the parliamentary 'men of business', who while they were politicians bound to the court, the Church and the individual privy councillors by ties of patronage and clientage, were also lobbyists against the Elizabethan bishops.¹² It was one thing for tracts and pamphlets from underground presses to attack bishops. It was quite another for Sir Francis Knollys, Queen Elizabeth's Treasurer, to campaign vigorously from 1590 against their status and resources.¹³ Even Sir William Cecil, the Queen's secretary, gave cautious support to this scheme against episcopacy. Scholars have often viewed Cecil as the patron of bishops and as the agent of episcopal selection, but more recent work stresses that Cecil could be a critic of episcopacy too and that anti-episcopal sentiments emerged from high in the government.¹⁴

Division and discord: Modern views

The exercise of episcopal power during the early seventeenth century has promoted a widely accepted modern interpretation of the Church. Scholars argue that during the late sixteenth and seventeenth centuries, Puritanism grew in opposition to the bishops of the English Church; it also grew in spite of the bishops. William Sheils posits that Puritanism, a term that for him is synonymous with non-conformity, was an alternative to episcopacy, a point most clearly made by his descriptions of efforts by politicians and courtiers such as Sir William Cecil to mediate between bishops and Puritans. Sheils also suggests that English non-conformist worship accrued a degree of respectability through the seventeenth century, because it was by then long-established as an alternative to control by bishops.¹⁵

Of course there is evidence of bishops contesting with dissenters. The manifestations of this conflict could also illustrate personal animosities and the importance of the control of the Church's fabric and property. For example, a fractious vicar locked Bishop Thomas Dove of Peterborough (1555–1630) out of a church in Northampton when he was attempting to enter to inspect it.¹⁶ Modern reconstructions of Jacobean religious controversies have identified strong demarcations between different religious factions, not least because of kingly efforts to negotiate between them. A. W. R. E. Okines argues that early Stuart religious policy attempted to find some common ground between different ecclesiastical groupings.¹⁷ Stephen Bondos-Greene argues that by the reign of James I, many English dissenters wished for 'peaceful co-existence' with the Church of England, meaning that they wanted to enjoy the freedom of reformed worship without requiring episcopal licensing and supervision.¹⁸ Bondos-Greene offers a detailed case study of a particular instance of Jacobean religious dissent, the controversy following the Christ's College election of 1609. He argues that by the beginning of the seventeenth century, ideas of further reform of the established Church had been abandoned by dissenters from the English Church who instead pursued 'peaceful co-existence' with the episcopate after the Hampton Court Conference.[19] Kenneth Fincham and Peter Lake argue that King James strategically negotiated between different factions of the English Church.[20] They deduce that James perceived that English religion was divided into three different categories: Catholic recusants, dissenters and the conforming clergy of the Church of England.[21] Their work charted King James's efforts to conciliate the different parties, and they challenge the more combative portrayal of James as an impartial adjudicator and the champion of the bishops.[22] In offering this newer appraisal of the Hampton Court Conference and James's participation, Fincham and Lake and other scholars have revised earlier assessments of the policies and conduct of James but have also endorsed earlier scholarly ideas of contestation between bishops and Puritans. James now appears impartial rather than a partisan of the episcopal party; bishops and dissenters remain as divided as ever.

Cataloguing bishops: Reformed and unreformed episcopates

Yet these modern works survey a period where the terms 'puritan' and 'dissenter' were subject to shifting and contested meanings, and these ambiguities are especially revealed in works which charted the recent history of the English episcopate. Harington's *Supplie or Addicion* can be read as indicating that Puritanism was found within the ranks of the episcopate. As the full title to his text indicates, Harington intended his *Supplie or Addicion to the Catalogue of Bishops to supplement the Catalogue of Bishops* to supplement a catalogue published by Bishop Francis Godwin of Worcester in 1601, which was issued in a revised edition in 1615.[23] Harington explained that his episcopal catalogue was a text written for Henry Prince of Wales, apparently at the behest of the Prince, and was designed to enrich his knowledge of the history of the reformed English Church.[24] Harington's text is thus a product of the scholars and clergy who surrounded Prince Henry until his death in 1612 and who may loosely be termed his 'court'. As an historian but also a noted wit and writer of epigrams, Harington was a leading figure in this circle. The work by Godwin that Harington augmented was itself an elaboration of *De Antiquitate Ecclesiae et Privilegiis Ecclesiae Cantuariensis*, written by Archbishop Matthew Parker in 1572. In Parker's catalogue, as would later be the case with Godwin and Harington, the material is organized bishop by bishop, much as medieval chronicles told the history of an institution through a sequence of church dignitaries.[25]

Royal, aristocratic and gentry lineages and genealogies and the tombs of royalty and gentry emphasized tradition and continuity in succession of titles and estates. Texts of this kind (and many tombs, with epigraphic and visual content that can be read as texts) stressed the shared memory of a family or even a kingdom. They illustrated family members succeeding each other and often memorialized and commemorated their predecessors.[26] In the early-seventeenth-century antiquarians including William Dugdale began to publish books about the history of the English Church. These texts, such as Dugdale's works on the medieval St Paul's Cathedral and the ruined English monasteries, catalogued and memorialized aspects of English history.[27]

Episcopal catalogues share some features with this broader body of works, notably their emphasis on tradition by showing the continuous succession of bishop after bishop and their construction of ideas of succession and continuity. But episcopal catalogues also functioned differently from other works which charted lineage and succession. Rarely did sons succeed their fathers in bishoprics, even after clergy were allowed to marry, and episcopal catalogues do not have the emphasis on familial lineage and genealogy as did many other types of catalogue.[28] Instead, the shared memory embodied by these texts was a memory of institutional office. Writings by Josias Nichols broke in on this shared memory, claiming individual bishops as fellow travellers. At stake in the recent history of the episcopate which both Harington and Nichols invoked was the meaning of conformity and non-conformity. By their nature, episcopal catalogues preserved and transmitted biographical data. They also revealed polemical impulses. Parker's history of his archbishopric stressed continuity and downplayed institutional or doctrinal change at the English Reformation.[29] Harington, while augmenting this work, travelled a different polemical path, stressing that Parker's office and authority originated in a reformed Church and charted the significant implications of reform for the authority and status of English bishops.

Harington indicated his awareness of the earlier works that he was augmenting. Addressing Prince Henry directly, he stated that 'my purpose from the beginning . . . [was] chiefly to enforme your knowledge, with a faithfull report of some things passed in Queene Elizabeths tyme'.[30] Harington repeated his purpose in compiling the catalogue in the passages which opened his account of the bishopric of London, where he observed: 'My purpose in this worke from the beginning and my promise to your highness [Prince Henry] being, to add to this Author a supplie of some matters (that he purposely omitted, writing in the latter yeares of Queene Elizabeth).' As an example, speaking of one particular bishop, Richard Vaughan of London, Harington indicated the necessity to enrich the biographical data given by Godwin, as Vaughan was 'the last man named in my Authors booke and of him he [Godwin] hath but two lynes'.[31] Harington therefore intended to supplement works that stopped in the sixteenth century.

Both Parker and Godwin saw the history of the English Church, as well as its apostolic authority, as being embodied in the English episcopate. Their works are not the only products of this period to catalogue bishops. A Jacobean scroll preserved at Lambeth Palace records 'the names and dates of consecration and translation of the Archbishops of Canterbury' from John Peckam in the thirteenth century to George Abbot, Godwin's contemporary, sailing through the period of the Reformation without pause and without suggesting that reform had any impact on institutional continuity.[32] Parker's work was confined to the see of Canterbury, from its Anglo-Saxon foundation until his own appointment in 1559. His *De Antiquitie Ecclesiae* remained largely silent on the implications of reform and change in his office and the institution upon which it was centred. Some episcopal catalogues, such as the anonymous *Catalogue of all the Bishops* from 1674, do point out that the Reformation did have some influence on the status and responsibilities of the episcopate. The anonymous writer recollected that, for instance, 'the Bishoprick of Bristol is of new erection', and similarly the diocese of Oxford was 'first founded by King Henry 8'.[33] One modern commentator, Edward Carpenter, goes so far as to argue that Parker's text failed to acknowledge that the Reformation had taken place at all.[34] Godwin's catalogue addressed a wider body of evidence: every English and Welsh episcopate then in existence from the early Middle Ages until the early seventeenth century.[35]

For both Parker and Godwin, one the Archbishop of Canterbury, the other the Bishop of Llandaff and later of Worcester, the continuous succession of English bishops and the ancient foundations of their sees were clearly reassuring and the changes they described at the Reformation were negligible. Harington's work operated with a different methodology and his catalogue gains its structural coherence and its subject matter from the Reformation; the long continuities charted by Godwin for the Church in general and by Parker for its primatial see make no appearance in Harington's work. It begins with the foundation of the reformed episcopate by Thomas Cranmer, Nicholas Ridley, Miles Coverdale and other Tudor bishops and then describes the reformed episcopate's consolidation by Matthew Parker. He was not alone in ascribing this reformist origin to the episcopate. Ralph Morice, Archbishop Cranmer's secretary, claimed that Canterbury Cathedral was 'newlie erected, altered and changed frome monckes to secular men of the clergie'. By this he referred to the dissolution of Canterbury Cathedral Priory and the establishment of rule by a dean and chapter and saw this as a fresh start and a reformed origin to this diocese and cathedral.[36] This strand of Harington's thought is fully explicated when the interplay of ideas between this work and Josias Nichols's *Plea of the Innocent* from 1602 is taken into account. Nichols's writings will be discussed more fully below, but it is useful to bring him into the argument at this stage. Nichols's text makes clear that he repudiated any suggestion that he was a dissenter or, worse, a Puritan, this declaration dominating the title page of his text which declared that the work was 'published for the common good of the Church' by Nichols, who was 'an humble seruaunt, of the English Church'.[37] Nichols examined the reform of the English episcopate and used the names and reputations of late-sixteenth-century bishops to account for his own rebellion from the Church. Harington's work strengthens this interpretation of the Reformation. For Harington, the reformation of the English episcopate was a battle, one that had been brought to a successful conclusion but was now again threatened by a rebellion emanating from nameless people within the bishops' own camp.

John Harington, the Prince of Wales and the episcopate

Although Harington's work supplemented catalogues by two bishops, readers of Harington's text in the seventeenth century had the impression that its writer was anti-episcopal. The seventeenth-century antiquarian Thomas Fuller (1608–1661) believed that the *Supplie or Addicion* contained 'some tart reflections' on the bishops of the late-sixteenth-century Church, a view later endorsed by the late-seventeenth-century historian and royal librarian John Strype when he encountered the text during his own researches for his lives of Elizabethan bishops.[38] His judgement had less to do with Harington's emphasis on the reformed rather than apostolic origin of the English episcopate and more to do with the frankly salacious tone of some of the episcopal *vitae*. Certainly, there is nothing as lubricous in this collection as the antics of the 'baby eating Bishop of Bath and Wells' who tormented Lord Edmund Blackadder in the BBC TV comedy before succumbing to blackmail. Nonetheless in Harington's text, one can read of the time Archbishop Edwin Sandys (1519–1588) was set up for blackmail after his host at a house he was staying at in Doncaster conspired to have a woman 'slip into my lords' [Sandys] bed in her smock' and leave the Archbishop to be found *in flagrante delicto*.[39] There are also criticisms of bishops for being fat or unshaven, or for having made bad marriages. Harington did hope that Prince Henry would not find a catalogue of 'grave greybeards', as he called the bishops collectively, too boring and did liven up some stories with gossip.[40] It is also the case that Strype, in particular, came to this conclusion because he had read an edited edition from 1653, where adjustments to Harington's catalogue meant it conveyed a more negative account of the Elizabethan and Jacobean bishops. Harington has gained an enduring reputation for writing an anti-episcopal text. For instance, in 1967, Phyllis Hembry suggested that Harington exhibited hostility towards English bishops in his catalogue.[41] However, it is not so much that Hembry interpreted the text in one specific way, but that she read a specific version. Hembry, like Fuller and Strype, read the edition of the text prepared by Harington's relative, John Chetwynd. Chetwynd was a Presbyterian, and he made alterations to Harington's original text accordingly. As R. H. Miller makes clear, Chetwynd detached from the original manuscript Harington's short treatise explaining his intention to defend the episcopate by highlighting some of the deficiencies of recent incumbents.[42] Shorn of this explanatory note we are left with criticisms of bishops without understanding Harington's reasons for being negative.

The apparent anti-episcopal emphasis in the *Supplie* has also been linked to Harrington's association with the court of the Prince of Wales. Prince Henry attracts attention from modern historians for having been the conduit for reformist aspirations and for dissent from the established Church, points drawn from both written and visual evidence. Roy Strong argues that the portrait by Sir Robert Peake of Prince Henry *à la chasse* mimicked the posture and stance of William Scrots's portrait of Edward VI, and even more of Hans Holbein's celebrated but now lost mural of Henry VIII, which decorated the Presence Chamber in Whitehall Palace from the Henrician period until the palace was burnt down in 1698.[43] The physical image of a gargantuan middle-aged monarch was imposed onto the frame of a teenage boy; likewise the reputation of the late King for having reformed the Church attached to his later namesake.

Prince Henry's reputation for religious radicalism largely was the product of the imaginations of some his contemporaries and reflected the appropriation of royal images throughout the seventeenth century, such as the creation of the cult of Elizabeth I in the seventeenth century which made her a champion of godly Protestantism.[44] Harington not only produced the text for Prince Henry, but also in writing his catalogue was reacting to this reputation that the Prince had gained for religious radicalism.[45] His catalogue directs attention to a fragment of textual evidence concerning Prince Henry of Wales's predicted reign as Henry IX:

> Henry the 8. pulld down abbeys and cells,
> But Henry the 9. shall pull down Bishops and bells.[46]

The rhyme, which Harington called a proverb, referred to the dissolution of the monasteries by Henry VIII. It then predicted that once the Prince of Wales acceded to the throne as Henry IX, he would abolish the English bishoprics. In textual material deleted by Chetwynd, Harington explained he had chosen to write of the English episcopate, in the period following the appointment of Matthew Parker to Canterbury, because of his concern that Prince Henry had become associated with expectations that he would enact religious change and actually abolish bishops.[47] The *Supplie or Addicion* concluded with a brief treatise on the entire work, which explained 'The occasion why the former worke was taken in hand.' Without the editorial treatment it received from Chetwynd in the later-seventeenth century, the *Supplie or Addicion* reveals Harington's indignation at the implication that Prince Henry was religiously radical and his intention to write his catalogue as a riposte to this interpretation of the Prince's religious intentions.[48] Yet Harington's narrower focus in his catalogue reflects his concern to describe the danger facing the Church of England from those he variously described as 'puritans' and 'novelists.' Harington also excoriated them as 'fanatical.'[49]

Battles fought and won: Protestant bishops and episcopal dissent

In the *Supplie or Addicion*, Harington conceived of the Reformation as a battle. Harington's metaphor argued that the battle of the Reformation was over and the triumph complete. A further episcopal catalogue, the *Catalogue of all the Bishops*, similarly stressed that since the Reformation, at which time the Church 'was manumitted from the Pope', it had been 'the most exact and perfect of the Reformation.' As with Harington, this anonymous author endeavoured to locate this perfection and completion in the Church's episcopate. According to Harington's formulary, reforming bishops such as Latimer, Cranmer, Ridley and Parker were the generals of the Protestant 'army'. Although the Reformation had been brought to a successful conclusion, other forces now threatened the battle.[50] Harington said: 'When I consider with my selfe the hard beginning, though more prosperous success, of the reformed Church of England, mee thinks it may be compared to a battaile fought, in which some Captayns and souldiers that gaue the first charge, either dyed in the field, or came bleeding home, but such as followed, putting their enemies to flight remained quiet and victorious.'[51] Invoking the names of the episcopal victims of the reign of Queen Mary, Harington said:

> For in such sort *Cranmer, Ridley, Latimer, Hooper, Rogers, Coverdall* and many others, induring great conflicts, in those variable tymes of Henry the eight, King Edward, and Queene Mary, suffering by fyre, by Imprisonment, banishment, losse and deprivation . . . theis that dyed, had the glorie of valiant soldiers, and worthie Martirs.[52]

He placed Parker in this company by noting that: 'Among the Survivors of theise first leaders . . . the first in tyme, and the highest in place was Doctor Mathew Parker.'[53]

Harington's account of Parker's place in history is strikingly at variance with Parker's own assessment of the historical precedents of his archiepiscopate. Harington's narrower focus in his catalogue reflects his concern to account for the danger facing the reformed Church of England from those he variously described as 'puritans' and 'novelists.' The nature of Harington's topic – bringing up to date a compendium of bishops from the time of Parker onwards – must inevitably have involved him in a more contentious set of biographies than Parker, since he was dealing with bishops who had been involved, one way or another, with all the religious disputes of the post-Parker period. His choice of topic made his work inevitably controversial in a way that was not the case for Parker's much longer episcopal catalogue.

This interpretation makes sense of his decision to locate Parker, as well as his immediate successors, as emerging in an institutional sense from the reforms of the sixteenth century. Harington indicated that the reformed Church of England was threatened by the activities of those who regarded themselves as more ardent Protestants than the episcopal hierarchy which governed the Church. Harington's conceptualization of the Reformation as a battle won against great odds was cited earlier; he expanded upon this idea and on his impression of a battle of ideas, for while he saw that Cranmer, Latimer, Ridley, Parker and other reformers secured victory for their side in the 'battle', there was now the danger that 'some mutinous souldiers of their own Campe' were intent on 'disturbing the peace at home', so as to 'giue hart to the enemy abroade'.[54] In recounting both the establishment of the reformed Church and the efforts of its clergy to defend that institution, Harington challenged the necessity to dissent from it while asserting the reforming actions of the Tudor bishops.

Loyalty in dissent: Episcopal puritans and puritan bishops

The dissenting minister Josias Nichols used the internal history of the episcopate to outline his conformity and his loyalty to bishops. He presented a vision of the episcopate in which dissent seemed to be linked to bishops who were known as patrons of godly clergy. His works were polemical texts, dedicated to senior figures in Church and State, including the Archbishop of Canterbury, and were arguments for Nichols's loyalty to the Church of England. In *Plea of the Innocent*, Nichols stressed that he was innocent of accusations of Puritanism or dissent; the work post-dated his deprivation. *Abrahams Faith* had a wider focus and examined religion from the time of the Old Testament Patriarchs, but swiftly moved to examine Nichols's immediate environment. In this work, Nichols exonerated himself and the Church of England from any suggestion of novelty or dissent. In both works, Nichols stressed his fidelity to the Church of England and its episcopal hierarchy by summoning up in writing an actively reforming English episcopate.

In 1603 authorities in the diocese of Canterbury deprived Nichols of his living and degraded him from holy orders because of nonconformity.[55] He came from the ranks of clerics who were deprived under the rigorous conformity enforced by Archbishop Whitgift.[56] Nichols's deprivation from the Church's orders was echoed two years later, when the clerics 'Hugh Tuke, Simon Bradstreet, John Jackson, Thomas Cotton and John More are, in hope of their conformity, dismissed'.[57] Similarly, the minister Andrew King was removed from holy orders and was sent to prison.[58] They were among many.

However, Nichols's writings reveal a different interpretation of his relationship with the Church of England and its disciplinary structures than his deprivation might suggest. He stressed his loyalty to the Church of England and his care for its good order. He used his arguments for the reformed episcopate to place himself within an orthodox and conformist framework. In *Plea of the Innocent* and *Abrahams Faith*, both from the turn of the seventeenth century, Nichols argued by association, raising rhetorical evidence against his deprivation from the seeming similarity between his ecclesiology and members of the episcopate. In doing so, Nichols's writings raise questions for subsequent readers regarding his audience. Both his texts, but especially *Plea*, addressed the meaning of 'Puritan' and discussed the historical reputation of an Elizabethan bishop, Edmund Grindal (d.1583), whose archiepiscopate remained controversial in the early seventeenth century.[59] In *Plea*, Nichols appealed to be exonerated from allegations of being a Puritan. We should note at this point that the bishops evaluated by Nichols, including Edmund Grindal (Archbishop of Canterbury 1576–83), are those whom modern scholars see as most tolerant of non-conformist preachers. As early as 1559, Grindal was lamenting the 'dearth of godly ministers' and pursuing reform at the Inns of Court.[60] Of Grindal, Patrick Collinson argued that his archiepiscopate reveals lines of tension and division in the English Church between Puritanism and orthodoxy that later became permanent.[61] According to Nichols' assessment of Grindal, during the few functional years of Grindal's archiepiscopate, he worked to protect and promote those clergy otherwise condemned by church leaders as puritans.

Nichols's arguments doubtless served their purpose as protests against his deprivation and as rebukes to those who had deprived him. But they are also significant for the assessment they offer of episcopal conduct and identity, and the way Nichols broke in on the shared memories of episcopal continuity and identity charted by episcopal catalogues by singling out godly bishops as his co-religionists. Scholars have already pointed to the existence of loyal dissenters or 'conforming Puritans' as present within the structures of the Church.[62] Alastair Bellany examines the trial for libel of the dissenter Lewis Pickering after he had disrupted Whitgift's funeral procession by pinning a libellous card to the coffin asserting the dead bishop's popishness.[63] Because he was known as a dissenter due to his very public affront to episcopal authority, Pickering fell victim to higher authority but at the same time he pledged his loyalty to the good order of Church and State. Bellany considers that Pickering exemplified a strategy of distinguishing between conformity to the State and to the Church. He draws upon the records of Pickering's trial for libelling the late Archbishop Whitgift, arguing that the dissenter's defence rested upon his efforts to demonstrate his simultaneous loyalty and dissent. Accounting for Pickering's defence, Bellany perceives that this dissenter drew upon what he calls a strategy of locating his dissent within the established Church.[64] Nichols's writings suggest nothing as coherent as a strategy, but they rejected the implications of the label 'Puritan' for being a rebel from episcopal authority and he stressed his adherence to the established Church and its episcopal leaders, arguing that he had been 'vncharitablie and vniustlie called by that odious and hereticall name of Puritane'.[65]

Nichols offered his own highly original definition of 'puritan', arguing that Catholic religious such as monks and nuns 'may & are properly to [be] called Puritaines, because they arrogate vnto them selues puritie and holiness'.[66] Having off-loaded the term onto the Church of Rome, Nichols highlighted his own moderation through asserting the differences between himself and the more extreme 'Martin Marprelate', whose pamphlets, in Nichols's view, 'slanderously abused' important figures in the established Church.[67] Persons such as the authors of the Marprelate Tracts were called, among other things, 'a contagious brood of Scismatickes' by conforming members of the Church of England, appellations that Nichols was anxious to avoid.[68] Nichols stands apart from a body of churchmen that Fincham recognizes as 'conformable Puritans', subscribing to escape deprivation while privately condemning aspects of the Church of England as unlawful.[69] Nichols did not escape deprivation and following his deprivation proclaimed his loyalty to the bishops. In contrast, 'Martin's' abuse of the bishops and archbishops was of great importance to Nichols, who stressed in *Plea* that his beliefs comfortably resided within an episcopal framework.[70]

Nichols's insistence that he was not a Puritan may have been a rhetorical strategy, but it gained additional meaning from the acceptance of this title by other dissenters.[71] For instance Henry Parker, a cleric deprived from his orders, asserted that those who objected to Puritans were 'papists, hierarchists, ambidexters and neuters in religion.' Any one of these was worse than being a Puritan.[72] Parker's commentary on Puritanism originated from a framework of texts that offered varying but often pejorative meanings of Puritanism. Works that originate in the Jacobean period indicate the comparisons drawn between Puritanism and separatist movements, an intellectual background especially encountered in James I's *Basilikon Doron* and which contributes much to understanding Nichols's repudiation of the label and his asserted loyalty to the Church of England.[73]

Nichols expressed his loyalty to the Church using names and reputations taken from the episcopal bench and argued that his ecclesial priorities accepted an episcopal hierarchy. Striking contrasts are discernible between Nichols and other apparent Puritans. The Elizabethan cleric John Field stressed his intention of remaining within the Church of England, yet argued that to do so he would have to purify it of popish remnants, including its bishops.[74] Field desired the establishment of presbyterial government and reformed worship and set down conditions for his continued membership of the Church. Nichols, by contrast, stressed his loyalty to the Church using the names of individual bishops and the office of bishop to substantiate his point.

Abrahams Faith was a product of the last moments of Elizabeth's rule. In the text, Nichols looked backed nostalgically at the achievements of Elizabeth's reign for the advancement of Protestant religion. Nichols placed himself firmly within the framework of the secure establishment of religion that Elizabeth achieved.[75] In *Abrahams Faith*, Nichols compared and contrasted the Elizabethan archbishops, suggesting that while Whitgift was repressive, the privations endured by some clergy during his time in office contrasted with the freedoms enjoyed under Grindal.[76] Nichols was particularly recalling the Three Articles introduced by Whitgift, which brought to an abrupt end the godly experiments patronized by Grindal.[77] Even before Nichols drew these comparisons, good and bad bishops had long been compared with each other and Nichols engaged with a much older tradition of contrasting good bishop with bad. While churchmen including Latimer (although a bishop himself) and Tyndale wholly condemned bishops and saw no positive qualities in good bishops to counterbalance the bad, their contemporary William Marshal contrasted 'a verye chrysten bysshop' with a 'counterfayte bysshop'.[78] By 1602, Nichols was using the tangible figures of actual bishops including Grindal and Whitgift to defend himself from the accusation of Puritanism. Throughout the *Plea*, Nichols's central purpose was to stress the unanimity between himself and the Church of England. For instance, he observed that Queen Elizabeth herself had 'suffered & endured great troubles and reproach' for the sake of reformed religion.[79]

In Nichols's assessment of the reformed episcopate, the career of Edmund Grindal was of greatest significance. Collinson's eponymous biography of this archbishop, tellingly subtitled 'The Struggle for a Reformed Church', established that Grindal's refusal to suppress the prophesyings, the melodramatically named meetings of clergymen to discuss scriptural passages and to practise sermons, angered the Queen.[80] Nichols was born in 1555 and lived through Grindal's archiepiscopate as a young adult, and from the early seventeenth century looked back to that period of his youth with affection. The time when 'the reuerend father Maister *Grindall* was Archbishoppe of Canterburie' was a golden age for him.[81] In Nichols's estimation, two features distinguished Grindal's archiepiscopate. First, it was a time when 'there was greate concorde among the Ministers', who were thus able to enact the 'moste godly proceedings'.[82] Second, after Grindal's death, clerics such as Nichols found themselves begging Grindal's episcopal successors for mercy: 'Yet doe we intreat our reuerend Fathers we be not held for rebels.'[83]

Grindal was perhaps the obvious choice of archbishop for Nichols to use in his work. Along with other bishops, Grindal was known as a patron of actively godly clergy and in his own way he was a victim of ecclesiastical authority, despite being the Archbishop of Canterbury. The stress that some bishops placed on godliness rather than ritual sheltered some clergy. For instance, dissenting clergy could retain their benefices when George Montaigne was Bishop of London, but not when he was succeeded by William Laud.[84] Expressions of episcopal authority, such as the Visitation Articles of Toby Matthew of York or those of his colleagues Henry Robinson of Carlisle and William James of Durham, emphasized the preaching duties and godliness of clergy, rather than demanding adherence to ritual.[85] If not Puritans themselves, the bishops tolerated clergy who otherwise would be deposed from their orders. Peter Lake argues that Matthew Hutton, the Elizabethan Archbishop of York, was reluctant to track down clergy who quibbled at vestiarian legislation, believing this would be a waste of strongly anti-papal talent in the Northern Province.[86] Hutton's contemporary, Bishop Still of Bath and Wells, preferred, where possible, to resolve ecclesiastical disputes without depriving ministers.[87] Neither Grindal's predecessor, Matthew Parker, nor Whitgift his successor, suffered sequestration or deprivation. Indeed, far from repudiating royal authority, Parker could more usually be found begging the Queen for assistance in implementing the royal policy.[88] Parker particularly requested Elizabeth to throw her weight behind his prosecution of the non-conformist clerics Sampson and Humphrey. Whitgift is usually portrayed by historians as a disciplinarian.[89] As with his analysis of the term 'Puritan', Nichols again dealt with the meaning of the religious terminology of his age. He was not a Puritan and neither was he a rebel. Instead, he invoked the memory of a reformed episcopal pastor to exonerate him and his contemporaries from any such accusations; episcopal authority which was reformed and Protestant accommodated, sheltered and encouraged the ecclesiology of churchmen such as Nichols.

Hampton court and its consequences

Nichols is only one clergyman, but the interpretation of his writings offered here can be placed in a broader and stronger set of circumstances. Nichols's efforts to show that he was compliant with episcopal rule reflect a broader body of thought which interpreted interactions between dissent and episcopacy. Nichols's involvement in the Church of England in the seventeenth century was peripheral; deprived from his living he could no longer officiate as a clergyman. He is known to have observed the Hampton Court Conference, a major ecclesiastical gathering in 1604, from the fringes and was not actively involved in this attempt to settle increasing tensions within the Church of England. The concerns of the participants in this conference, the King, bishops and lower clergy, show how the interpretation that both Harington and Nichols offered of the recent history of the episcopate was shaped by contemporary concerns to set the parameters of orthodoxy and dissent.

The Hampton Court Conference began in 1604 and ended the same year with the promulgation of ninety new canons regulating doctrine, liturgy and clerical apparel, to which the English clergy had to conform and which were enforced by episcopal authority.[90] As later accounts of the conference indicate, both attendees and observers of the Hampton Court Conference debated the meaning of 'dissenter' and 'puritan', and were preoccupied with establishing parameters of obedience and authority. As the seventeenth century progressed, this terminology lost much of its nuanced and controversial meaning, at least as far as church leaders were concerned. By the Restoration, Archbishop Gilbert Sheldon of Canterbury divided the population of England into members of the Church of England, Roman Catholic recusants and Protestant dissenters. Sheldon's census of 1676 undoubtedly lacks any attempt to define religious groupings with precision, and its purpose at any rate was to provide Sheldon with a debating point that the bulk of English people were loyal to the Church of England. Nonetheless, Sheldon's census shows how the meanings of dissent and puritan gradually contracted over the seventeenth century in contrast to the contested and controversial meaning attached to this terminology earlier in the seventeenth century. Contemporary with Sheldon, the dispossessed minister Richard Baxter defined a Puritan as one outside the episcopal oversight of the Church and the label 'non-conformist' was used as a self-generated title by writers who had lost their licenses by the 1662 Act of Uniformity.[91]

Earlier in the seventeenth century, a dissenter could be easily defined for members of the clergy at least: had their licence to preach been withdrawn by their bishop? Being a dissenter was on this level an aspect of ecclesiastical polity and the dissent was from the canons and regulations of the Church. Being a dissenter was therefore understood as being a set of circumstances, whereas being a puritan was the label to describe the religiosity underpinning these circumstances. The circumstance was being a minister without a licence or a living. Puritan was an associated pejorative term used to describe the religiosity behind the circumstance of dissent. These meanings can be teased out from statements by clergy who retained their episcopal licences. The Cambridge theologian Oliver Ormerod (1580–1626) argued that Puritanism originated in the lower orders of society, although James I preferred to restrict the label to a specific religious extreme of society, namely the Anabaptists. In making this claim, it is unlikely that James was ascribing actual Anabaptist characteristics (such as polygamy or adult baptism) to English churchmen but was rather invoking a general reputation for disorderly conduct and repudiation of Church authority.[92] Certainly Anabaptism remained a byword for revolt against ecclesiastical order courtesy of the widely known rebellion of 'King' Jan van Leyden against the Bishop of Munster in the 1530s.[93] Such a reputation is suggested by the writings of Bancroft's chaplain Thomas Rogers, who described Anabaptists as holding that 'an equality must be made of ministers'.[94] James I's archbishop, John Whitgift, used the less specific term 'puritan' and used a series of disparaging adjectives to describe Puritans, arguing that they were 'spiteful' and 'tumultuous'.[95] The martyrologist Samuel Clarke noted that the dissenting Stuart cleric, William Bradshaw, was reported to his bishop for being 'not conformable to the *Rites* of the Church' and through his dissent was known as a Puritan.[96] In these statements, Puritanism became bound up with opposition to episcopacy.

Yet set against this apparently simple meaning were other assessments which argued that Puritanism did not imply existence beyond the authority or structures of the Church, a point which Nichols advanced and which worried Harington. The historian of the Cecil dynasty, Pauline Croft, argues that the godly minister Sir Robert Cecil distinguished between religious dissent and political dissent, telling the Privy Council that dissenters from the Church of England were nonetheless loyal members of the State: 'among all those malcontents, papists and atheists, not one of those called Puritans did offer up a hand against Her Majesty'.[97] According to Peter Clark's analysis of Nichols's career, Nichols's moderate non-conformity was partly exhibited in his adherence to monarchical if not ecclesiastical authority and Clark points to the reproving opinion of Nichols's dissenting contemporary William Covell (d.1614?), who identified Nichols's acceptance of the Elizabethan government but not the Church's hierarchy, and who according to Covell 'slubbered over vnhamdsomely' the issue.[98] For Covell, Nichols's dissent was not taken far enough.

Nichols constructed a particular definition of dissent which harmonized with his ecclesiology and illustrated the view of many of his contemporaries who argued that they remained in conformity with the Church and its bishops. One contemporary, the dissenting minister Dudley Fenner, protested against the 'false accusations and slanders of their adversaries'. In his case the adversary was William Fulke (1538–1589), a clerical participant in the Elizabethan vestiarian controversies about the surplices worn by ministers.[99] Like Fenner, Nichols moved swiftly to stress his fidelity to the Church of England and his care for its peace and good name.[100]

But there was another form of interaction between episcopacy and dissent. Sometimes the bishop could obscure the Puritan in a clergyman. It is noteworthy that when James made the Oxford don Henry Robinson a bishop, Robinson was transformed to become 'a bishop, and therefore no puritan', as King James put it, suggesting, as his minister Robert Cecil had not, an outright dislocation between Church authority and dissent.[101] Likewise, in 1624 Richard Montagu published *A Gagg for the New Gospell?* and in it expressed his anxiety that in Roman Catholic writings 'puritan positions [are] maliciously imputed to protestants'.[102] For Montagu, as apparently for James, Puritanism existed beyond the structures of the Church. While Montagu believed that distinctions between dissenters and orthodox churchmen like him were dangerously blurred by Roman Catholic controversialists, he also acknowledged that the Church of England did itself no favours in this regard, ascribing Puritan beliefs to those high in the Church's hierarchy. Writing to John Cosin, he requested his book be licensed 'but of no puritan', a point which stresses his anxiety that Puritanism might have existed on the episcopal bench.[103]

Samuel Clarke's catalogue of victims of episcopal malevolence further contributed to efforts to understand Puritanism's forms and expressions. He included a puritan bishop among the thirty-two eminent divines whose lives he recounted.[104] Another of the bishops was Barnaby Potter, who became the Bishop of Carlisle yet was known as a puritan.[105] An exchange between James I and Bishop Godfrey Goodman (1583–1656) also makes clear James believed there were bishops who were also puritans. While the King complained of the number of Puritans in his English Kingdom, Goodman pointed out that the James made bishops out of Puritans. Goodman did not indicate if he had specific bishops, such as Potter, in mind, but his frank comment to James suggests his belief that the ranks of the episcopate could be filled by churchmen recognizably puritan in outlook.[106] In this way, 'puritan' and 'dissenter' were not synonyms for each other, and Goodman and Clarke both recorded a sense of puritan as meaning godly activity within, not beyond, the structures of the Church. James's archbishop, George Abbot, seemed to bear this comment out, as contemporary gossip about Abbot alleged that Richard Bancroft, Abbot's predecessor, 'held his Grace Abbot for a Puritan'.[107] Patrick Collinson placed Bishop Rudd of St David's within an even more obviously Puritan framework. For Collinson, Puritanism could be defined by its association with compromise, as he highlights this Bishop's belief that Puritans and members of the Church of England were able to agree in 'substance of religion'.[108] Later in the seventeenth century, William Laud suspected that bishops such as Joseph Hall of Exeter favoured Puritans. He even suspected Archbishop Ussher of Armagh of such views.[109] The character of the episcopal bench remained complex later into the seventeenth century. Richard Baxter, a dissenting cleric, divided bishops and episcopal sympathizers into 'old orthodox' and the 'new party'. The former carried some beliefs and principles in common with Puritans; the latter was taking the Church of England towards Rome.[110] If not exactly patrons of godly clergy, reformed bishops were at least lukewarm persecutors of Puritans and some were active supporters of clergy who could have been called *Puritan*. Later in the seventeenth century, in 1673, Baxter claimed the Tudor Bishop Thomas Bilson (d.1616) as his ecclesial kinsman, arguing that had this sixteenth-century prelate been alive a century later, he would have been a dissenter.[111] Baxter's alternative strategy brings Nichols's work into sharper focus. Nichols did not wish to claim Grindal and other bishops as dissenters but to show himself as a conformist.

The complexity of the seventeenth-century episcopal bench reveals itself particularly in the enforcement of ceremonial conformity, which was a distinguishing characteristic of some bishops but not others.[112] Even the primates were markedly different. Archbishop Abbot was more concerned about the so-called 'scandalous living' of ministers than about their conformity to the ecclesiastical articles and canons.[113] In contrast, Laud vigorously enforced the canons regulating liturgy and clerical apparel, while his subordinate clergy such as John Williams, the Bishop of Lincoln, displayed a lukewarm response to similar tasks. Bishop Williams even ventured into print against his primate, Archbishop William Laud, publishing a tract against the liturgical practices that Laud wished to see in every English church.[114] Likewise, the religious controversialist William Prynne stated that Archbishop Laud (in office 1633–44) had included the late Bishop of Winchester, John Ponet (1516–1556), among a list of notorious Puritans, even though Ponet was cut from the same cloth as Laud, being 'one of your owne rochet, and a bishop Puritan, if a Puritan'.[115] Gossip of their alleged Puritanism would have been received negatively by some churchmen, and Prynne deliberately meant to affront Laud. But at the time of the Hampton Court Conference, Nichols rejected the idea that the term *Puritan* implied disobedience when he asserted his own status as the loyal servant of godly bishops.

Thus, the issue of conformity is far from clear-cut. Some scholars now argue that common ground existed between dissenters and conformists, an interpretation which would seem to make sense of Nichols's insistence to have been sheltered by the episcopate.[116] Nicholas Tyacke points to a 'bond' between conformists and dissenters, one that he sees as expressed through commonly accepted Calvinist doctrines of salvation.[117] For Tyacke, common features existed between the nebulous groups of conformists and nonconformists relating to doctrines of salvation. His argument is an important indicator that members of the English Church cannot be easily categorized. Maurice Lee offers a similar reading, arguing that a 'broad consensus' existed in the early-seventeenth-century Church which made separatist agitation less likely.[118]

The discipline exercised by bishops further complicates modern scholarly tendencies to demarcate between dissenting and orthodox clergy. Through studying the career of Stephen Denison, the seventeenth-century minister and incumbent of St Katherine Cree in London, Lake points out that he was both a victim of the Star Chamber, an instrument of episcopal control, and a star witness there against dissent.[119] Similarly, apparent puritans such as William Whitaker were fully conformant to episcopal authority.[120] Lake therefore sees distinctions between the victims and the agents of episcopal authority as blurred. To have been both victim and episcopal favourite, in Denison's case, indicates the priorities of the political forces behind episcopal authority, in publicly exhibiting a de-radicalized clergyman. Nichols's assessment of Church authority emerges from a similar fusion of the dissenting and the orthodox, although his intention was not to show clergy as de-radicalized servants of the Star Chamber, but rather to suggest that the careers of former bishops showed that perceived radicals were not radicals at all.

Conclusion

Nichols set himself the task of identifying the actions and defining characteristics of the godly episcopate. As one of many deprived clergy, he was on the fringes of the Church of England yet viewed himself as operating according to the demands of episcopal government. Previous interpretations of Nichols have left him outside the Church of England; in particular Peter Clark's interpretation of Nichols has, in a more general analysis, been endorsed by the important new study by Susan Brigden, who argues that dissenters from the Church of England moved to convert it 'by stealth', by planting 'presbytery within episcopacy'.[121] Yet Nichols is part of a longer trajectory of thought which attempted to define the actions which gave meaning to reformed episcopacy. In 1642, a parliamentary tract complained that 'The Bishops neither can nor will be diligent preachers themselves, so long as besides their Ministerial functions, they have a diocese to rule'.[122] While calling for the abolition of episcopacy, the tract actually identified the duties and defining characteristics of a reformed ecclesiastical hierarchy – preaching and ministry – and contrasted them with the obligations of 'a diocese to rule'. Here Puritan agitation pointed to the functions of bishops, for while their diocesan authority seemed inimical to pastoral oversight, it was still possible to think of bishops as reformed preachers.[123] One of the agitators of the period, William Prynne, argued that the bishops of the seventeenth century were concerned more with their disciplinary powers and less with their pastoral responsibilities. Prynne listed those bishops who were non-preachers.[124] While generally condemning bishops, Prynne also expressed, if only as a stick with which to beat other bishops, his expectation of the godly activities that bishops could undertake. A contemporary anti-episcopal tract asked 'And how negligent are our Lordly Bishops, that do not preach once in a whole year, when as Bishops should be preaching Bishops, and not Lording Bishops'.[125] Bishop Williams of Lincoln, in office during the reign of Charles I, recorded the expectations held of reformed bishops, again in relation to the provision of preaching clergy. When engaged in a dispute with the vicar of Grantham over altar policy, Williams indicated his episcopal duties lay in providing 'grave and painfull' lecturers for townsfolk.[126] Williams's stance was likely to have been influenced by animosity to Laud, but his statement stressed the duties of bishops in supporting godly activities.[127] Members of the reformed episcopate patronized those clergy who were effective preachers and lecturers. In these instances, the animating characteristics of the godly episcopate were simply a means to urge for the episcopate's abolition; Prynne may have outlined the possibly godly actions of bishops, but only to show the inadequacies of the bishops who actually governed the Church. Nichols's purpose was different, showing the godly episcopate actually in action. His intent was to exonerate himself from the charge of Puritanism, an allegation which had brought with it the unwelcome and inconvenient circumstance of deprivation: unemployment. Nichols therefore gives an indication of what was at stake in these different assessments of the godliness of bishops. Nichols was a victim of episcopal authority, yet his conception of godly episcopacy cut across self-generated images of episcopacy, particularly catalogues which stressed the continuities and traditions of episcopal rule. He reconfigured the meaning of authority in the early Stuart period, showing bishops who governed the Church but who did not regard clergy of his kind as dissenters, or who did not expel them from the Church's orthodoxy.

The association that Nichols drew between the episcopate and his dissent resonates with other accounts of the reformed episcopate. The Jacobean minister Sir Robert Cecil attempted to moderate the severity shown against Puritans by stressing the King's love for them. He argued that James 'loved and reverenced' Puritans, to the extent that he would 'prefer [them] to the best bishopric that were void' if they would only conform.[128] An influential modern interpreter of Robert Cecil, Pauline Croft, believes that such sentiments and promises were intended as a 'lure' for Puritans and dissenters and that the seduction of ambition was a substitute for discipline.[129] However, it seems unlikely that the ambitions of dissenters would have been especially lured by a solitary promise of ecclesiastical preferment; if Croft is to be believed, then Cecil was offering a particularly feeble and implausible inducement to conform. Instead, Cecil's comment is important because of the light it can shed on Nichols's writings. According to Nichols, dissenters did not have to be seduced into accepting bishoprics; they were already there.

Surveying Nichols's writings, it does seem that he protested too much about his loyalty to the Church of England. The downfall of Archbishop Grindal was a convenient excuse for Nichols to argue away his dissent. It should be stressed that Nichols was alert to the less sympathetic policies of Archbishop Whitgift and the repressive measures of the Tudor and early Stuart episcopate. Nichols also argued he was not a Puritan and expressed his anxiety for the well-being of the Church. His writings turned the Church of England against itself, allowing Nichols to conform, if only rhetorically, to a godly episcopate. As much as these are rhetorical aspects of his text, they also inhabit a similar ecclesial world to the episcopal battleground of John Harington's supplementary catalogue. Harington asserted the reformist attributes of the episcopate but also the dissent that grew up within the reformed Church of England. For Harington this dissent was worrying; for Nichols, Puritan bishops were a source of support and patronage. In arguing away his dissent, Nichols resorted to the reputations of Protestant bishops; according to Nichols's understanding of episcopal authority, if the bishops were not dissenters, then neither was he.

3

Exorcising Demons and Defending Episcopacy

Introduction

If Nichols looked back nostalgically to Archbishop Grindal, then Grindal's successors Whitgift and Bancroft will have presented fewer happy memories to deprived clergy. Richard Bancroft in particular has earned a posthumous reputation as a harrier of puritans and a defender of episcopacy. One avenue for Bancroft to polemically outline his defence of episcopacy was through the prosecution of exorcists.[1] Bewitchment and exorcisms were important sites of anti-episcopal activity but their significance in this regard has been underestimated and underexplored in the literature. Analysis of Bancroft's activities as an opponent of exorcism deepens the understanding of episcopal responses to the challenges they faced. A number of bishops were assiduous investigators of cases of exorcism. The Bishop of Coventry and Lichfield became involved in the notorious case of the Bilson Boy,[2] and Dr Richard Vaughan, the Bishop of London, also investigated cases in his diocese.[3] However, Vaughan's predecessor in the diocese of London, Richard Bancroft, merits particular attention, as do some of the exorcisms he investigated and debunked, especially those performed by John Darrel. Bancroft was successively the Bishop of London (from 1597) and then (from 1604 to his death in 1610) the Archbishop of Canterbury. One of Bancroft's earliest episcopal acts was to make Samuel Harsnet (d.1631) his chaplain.[4] As Bancroft's chaplain, and later as a bishop, Harsnet was responsible for licensing or prohibiting books, but also for conducting investigations into alleged acts of *maleficium* and in taking action against exorcists, including degrading clerical exorcists of their orders and writing propaganda against them.[5]

Harsnet was well rewarded by Bancroft for his energetic service, becoming an archdeacon and then rising through the ranks of the episcopate to the high office of Archbishop of York.[6] For the purposes of this chapter, the bishop and his chaplain form an unlikely trio with John Darrel, a clergyman active as an exorcist in the late sixteenth century and whose exorcisms were investigated by Bancroft and Harsnet. They declared Darrel an imposter, degraded him from holy orders and committed him to the Gatehouse prison in London.[7] The interactions of these three clergymen and the pamphlets and tracts they wrote about one another speak of broader concerns not only with the detection of witches but also with the contestation of episcopal authority. Examined together, they suggest how witchcraft cases in sixteenth- and seventeenth-century England became embroiled in debate over church government and provided ways to argue for and against the necessity of bishops, arguments expressed in tracts which discussed the expulsion of demons from the bodies of the possessed.

Together Bancroft and Harsnet investigated cases of possession and bewitchment. These were dispossessions performed by Darrel (1599), the possession of Mary Glover (1602) and finally the possession of Anne Gunter (1605). These concerned a particular type of possession, whereby it was alleged that the human agency of a witch had facilitated the bewitchment by the devil.[8] They came to the notice of such high officials because of the notoriety they attracted among observers; they were replete with suggestions of preternatural appearances by strange black creatures, wild prophetic utterances and sudden linguistic facility and frothing at the mouth by the possessed persons. The exorcisms, especially Darrel's, were also public spectacles; they attracted people in the hundreds to watch and to participate as prayerful agents of dispossession. As many as 150 people joined in prayer to help Darrel dispossess Will Somers, a musician's apprentice, before 1599.[9] But the exorcisms could also be experienced vicariously as they had a literary afterlife. The behaviour of the possessed and the exorcisms performed on them appealed to the writers of cheap texts on bizarre cases because of the level of picaresque detail they included.[10] However, a range of tracts about exorcism also focused on bishops and church government.

Interpretations of exorcisms, which after all were statements of an exorcist's singular religious authority, intersected with long-standing anti-episcopal propaganda. As Keith Thomas points out, cases of possession in England frequently occurred in godly households.[11] While this point has led to much psycho-historical speculation by some historians about emotional repression and the reasons for the demoniacs' behaviour, the significance here is that these households were also centres of a form of piety and churchmanship often inimical to episcopacy. Darrel's operations in and around Leicestershire placed him in an area among people sympathetic to his godly activities and to the prayerful forms his exorcisms took whereby he prayed intensively over the possessed person but also in an area likely to promote opposition to episcopacy.[12]

In the cases of 1599, 1602 and 1605, Bancroft actively investigated, propagandized, defended the accused and combatted with the claims of puritan ministers to be the prayerful instruments of dispossession. Bancroft was clearly the agent entrusted by Archbishop Whitgift of Canterbury with the defence of the episcopate in multiple arenas, including the challenges raised by exorcism. Later as the Archbishop of Canterbury himself, Bancroft retained his active interest in dispossession. This again suggests the importance of tracing this aspect of his career as public defender of the episcopate, particularly his use of exorcisms as vehicles of pro-episcopal propaganda. Viewed in this light, Bancroft the expert on witchcraft harmonizes with the more familiar vision of Bancroft in the scholarly literature on the Jacobean Church, which reveals him as a combative opponent of puritanism and an active defender of episcopacy.[13]

For a moment let us consider Bancroft's rise to prominence. Bancroft was very much a star of the generation of clergy who emerged from Cambridge in the 1570s and gained rapid preferment in the Church. He was ordained in 1574 and made an immediate impact, being praised by the strongly Protestant Bishop Cox of Ely as 'very well learned ... & a very good preacher'.[14] From the beginning of his career, the Church hierarchy valued Bancroft as an articulate and educated defender of the episcopate; his reputation led Archbishop John Whitgift to entrust Bancroft with the investigation into a number of affronts to episcopal authority, including the uprising inspired by the messianic William Hacket and the publication of the anti-episcopal Marprelate Tracts.[15] He was also tasked with preaching in defence of episcopacy at Paul's Cross in 1589.[16] One historian of the archbishopric of Canterbury, Edward Carpenter, likens Bancroft to both Sherlock Holmes and Senator McCarthy; while the comparison is flamboyant, it does testify to Bancroft's recorded abilities as an investigator and a propagandist, as well as his capacity to collaborate with colleagues including his chaplains and Queens' Counsels, and his use of the prerogative courts of High Commission and Star Chamber as instruments of punishment.[17] In 1604, he was a notably combative participant in the Hampton Court Conference and was the chief representative of the episcopal party, in place of the ailing Archbishop Whitgift.[18] Harsnet also enjoyed career preferment, and embarked on his investigations after his collation to the archdeaconry of Essex.[19]

The cases Bancroft and Harsnet investigated had a number of other notable witchcraft cases going on around them, including the Warboys case of 1593.

These were part of a wider problem; in England, over 100 cases of possession are counted for across the sixteenth and seventeenth centuries.[20] The Bancroft cases also conformed to a clear pattern of a person being cursed by a bystander, very often an old woman, and then bringing an accusation of *maleficium* against the person who had uttered the curse.[21] In 1599 local authorities in the Midlands asked Bancroft to investigate the exorcism of Will Somers, a fiddler's apprentice. Somers claimed that after an old witch, Alice Goodridge, had possessed him after he broke wind near her. He had then been dispossessed by Darrel, who had been active as an exorcist since the 1570s. Bancroft extracted from Somers a confession that his symptoms of possession were faked, and, using this confession, Bancroft and Harsnet declared Darrel to be a fraud. In 1602 Bancroft, again working with the energetic Harsnet, was called in to review the case of Mary Glover's bewitchment by Elizabeth Jackson, another old woman. Although Jackson was remanded and sentenced to the pillory, Bancroft adduced medical evidence which he hoped would disprove the authenticity of Glover's possession and her accusation against Jackson. In 1605 Bancroft, by then the Archbishop of Canterbury, investigated the bewitchment of Anne Gunter, and as a result of Bancroft's intervention, Gunter and her father were tried in Star Chamber for laying false accusations.[22] In this last case, much of the work was delegated to Harsnet.[23] Harsnet energetically investigated, placing Anne Gunter under his custody at Lambeth Palace and extracting from her a confession of fraud.[24]

The major contours of the reported cases, including the mysterious appearance of old women as the instigators of possession, reflect others of the period, including the Boy of Bilson,[25] and more broadly reflect the social characteristics of many of the women accused of *maleficium*[26] as well as the physical symptoms of the possessed, such as preternatural strength and knowledge of hitherto unknown languages.[27] These cases were also part of a 'plague' of possession cases throughout Europe which intellectual elites assiduously investigated.[28]

The three cases which preoccupied Bancroft and Harsnet thus took place against a backdrop of continental cases of possession of individual demoniacs, such as the notorious French demoniac Marthe Brossier who, like Anne Gunter, was shown off before monarchy; Gunter met King James I, as Brossier had been paraded in front of the King and Queen of France,[29] just as another continental demoniac, Nicole Obry, was carried in religious processions through Laon.[30] There were also group possessions, such as the convent possessions at Loudun and elsewhere.[31] Cases of this nature suggest that exorcisms had the capacity to become sites of both flamboyant activity and religious competition, a point borne out by the Bancroft cases. The pamphlets published about them relate the startling behaviour of other possessed persons, including Gunter and Somers. As with demoniacs in Europe, descriptions allude to obscene language, prophetic utterances and physically outrageous behaviour, as well as preternatural physical events, such as a moving lump on Somers's body.[32] They were therefore occasions where not only was the possessed in dialogue with his or her internal demon, and the demon in dialogue with the exorcist, but also the possessed person was engaged in a performative act. Up to a hundred people could gather at a time to see the demoniac in action and to participate in prayers and the singing of metrical psalms.[33]

Attracting high levels of attention, exorcisms were potent opportunities to propagandize, both on the spot while the exorcist confronted the demon, but later through the issuing of interpretative tracts.[34] Darrel's dispossessions and those of other puritan ministers were recorded in widely read tracts and pamphlets. Ultimately Darrel became well enough known as an exorcist for him to be mentioned by name (albeit mockingly) in Ben Jonson's *The Devil is an Ass*.[35] For this reason, the cases of possession could become sites of confessional competition and are natural places to look for arguments between anti-episcopal and episcopal forces being played out. As exorcisms were attention-grabbing events and an opportunity for puritan ministers to show the efficacy of their prayers, they were also opportunities for ministers to issue propaganda against the episcopate, a point that emphasizes why investigating these cases mattered to the episcopal hierarchy of the Church of England.[36]

Cases of exorcism became a means for Bancroft to resist claims that his order was ungodly and he used writings against exorcisms and exorcists to promote episcopacy. His energies in this arena confronted anti-episcopal propaganda, especially that promoted by John Darrel and his associates. In these instances, Darrel not only challenged the demons supposedly inhabiting the possessed, but also confronted the Bishop of London, who ridiculed his capacities as an exorcist. According to Darrel, to disbelieve in his exorcisms was to be identifiably popish, for it was 'Papists who deny any such power to be in our Church'.[37] Implicitly, bishops were among the 'friends of Rome' for denying that Darrel had the power to cast out devils.[38] Darrel and his sympathizers took this point further, suggesting explicitly that not only was it popish to disbelieve in exorcisms, but that bishops were popish for their actions against exorcists. *The Trial of Maist. Dorrell*, of unknown authorship but clearly written by a person close to Darrel, takes up the question of episcopal identity. '[A]ll the learned Preachers of the

Gospell in England, France, Scotlande, and the Low Countryes' stood opposed to the disbelief of bishops in bewitchment and stood in condemnation of their treatment of exorcists in the High Commission. This comparison located bishops among the 'Romish Hierarchy and Ceremonies enforced' by the ungodly at the expense of the godly. In declaring the power of his exorcisms, Darrel was not so much concerned with the reality of miracles, but with separating the godly from the ungodly.

By the late sixteenth century, investigations into exorcisms followed a trail that led back to episcopal circles and very often back to Lambeth Palace itself, home of the archbishops of Canterbury. At the end of Elizabeth I's reign, Archbishop Whitgift's chaplain Abraham Hartwell published a translation of a French tract which poured scorn on the veracity of Marthe Brossier's possession, a famous French case that had been widely reported in England.[39] He also assisted in assembling and promoting the evidence against Darrel.[40] By early in the next century, Hartwell's place at Lambeth had been taken by Harsnet, but the significance of episcopal patronage of the agents against puritan exorcists remained.

The focused nature of episcopal involvement meant that in hunting the hunters of witches, Bancroft and Harsnet, had by 1605 developed a consistent approach to overturning or challenging a case of possession and exorcism. Although he was a central figure in these cases, the sources for them do not let us hear Bancroft's own voice or gauge his actual perceptions on exorcism and witchcraft. The legislative history of the Church of England testifies to Bancroft's concern with witchcraft, notably the promulgation of Canons in 1604 under his direction which included the proscription of precisely the kind of godly exorcisms that he disputed in the three cases, forbidding 'privatt fasting and prayer under pretence of Castinge out Devilles under payne of suspension and deprivation from the minister'.[41] Bancroft did not stop with simply the promulgation of the canons. He and Harsnet followed the steps including active investigation, with the contestation of the credibility of the accusers, the defence of the accused, and the publication by Harsnet of tracts decrying the circumstances of the case and dismissing the reputations of the puritan clergy involved. The involvement of Bancroft and Harsnet ensured not only the defence of the accused, but also the punishment of the accusers. Extensive propaganda, dutifully written by Harsnet, also appeared in the wake of these cases, dismissing the authenticity of the accusations but more broadly taking issue with the systems of belief underlying these accusations and disputing the efficacy of exorcists' powers to dispossess the bewitched.

Darrel's 'career' as an exorcist extended over 20 years and in that time he attracted extensive literary attention from pamphleteers and polemicists and ultimately from Bancroft and Harsnet. Harsnet's energies extended to delving into Darrel's earlier cases, for instance extracting from Katherine Wright, exorcised some years earlier, a confession that she had faked her possession and thus discrediting Darrel's exorcism from the 1580s.[42] He also discounted the claims that the accused elderly women were really witches. For example, he stated that Margaret Roper, accused by Wright of bewitchment, was only a 'pretended witch'.[43] He even re-examined cases involving Darrel dating back to 1574 to adduce evidence of fraudulent practice.[44]

The cases Bancroft investigated occurred at a particularly sensitive time for the episcopate, and to conduct an exorcism in Tudor and Stuart England meant to become engaged in a complex relationship with ecclesiastical hierarchy. Historically, the position of exorcists in relation to diocesan structures was ambiguous and they were often unwelcome as bishops could resent the presence of exorcists or inquisitors in their jurisdictions. This was as much a problem in Europe as in England. Even the famed Heinrich Kramer (or Institoris), author of the *Malleus Maleficarum*, ran foul of Georg Golser, the Bishop of Innsbruck, and was eventually ordered to leave the town.[45] In England, bishops could also significantly complicate the actions of exorcists and challenge their credibility. Protestant exorcists, especially Darrel, engaged at length with the putative popish identity of the English episcopate. From the middle of the sixteenth century, a range of publications and agitators had protested against the ungodliness of bishops and the imparity of ministers within the Church of England.[46] Bancroft's predecessor at Canterbury, John Whitgift had proclaimed that the imparity of ministers and the superiority of bishops were instituted by God.[47] In making these points, Whitgift drew on earlier bishops, such as Thomas Thirlby, who had insisted on the sacramental significance of bishops, reminding contemporaries during the reign of Henry VIII that in terms of the Ordinal only a bishop could make a priest.[48] By the time Bancroft and Harsnet came to investigate the cases involving Darrel and other exorcists, their actions participated in a much wider process of debate and contestation in which bishops attempted to demarcate the scope of their powers and to neutralize anti-episcopal propaganda.

The evidence left by both Darrel and Harsnet (reporting on behalf of Bancroft) suggests that in cases of possession and exorcism, identity was central to disputes over bodily possession and church government. The identity of the demoniacs themselves as possessed persons, temporarily beyond the bounds of polite and godly conduct, was a defining feature of cases of possession throughout Europe, from sexually precocious nuns to Protestant children who swore at ministers during church services. English cases, such as the Throckmorton children in Warboys, show that those who claimed to be possessed exchanged one identity – the offspring of a godly household – for another – the raucous and foulmouthed victims of bewitchment.[49] But the claiming of identity was also central to those puritan ministers who took on the mantle of persons with the power to dispossess people from their demons, and who depicted bishops as ungodly. Exorcisms reveal themselves as sites of contested identity and the contestation over episcopal identity was one aspect of this. Challenging exorcisms was a means to counter this iteration of episcopal identity. In a world where polemicists contested the necessity and usefulness of bishops, and where polemical exchanges were intensely sharpened by decades of debate, bishops invoked a reformed identity that was complex in nature and subject to shifts in meaning and emphasis. The language of debate was confessionally charged, and turned upon disputed identities as Protestant or popish. According to Bancroft and Harsnet, it was popish to believe in 'anie Possession since Christs time'.[50] By labelling the Puritan Darrel popish, Bancroft and Harsnet turned on its head Darrel's anti-episcopal polemic which had portrayed bishops as agents of popish authority. For example, Thomas Darling, a Darrel supporter, had accused Bancroft of having 'made the way for Papistry'.[51] An anonymous tract written in defence of Darrel castigated bishops as being of 'ye Romish synagogue'.[52] Cases of exorcism permitted this inversion. Darrel realized the intention, stating that his opponents sought to discredit him through speaking 'at randome of Poperie'.[53] Contests over the meaning of reformed episcopacy and the extent and necessity of their powers took place in a variety of ways, including debate at court and in parliament, through the exchange of polemical texts and through arguments over exorcisms. However, they commonly turned on this issue of identity.

The detail of Darrel's encounters with Bancroft illuminates broader realities of contestations over the identity of episcopacy. Hitherto scholars have noted that Darrel's exorcisms brought him to the notice of and into conflict with the members of the episcopate. Walker acknowledges that Darrel's treatment by Bancroft was part of a broader anti-puritan campaign that Elizabethan and Jacobean bishops were conducting.[54] However, these points tend only to be noted in passing by scholars, as part of broader surveys of the cultural history of exorcisms, when in fact the point can be more cogently argued. Darrel's exorcisms took place in a period when the godly argued that English bishops were agents of the Devil.[55]

Samuel Clarke, the martyrologist and biographer of puritan divines whom we encountered earlier, saw the Devil at work in his episcopal-led prosecution for nonconformity in 1627, whereby the Devil raised up 'instruments' against him, in this case in the ecclesiastical infrastructure of a bishop's court.[56]

Darrel experienced the same episcopal censure as Clarke. Darrel himself narrated the circumstances of the Will Somers case, explaining in the justificatory tract from 1599 *A Brief Apologie Proving the Possession of William Sommers* that Somers confessed to the Bishop of London that both his symptoms and his accusations had been false.[57] A concomitant of Somers's *volte face* was to expose Darrel as a fake exorcist who had presided over a fake exorcism. Darrel's treatment by the Church hierarchy was thought of in highly personal terms by Darrel's supporters, who argued Bancroft had a violently personal antipathy towards Darrel. Darrel's own *Apologie* reports his belief that he had incurred Bancroft's displeasure. The text is in fact structured as a series of anti-episcopal arguments, presenting a counter-case to the arguments that Somers had faked his possession; for instance, Darrel insisted on Somers's preternatural strength and the appearance of a strange moving lump on his body against Bancroft's attempts to rationalize these events.[58]

There is a further division apparent in the text, as Darrel repeatedly positions himself as counterposed against the Bishop of London, and the value of his text to analysis of episcopal authority is how Darrel constructs his narrative as case of episcopal opposition to godly ministry. Importantly, the impression of the episcopate ranged against Darrel is reinforced by other apologetical texts. The *Triall of Maist. Dorrell* from 1599 positions Bancroft not only as an investigator of the exorcisms, but also as exhibiting a specific antipathy towards Darrel, for example, raising the highly embarrassing point that one aspect of Darrel's methodology for exorcizing Katherine Wright had been to lie down on top of her, a point that left even Darrel's sympathizers scrambling to find cogent reasons for this unusual method of dispossession.[59] These texts are shot through with reference to the 'L.B of London' and his energies in bringing Darrel into disrepute. Darrel proclaimed his own status as a member of the godly ministry, placing himself in the company of 'M. *Hildersham*, M. *More*, and M. *Brincesley*, all godly preachers, and some of them of great renowne for learning'.[60] This company of godly clergy stood in diametric opposition to 'the Bish. of Lond'.[61] Defences written for Darrel placed him in the company of the godly, proclaiming him to be 'a godlie, and faithfull man' who was among 'the best Christians'.[62]

Throughout the *Apologie* the Bishop of London appears as a repressive force, extracting confessions of counterfeit possession from Somers, who had 'bin examined vpon their othes by the aforenamed Bish'.[63] Bancroft is also an investigating agent, for instance re-examining Darrel's earlier exorcisms of young people in Ashby-de-la-Zouche in Leicestershire,[64] where Darrel was among sympathetic co-religionists, as the gentry there were strongly Protestant.[65] Once Darrel had been brought to London, Bancroft initiated an intensive investigation, using Harsnet as an investigator to interrogate earlier subjects of Darrel's dispossessions and leading the work of the High Commission in London himself.[66]

The language of the competing tracts is charged with confessional meaning. In his apologetical tract, Darrel positions himself in opposition to Bancroft and the Commission, commenting that in publishing his apology, he is bracing himself for the accusation that 'I goe about to raise mutinies among ye Queenes subjects, or to discredit the Ecclesiastical state, or hir Majesties commission for ecclesiastical causes'.[67] Darrel wrote of the powers of that Commission in a highly charged way. According to Darrel, Bancroft and Harsnet were 'our two English inquisitors', thus linking them polemically to the continental and Catholic inquisitions.[68] His comment is the result of the doubtless unpleasantly intense questioning to which both men subjected him, but its import is wide-ranging. In making this association, Darrel identified bishops, in this case Bishop Bancroft specifically, as forces of ungodly authority. His comment is explained by surrounding discourses of authority which denied bishops an identity as agents of godly authority and instead located them among the ungodly and popish.[69] This point resonates through much anti-episcopal polemic in the seventeenth century, for example, the puritan polemicist William Prynne's assertion that episcopacy and its instruments of justice were inquisitorial.[70]

While Darrel's apologetical tract makes direct reference to bishops and to Bancroft's opposition to his exorcisms, his discussion of authority goes beyond this strictly institutional level to a deeper evaluation of authority. Darrel insists on the supernatural evidence of the possessions, referring to, for instance, the appearance of the Devil in the shape of a black dog,[71] of a 'thing like a rat', or the effusion of blood out of the possessed person's mouth.[72] But it also clearly mattered to Darrel that other people believed him. For example, in the Somers case, he referred not only to the great crowds who apparently saw the blood spurt or strange creatures scuttle around, but also to witnesses who included the commissioners themselves, who apparently saw 'the divers fits he [Somers] had'.[73] Elsewhere he placed himself among the company of not only the godly, but the socially exalted as well, noting that he acted at the request of the Mayor and aldermen of Nottingham.[74] Most significantly of all, he attempted to turn the authority and the judgments of the episcopate against itself, insisting that a commission assembled by the 'arch B of Yorke' had respected his actions.[75]

Writings by and in support of Darrel contributed to a fractious exchange of tracts between those sympathetic to Darrel and those who sought to discredit him. The most substantial contribution was Harsnet's, who at the behest of Bancroft wrote the *Discovery of the Fraudulent Practices of John Darrel*, which came out in 1599. Over 300 pages in length, Harsnet's tract systematically assembled evidence to discredit Darrel's exorcisms, not only of Somers, but of earlier cases in the Midlands such as Katherine Wright's. Extensively researched – he quoted at length from tracts sympathetic to Darrel in order to fill in the major contours of the narrative of Darrel's career – the tract also showcases Harsnet's abilities as an investigator. Original witnesses were dragged out to re-testify and Harsnet adduced confessions of fraudulent practices from decades earlier. But the text also makes clear that Harsnet was an investigator working for the episcopate. The tract, especially its opening chapters, is shot through with reference to bishops and their authority, and it is clear that Harsnet read the exorcisms as cases promoting the expression of anti-episcopal sentiments.

The setting of the action for Harsnet's tract is Lambeth Palace, where the High Commission sat in order to call Darrel's practices into question. The bishops sitting there also appear in Harsnet's work as instruments for uncovering the truth[76] and for seeking rational explanations for apparently preternatural events.[77] Other sources suggest Bancroft's centrality in these proceedings; a tract in defence of Darrel quoted Bancroft's more challenging questions, such as his demand that Darrel produce scriptural evidence to support his actions.[78] From the outset, Darrel appears in Harsnet's narrative as an opponent not of the Devil, but of lawful authority. He is thus introduced as 'no minister'.[79] He also operates 'unskilfully'.[80] Writings sympathetic to Darrel endorse this emphasis, implying that Darrel was singled out for punishment and suggesting his role in the proceedings as a victim of episcopal investigation.[81] Much of Harsnet's text is overtly sarcastic in its approach to Darrel's exorcisms, for instance pithily describing Somers as having been 'possessed, dispossessed, and repossessed'.[82] The sharpness of his text is possibly one factor that may have led later readers to infer that Harsnet was sceptical about diabolic intervention in the world. However, Harsnet took the application of authority very seriously. Exorcisms were not concerning because they suggested that the Devil was intervening in the affairs of humans, but because they were sites of disorder. For the 'pulpits also rang of nothing but Devils, and witches' after Darrel had conducted an exorcism and disorder followed in his wake.[83]

Contrasted with this disorder were the bishops of the Church. Agents of order, and equipped with the power to condemn Darrel as counterfeit, bishops appear in the *Discovery* as existing in tension with Darrel. Because Harsnet cited so extensively from tracts sympathetic to Darrel, much anti-episcopal commentary runs through his tract. Accordingly he repeated (but clearly disagreed with) the idea that bishops have given '*gentle audience to Papists, Arrians, Atheistes, and Blasphemers*' but who '*wold not permit M. Darrell to speak anie thing almost in his own defence*'.[84] The idea expressed here of episcopal severity is generalized. What is important is that, according to Harsnet, both Darrel and those who wrote in his defence were calling into question the very validity of episcopacy. Thus, he recorded from a treatise in favour of Darrel that the question was asked '*Whether a Bishop and Elder be all one in Scriptures*'.[85]

It is significant that this question was raised again in a tract about the punishment of an exorcist by the Bishop of London, and which was written in the midst of this long-standing disagreement over the range of episcopal authority. Darrel's sympathizers constructed accounts of his acts and of his punishment which were intended to exclude bishops from the line of godly ministry, questioning not only the imparity of ministers (hence the question about bishops and elders) but also the identity of bishops as Protestants. According to one (again quoted by Harsnet in order to refute it), it was the case that '*the faith of the Church established under the Pastors and Teachers etc shall bring forth this fruit: namely to cast out Devils*'.[86] Understood on these terms, division was proposed between the godly exorcists who continued the work of early Christians in conducting exorcisms and the bishops who denied the efficacy of exorcisms and who thus excluded themselves from these godly linkages.

The importance of this point to Harsnet is suggested by the sustained attention which he gave it. Reading the tracts of episcopal opponents, Harsnet encountered substantial discussion of episcopacy, including the assertion that contemporary bishops were dislocated from the godly order of the apostolic age, or the period of '*Apostles* and *Disciples*', when bishops had allowed exorcisms to take place.[87] For Darrel's supporters, different attitudes now prevailed, with bishops functioning as the suppressors of exorcists and therefore placing themselves beyond the ranks of what one of Darrel's sympathizers called the 'many scores' of the godly, who outnumbered Bancroft and who testified to the authenticity of Darrel's work.[88]

These arguments directly intersect with many decades of anti-episcopal polemic. Because he incurred the displeasure of Bancroft, Darrel in many ways found himself swept up into a different level of argument that went beyond the fact of his exorcisms. By disputing the reality of these exorcisms, Harsnet was also pushing against the idea propounded in texts sympathetic to puritan exorcists that bishops were beyond the fold of the godly. Instead he inverted these claims, arguing that the ability to exorcise could not be a hallmark of godliness and excluded Darrel from the ranks of the godly ministry.

Conclusion

Exorcisms were occasions where Bancroft and his chaplain actively clashed with self-proclaimed godly exorcists who viewed bishops themselves as agents of the devil. Bancroft became involved in these cases because they allowed for propaganda against the episcopate to be disseminated, and it was important for the reputations of the exorcists to be disputed. Within Bancroft's approach to investigation lay a strongly consistent rhetorical strategy, intended to elevate the authority of the episcopate at the expense of the puritan ministers involved. In this way, these cases of possession move beyond the history of witchcraft as they participated in broader contestations of the period concerning church government and the extent to which the English Reformation had developed. Disputing the efficacy of puritan exorcisms was an opportunity for Bancroft to claim against the godliness of the ministers, and to neutralize propaganda which suggested bishops stood among the ranks of the ungodly by virtue of their actions against exorcists.

Exorcisms were also events when identities were in flux and indeed at stake. As a godly child turned into a foul-mouthed demoniac, so too did exorcists take the opportunity to play with identity. An exorcist such as Darrel proclaimed his self-generated identity as one of the godly. The aftermaths of exorcisms were opportunities to reignite arguments about the ungodliness of bishops. These contestations emerge from a context where episcopacy and the powers of bishops had been challenged for a number of decades. It is not so much the case that exorcists began to complain about bishops after their exorcisms, but rather that bishops became involved because the exorcisms were inherently anti-episcopal, taking place in parts of England known as the abode of the godly and promoting propaganda unfavourable to bishops.

Bancroft was dead by 1610, and he was therefore not alive to worry about the spike in witchcraft accusations that accompanied the worsening relations between monarchy and parliament as the kingdom of England moved down the path to civil war. By then his place at Lambeth had been taken by Archbishop William Laud. Bancroft would doubtless have been surprised by Laud's position. Here was not an archbishop intervening in criminal cases, but in the dock and subject to the law. Laud would find himself on trial for the full spectrum of his career in the Church, from the time of Bancroft up to his fall from power in 1640. By then, bishops were no longer able to intervene in trials of witches; the episcopate was on trial instead.

4
Reformed Episcopacy Under Pressure

Introduction

We have so far seen that a recurrent preoccupation of sixteenth- and seventeenth-century episcopal writers was to neutralize claims that the episcopate was popish and to substitute an alternative identity for bishops as agents of reform. Many factors animated this preoccupation and one of the important players was William Laud (Archbishop of Canterbury, 1633–45) who was a polemical target accused of innovation and deviation from godly Protestant precedents. Attacks on Laud extended far beyond written or spoken polemic: he was arrested, tried by Parliament, attainted and executed for treason. The focus of this chapter is not so much Laud himself, but a wider body of thought which developed around him, prompted by the exceptional pressures against episcopacy in this period. Laud advanced a self-conception of his archiepiscopate that was at once personal and wide-ranging. While defending himself from personal attack, he used the example of his predecessors to argue that episcopacy in general adhered to benchmarks of reformed authority.

By 1645, Laud was dead and his palace in Lambeth had been sacked and converted to a prison. He was not the only bishop to suffer during the 1640s; for example, Matthew Wren of Ely (1585–1667) was imprisoned and other bishops lost revenues and status and were exiled from their cathedral cities. These lethal circumstances strongly indicate the disfavour in which bishops were held, and Laud's administration of the Church is more easily tested through the writings of his detractors than those of his admirers. Much recent research into Laud has concentrated on what his opponents had to say about him and the clergy associated with him. Laud's detractors contributed to a representation widely reflected in modern scholarship, of Laud the Laudian or of Laud the Arminian. Either label indicates his innovations in religious doctrine and liturgy and his reaction in various spheres of influence (including as college president in

Oxford and as dean, bishop and archbishop) against austere Calvinist doctrine and worship. Modern scholarly interpretations of the Caroline Church and the Civil Wars have painstakingly reconstructed the ecclesiastical characteristics and priorities of 'Laudianism' and 'Arminianism'.[1] The terms are not cognate, but neither are they precise. Laudianism is an impressionistic label, anti-Laud in import, based on reactions to church practices such as music, vestments or the positioning of holy tables in chancels so that they resembled pre-Reformation altars. Arminianism suggests that Laud and a large body of clergy associated with him were both adopting an anti-Calvinist theological position This latter title is both misleading and confusing, in that Laud's policies or churchmanship were by no means modelled on those of the seventeenth-century Dutch theologian Jacob Arminius.[2]

The concept of 'Laudianism' is equally unhelpful to understanding the Church in this period, serving to strongly personalize the Church of England and to suggest that the religious policy of the period was solely Laud's creation. More recently, research into the Church of England before the Civil Wars has taken note of these limitations, shifting responsibility for the intellectual cohesion of English Arminianism or Laudianism from Laud to King Charles I or to other clergy including John Cosin (1594–1672), Matthew Wren and Lancelot Andrewes (1555–1626), all bishops who emerged after Bancroft's death in 1610.[3] These points provide a useful reminder that even considerations of Laudianism should not imply a singular focus on Laud himself but rather on a broader set of surroundings and personalities.

In this chapter, I build upon this emerging scholarly approach to examine both Laud and his associated clergy in a much more general way than has been usual in assessments of the Caroline Church which fixate on Laud. I argue that the works of Peter Heylyn (1600–1662), Laud's chaplain, John Cosin, a clergyman linked with Laud in much polemical literature, and Christopher Dow (dates unknown), a pro-Laud apologist, as well as the accounts of Laud's trial preserved in Laud's diary reveal an aspect of the seventeenth-century Church hitherto largely ignored in modern scholarship: Laud's attempts to portray himself as a reformed bishop.

I will study evidence which while meaningful to Laud's personal story also directs attention to themes of more general significance. I first survey the modern historiography on Laud, challenging modern preoccupations with Laud as an Arminian or a Laudian and instead I situate him in a broader and older setting of pamphlet attacks on the episcopate. I secondly examine what Laud and his supporters said about bishops, first in works from the late 1630s when the episcopate was ascendant and then during the time of his arrest and trial in the 1640s. I particularly study one event from his trial, where the evidence turned on the decoration of episcopal chapels and Laud built up a defence based on the conduct of the 'zealous' Archbishop Cranmer. In his defence, Laud protested that a reforming archbishop matched his own intentions and actions. The chapel in question was Laud's, but this evidence directs attention to a much wider world, as other clergy of this period were accused of the same offence: innovation away from the Reformation, as evidenced by putatively Romanist practices such as the installation of religious art. Bishops in Oxford, Durham, Winchester and elsewhere stood accused of innovation.

An episcopal chapel does not make a case for a reformed episcopate, but Laud's defence indicates where two much broader themes of the period converge. Laud appealed as one bishop to another bishop, Cranmer. But he did so in response to broader currents of polemical thought. First, Laud worked, wrote and was condemned to death after many decades of argument that the English Reformation was incomplete, and that bishops were a major manifestation of this inadequacy. Laud was subject to criticism as a bishop on these terms as other contemporary and earlier bishops had been. Laud's opponents beheld the Reformation not as a fixed point in time, but as a yet-incomplete process. However, a second and at times contradictory theme is also apparent in what was written against Laud: that earlier episcopal reformers conveyed to posterity a set of precedents and that Laud was guilty of innovation away from these precedents. As such, reform could be both mutable and immutable and in both guises served as a stick to beat the episcopate.

The accusation that Laud had innovated against and diverged from the heritage of the Reformation is a central issue accounting for attacks against the episcopacy during Charles's reign. While earlier bishops and the episcopate in general endured criticism as showing the inadequacy of the English Reformation, Laud's putative innovations meant that attacks against the episcopate became sharply personal, as he seemed to be not only holding an unreformed office but also actively taking the Church of England to Rome.

In his writings, Laud reacted to both presentations of reform, as incomplete and as providing timeless standards of reformed religiosity. His works are of broader significance beyond his immediate circumstances and personal history, for the issue of innovation was part of wider political currents of the 1630s and 1640s when the episcopate in general stood accused of innovation. Laud picked up on the implications of these contrasting impressions of reform, arguing in his defence that reforming bishops were capable of disagreement with each other and that he could locate precedents which vitiated any sense that the Church under his leadership was guilty of innovation.

Laud among the bishops

While I place Laud in a broader setting of the Church and political life of his period, I am also alert to the fact that during his archiepiscopate attacks against episcopacy came to focus singularly on Laud and he was a conspicuously unpopular figure. At the same time, study of Laud directs attention to a broader body of anti-episcopal writings, which focused on Laud but which also transmitted the impression of Laud as one popish bishop among a host of other popish bishops. The nature of the attacks against the popishness of bishops exhibited a new sense of urgency and peril. The attacks also expressed a greater sense of alarm; strong rumours that Laud had been offered a cardinal's hat suggest greater and more immediate peril to the Church of England than the more nebulous claims that Whitgift or Bancroft, among others, leaned towards the papacy.

Allegations of the popish leanings of individual bishops and the general popishness of the episcopate were intended to undercut and weaken episcopal authority. Bishops were responsive to these claims. Important seventeenth-century commentaries by Laud and his satellite clergy show they defended episcopal office by delineating the reformed identity of English episcopacy. Justification for the actions of Laud and his fellow bishops came from earlier reformers.[4] An insight into this strategy in fact comes from Laud's opponents. William Prynne (1600–1669), a lawyer and controversialist who wrote much against Laud, reported that in publishing his *Book of Devotions*, John Cosin, a clergyman associated by his contemporaries and subsequently by modern scholars with Laud's liturgical policies, endeavoured 'to make Queene Elizabeth of *euer blessed Memorie*, the Patronesse of this his Poperie; and to harbour it vnder her Protection'.[5] A specific instance demonstrates the nature of Cosin's alleged 'Poperie'. Peter Smart, the senior prebendary of Durham Cathedral, left a record of his impressions of the innovations introduced by John Cosin in the late 1620s. At that time, Cosin was the junior of the ten cathedral prebends, and his changes to the worship in the cathedral were literally not music to Smart's ears. Complaining in a sermon of 1628 of the noise created by the Sackbuts and

Cornetts played during the Sunday morning services, which made 'an hydeous noyse', Smart showed that not only was the noise of these instruments unfamiliar to him and their use in worship unprecedented at Durham Cathedral, but also more significantly, that in encouraging their use, Cosin was deviating from the established reformed customs of the Church of England.[6] Prynne used the term 'cozening' to describe Cosin's apparently unProtestant prayer rituals, the implementation of which distinguished his time as a prebendary and then as a dean of Peterborough Cathedral.[7] Prynne was therefore using a term which had contemporary currency as signifying preternatural as well as deceitful actions.[8] Prynne re-iterated his complaint in the same text, arguing that 'our Religious and renowned Queene *Elizabeth* [sic]' was '*Prophaned*' by Cosin's citation of her patronage.[9] According to Prynne, Cosin's text 'stinkes of Poperies', but his popish tendencies were rendered worse as the memory of the Tudor queen was used to give a Protestant authority to the text.[10] Prynne was alert to and objected to Cosin locating Protestant underpinnings for his Church.[11] Again, in Prynne's writings the reform could be both mutable and immutable. Cosin personally represented practices that showed that English reform was insufficiently developed and which further reform would eradicate. Yet Cosin also stood accused of innovation from reformed precedents and in this case the Reformation was understood as both requiring development and offering unchanging precedents.

Laud's expression of the reformed precedents of his office must be placed in this atmosphere and in a particular setting: the destruction of the English episcopacy; the abolition of the English bishoprics and cathedral foundations by the Long Parliament in 1646; and the arrest or exile from their cathedral cities of individual bishops.[12] The function and necessity of bishops was sharply questioned throughout this period. The parliamentarian Sir Thomas Aston (1600–1645) compiled a diary of proceedings in the Short Parliament in the early 1640s. He reported questions in parliament which proposed alternatives to episcopal control and oversight, such as the proposal for 'The making & inioyning of the Articles at vizitations without any authority then the Bishops of the Diocese'.[13] This parliamentary debate reveals the authority of bishops as being supplanted and dismantled. More explicitly the Grand Remonstrance of 1641 called for the destruction of the episcopate, an aim accomplished by the Long Parliament by 1646. Laud's execution in 1645 was carried by the same momentum that resulted not only in the death of an archbishop but also in the destruction of the entire episcopate which collapsed under the weight of this odium.[14]

Archbishop Laud and the episcopate: Arminianism and Laudianism

After sustained attacks throughout the sixteenth and seventeenth centuries, the Church of England and its episcopate had been brought to a state of ruin. Laud's arrest, trial and execution were a part of this ruination. The attorneys prosecuting Laud in 1644 used textual evidence from his diary against him.[15] Since then scholars have reconstructed this work from the malicious editing of William Prynne, but the diary is still used by many scholars to portray Laud as variously inept, full of superstitious dread, vindictive or unaware of the resentment that his ecclesiastical policies caused among members of the English Church.[16] His correspondence with Lord Strafford, when the latter was Lord Deputy in Ireland, has been used for a similar purpose, especially the exultant tone Laud assumed when complimenting the Lord Deputy on his suppression of Protestant non-conformity in Ireland.[17]

Historians have inscribed the practices recorded in Laud's diary within a precise framework. Modern scholarly accounts of the Caroline Church and the Civil Wars have painstakingly reconstructed the ecclesiastical characteristics and priorities of 'Laudianism' and 'Arminianism'. Not only William Laud, but also Bishop Lancelot Andrewes (Bishop of Winchester 1619–26), John Cosin and his book of devotions, and a host of lesser clergy including John Buckeridge and Peter Heylyn fill out the modern scholarly reconstruction of Arminian clergy and their attendant innovations and affronts to English Protestantism. While Hugh Trevor-Roper condemned Laud as an uninspired plodder and an unoriginal thinker, contemporary responses to his archiepiscopate, or earlier to his tenures as Dean of Gloucester and successively Bishop of St David's, Bath and Wells and London, make clear that some of his actions at least seemed startlingly original to contemporary observers.[18] These included not only his introduction of more elaborate ceremonial and his stance on doctrines of salvation, but also his insistence on the status and superiority of episcopal office.[19]

Much of the evidence adduced by modern scholars for the existence and priorities of the Laudian Church in fact comes from Laud's detractors, such as arguments made by non-conformist clerics and laymen such as Henry Burton (1578–1648) or Prynne.[20] The impression they convey of Laud and his ecclesial priorities have often dominated modern scholarly accounts of the Church in the lead up to the Civil Wars.[21] As Kevin Sharpe points out, William Prynne still commands a wide and sympathetic readership.[22]

Certainly the terminology and characteristics of practices labelled as Arminian and condemned by Prynne, Burton and others were discernibly in use early in the seventeenth century. As early as 1628 the House of Commons had warned Charles I that 'Arminianism' and popery threatened the Church of England, a warning Charles chose to ignore and certainly disagreed with.[23] Prynne also used the term to describe the theology of Laud's chaplain, Dr Martin, who 'preached Arminianism at S. Paul's Cross'.[24] Long after Laud's execution the label 'Arminian' remained current; as late as 1691 the millenarian clergyman John Mason used it as a term with implications of falseness and corruptions and as shorthand for Roman Catholicism.[25] Caroline controversialists, writing in the lead up to the first Civil War, had criticized Laud for leading the Church of England away from reformed precedents and an association arose between Laud and Catholicism.[26] I. M. Green characterizes the allegations made about Laud and his satellite clergy as being preoccupied with 'English Popery'.[27] The activities which Green sees as English Popery' characterize for him the liturgical priorities of the Laudian Church, manifested in works such as John Cosin's *Book of Devotions*[28] or the construction and consecration of pseudo-medieval churches such as St Katherine Cree or the chapel of Lincoln's Inn and the restoration of St Paul's Cathedral.[29]

Over the last two decades, a scholarly point has been debated which perceives the seventeenth-century episcopate as dominated by Arminianism or Laudianism and therefore in conflict with Calvinist clergy and doctrines. The notion of there being 'anti-Calvinists', a terminology which belongs to the influential work of Nicholas Tyacke, immediately draws attention to contestation between bishops and their Calvinist opponents. Modern surveys of the seventeenth-century Church have charted the re-orientation of the episcopal hierarchy along Arminian lines and the subsequent conflict between bishops and puritans.[30] Tyacke uses the term 'Arminian' to refer to a body of beliefs that rejected Calvinist theology. Laudian may also be understood in its opposition to the Calvinist orthodoxy of the Church of England, although the term may be used with more precision to reflect the more elaborate vestments, music and liturgy which Laud favoured. The terminology used to describe doctrinal groupings within the English Church has been refined in recent years. Collinson has used the term 'Calvinist' to bring greater precision to understandings of the post-Reformation Church than the labels associated with Puritanism which he has previously used.[31] Tyacke similarly argues that the beliefs concerning salvation articulated by Laud rejected the Calvinist beliefs but that many bishops found themselves in disagreement with Laud.[32] Tyacke expressed his view in his monograph *Anti-Calvinists*. As his title suggests, Tyacke conceives of Laud and his beliefs by means of a negative definition, in that Tyacke demonstrates how they differed from the Calvinist orthodoxy of the Church.[33]

Modern accounts of Laud

Modern scholarly contestations over the Caroline Church, especially those between Tyacke and Peter White, have been preoccupied with Laud's Arminianism. These scholars differ markedly in their interpretations of Arminianism; Tyacke indicates its innovative and affronting elements while White argues for the mainstream acceptance of Arminianism. Both fixate on Laud the Arminian.[34] There are two contrasting points here. First, Arminianism is too narrow a term; prelates like John Williams of Lincoln followed liturgical practices which seem to have conformed to Arminian principles, such as installing stained glass windows in churches and using organs and elaborate choral music.[35] Yet Williams was not an Arminian and was more often found in contestation with Laud than falling into line as a Laudian or Arminian bishop.[36] Williams's own liturgical policies seem Arminian, but cannot be by the estimate of modern scholars who see Laud as Arminian and Williams as his opponent. Second, it can be argued that contemporary reactions to Archbishop Laud do not so much stress his Arminianism but focus on him as simply as a member of the episcopate and fail to differentiate him on any other terms.

Laud the Arminian or even Laud the Laudian has obscured Laud the bishop from modern historians' eyes. Recent scholarly explorations of the Caroline period have considerably complicated ideas of Laud as the architect of Arminian theology. Both Kevin Sharpe and Julian Davies argue that Charles I, rather than Laud, inspired and enforced the liturgical and devotional changes which are thought of as Laudian, including enclosing altars with rails.[37] James Turrell's study of doctrines concerning confirmation has led him to conclude that some clergy were more Laudian than Laud himself. His study valuably points out that viewing Laud as 'Laudian' has significant methodological drawbacks for interpreting his own policies and thoughts.[38] The ideas of these historians liberate Laud from many older ideas of his Laudianism or Arminianism; instead they leave the way clear for the study of Laud the bishop, as an example of episcopacy under attack.

Laud and the bishops: Episcopacy under attack

Peter Heylyn's apologetical works in defence of Laud indicate that Laud can be liberated from modern scholarly constructs of Arminianism or Laudianism, instead showing that Laud's episcopal office preoccupied his contemporaries. He quoted from the 'Proclamation, and Declarations against all innovations of religion', which declared that 'They [bishops] are dangerous innovation, hinderers of the Gospell, opperesers of his Majesties lawes'.[39] According to the work refuted by Heylyn, who was Laud's chaplain, Laud and his colleagues were condemned simply for the fact of their episcopal office.

Laud himself indicated the nature of allegations made against him. During the period of his ascendancy, he spoke in 1637 in the Star Chamber over which he presided. He complained that he and his supporters had been the recipients of abuse from radical Protestants. He bemoaned the fact that he and his brethren 'have been very coarsely used by the Tongues and pennes of these men'.[40] Importantly, Laud asserted that these criticisms extended to the episcopate, for the chief crime of which he and his brethren were accused was that 'they are bishops'.[41] At the censure of Prynne, Bastwick and Burton in 1637, Laud complained that 'Our main crime [in Prynne, Burton and Bastwick's view] is that we are bishops'.[42] Laud expanded on the implications of this comment, alluding to the widely held fear that the episcopacy was a bridgehead for the reintroduction of popery into England. He referred to the claim by the dissenting writer Henry Burton of the existence of 'Dangerous plots' to 'change the orthodox religion and bring in popery'.[43]

It is also worth remembering that the entire order of bishops, not only Arminian or Laudian bishops, came under both physical and verbal attacks in both the Short and Long Parliaments. In December 1640, Sir Harbottle Grimston led an attack in the House of Commons against the episcopate.[44] An anti-episcopal mob perceived Bishop Williams, while an opponent of Laud, to be sufficiently odious to attack him in the street, rip his clothes and besiege him in the deanery of Westminster Abbey.[45] In 1641, Lord Falkland urged on parliamentarians the point that 'bishops may bee good men.' James Ussher, an opponent of Catholicism, a moderate Calvinist, and, coming from Ireland, untainted by the innovations of the English episcopate, was living proof that some bishops could be good men.[46] However, Falkland's comment indicated that a search for a good man among the English bishops took place among all English bishops, not simply a Laudian subgroup, a point stressed by the only available instance coming from Ireland. His point was polemic, as some bishops like Ralph Brownrigg enjoyed good relations with parliamentarians. Nonetheless, Falkland returns attention to the general traducement of the episcopal order, rather than any specifically Arminian bishops. The order of bishops was entirely abolished by 1646, a circumstance which draws attention to Laud the bishop, rather than Laud the Arminian or Laud the opponent of other bishops such as Williams. Any distinctions which Laud's contemporaries drew between bishops related more to their personal qualities than any liturgical distinctions between Laudian bishops and other bishops.

Although Laud ascribed a general feeling of opprobrium to all bishops, not simply those closely associated with him, certain bishops were in fact regarded more positively by Laud's opponents.[47] The Westminster Assembly of Divines even invited a number of bishops to attend its sessions, contrary to Laud's sense of there being a blanket denunciation of the episcopate.[48] But the significance of Laud's assessment of the reputations of all bishops is that it clearly demonstrates his thoughts on episcopacy. Laud rhetorically placed himself in the midst of an order which he insisted incurred general displeasure.

Words put into Laud's mouth also made this point. In 1641, a fraudulent document, which purported to be correspondence between the politician Lord Finch and John Cosin, later the Bishop of Durham but then the Vice-Chancellor of Cambridge and the Dean of Peterborough, traduced English episcopacy. The document attacked the English episcopate, but not for being Arminian or Laudian.[49] The fraudulent correspondence between Lord Finch and Cosin contained by then familiar points of innovation against Protestantism, such as Cosin 'letting me kisse the Virgin Maryes Picture and the Popes head'.[50] But while the controversial ceremonies, church furnishings and musical instruments that form part of the modern reconstruction of Arminian worship were all alluded to in this text, it condemned Laud for introducing these innovations not as an Arminian, but as a bishop contributing to the dominance of universal episcopacy.[51]

Three works in particular further illustrate the nature of the charges against Laud and the legitimacy of the reformed episcopacy which he beheld in his own office. One is Peter Heylyn's *A Briefe Answer to the Challenges of H.B.*, the 'H.B.' being Henry Burton. As Heylyn reported it, the burden of Burton's dissent from the Church of England lay with the bishops' alleged efforts to introduce popery to England and Heylyn's work was a point-by-point defence of the episcopate in general. His work reflected a strategy which would be seen also in Laud's defence at his trial, matching precise detail with detail. So Heylyn shifted responsibility from the bishops to the late King James for the proscription of some of Calvin's writings, dealing in detail with the works themselves and the precise circumstances of their proscription.[52] Heylyn also dealt with an old issue that would not go away, the apparently popish Book of Devotions which belonged to John Cosin.[53]

The second is a summary of the complaints made against the episcopate which is found in Henry Walker's 1641 polemic *The Prelates Pride*, which enumerated the complaints against the established Church which Heylyn iterated. There are few original features of this work, which re-stated well-trod complaints against the episcopate. Walker's principal cause of contention was the fact that Laud was a bishop. As Walker saw it, the episcopate was an agent for promoting the power of 'the chaire of Rome'.[54] Walker did exhibit some originality in his analysis of the episcopate. He repeated the call, by then familiar, that the Scriptures made no allowance for government by bishops and instead authorized presbytery, but unusually among his contemporaries he did not call for the abolition of the episcopate.[55] Instead it was his perception that English bishops were caught between two churches, England and Rome, and needed to make a choice between the two. It is striking that Walker's text indicated the capacity of English bishops to choose reform, raising a point which Laud would echo.

The third work, a remarkable series of documents known as 'Rome's Masterpeece', amplified Walker's thesis.[56] 'Rome's Masterpeece' reads as a farrago of conspiratorial hysteria only exceeded by Titus Oates's Popish Plot some forty years later. The text is a concatenation of several fraudulent sources, chiefly the letters of the Privy Counsellor Sir William Boswell, works from Laud's pen and marginal addenda allegedly by Charles I himself. These documents purported to outline the discovery of a master plan on the part of Jesuit priests to effect religious revolution in England. 'Rome's Masterpeece' traduced the English episcopate in general by claiming that it served as an agency for papal infiltration. The author or authors of 'Masterpeece' made an original contribution to this idea, bringing the families of the bishops into the realm of this accusation. In one section of 'Masterpeece', the textual and marginal comments together united to stress the danger not only of bishops but of bishops' sons. The text described Sir Tobie Matthew, the recusant son of Dr Toby Matthew, the Archbishop of York, as 'noxious'. The marginal comment made this point more explicit, for just as vicar's children traditionally have an unfavourable reputation, the marginal addenda points out that bishops' sons are 'ofttimes the pope's greatest agents'.[57]

'Rome's Masterpeece' offered more explicit condemnations of bishops in general. One of the worst criticisms made of Laud and the King was their dithering inactivity. On the question of converting to Rome, the King's mind was 'pendulous', while Laud allegedly equivocated when offered a cardinal's hat.[58] The letters purportedly by Laud discussed the temptation of the cardinalate at length.[59] The presentation of Laud is clear and damning: the offer of a cardinal's hat tempted him and he only disclaimed it conditionally.[60] The text stressed further evidence of Laud's papal sympathies. The Scottish Prayer Book was said to smell 'very strongly of popery', for its Eucharistic theology implied the corporal presence in the Sacrament.[61] Laud's authentic writings from this period included reflections on textual material, repeating the accusation for instance that he was associated with the publication and sale of a Bible which had a 'popish table' (meaning a genealogy) at the end of it.[62]

These ideas continued to appear in print during the period of Laud's arrest and trial. In 1643, a *Confession* was published which purported to be a letter from Laud to the Pope, in which Laud abjectly apologized for failing to introduce popery to England. The *Confession* covered every aspect of 'Laudian worship' as understood by modern scholars, essentially a checklist of the typical apparatus, including such items as ritual and the use of musical instruments in worship. Thus, Laud had 'introduced something of the Roman Religion: and I brought in Ceremonies . . . besides Organs were heard in every Church on Sundayes.' But the document is significant for the words it placed in Laud's mouth pertaining to 'us bishops'; the anonymous author was preoccupied with Laud not as an Arminian or a crypto-papist, but simply one bishop among 'us bishops'.[63] This author conceived of the papacy as 'Vniversall Episcopacy'; while he therefore indicated the domination of one particular bishop, the English episcopate was inevitably complicit in this ecclesiastical order.[64] Laud operated against the King, Parliament and English Protestantism in concert with 'my other fellow Bishops'. Laud also 'confessed' to undermining Protestantism, but only of having the power to do so 'when I was firmly seated in the Episcopal dignity'.[65] Laud's putative *Confession* appeared in 1643. The following year the equally fraudulent *The Last Advice of William Laud, late Arch-Bishop, to his Episcopal Brethren* appeared. Laud's purported work reflected a similar argument about episcopacy, and the work indicates the continued agitation and activity against Laud after his fall from power. The text observed of the episcopate in general 'I feare Heaven and Earth have combined against us all', meaning the bishops the general.[66] Laud was notably preoccupied with portents and providences.[67] One incident from late in his career reinforces the impression that Laud was attacked as one bishop among many. During a severe storm, Laud's coat of arms was blown from the central tower of Canterbury Cathedral. As it fell, the stonework crashed into the coat of arms of the archbishopric of Canterbury and both were brought down. The storm was in 1639 and by the time of Laud's arrest in 1641, lines of contemporary doggerel recorded:

> The Quire and Cloister do want a plaister
> And so doe the Arch-Bishops Armes
> The heavens just stroake the Prelates Armes broke
> And did the cathedral maule:
> 1.6.3.9. Brought forth this signe
> Heaven foretells Prelates fall.[68]

The event and the verse interpreting it were personal and at the same time wide-ranging in their implications. The fall of Laud's coat of arms prefigured his own downfall, yet the fall of the arms of the entire archbishopric took this portent beyond the personal, foretelling the end of the entire order of bishops, or 'Prelates fall', as the archbishopric of Canterbury fell. These lines of verse reinforce the impression from other sources of evidence that his detractors condemned him not as an aberration from long-standing traditions but because he was a bishop.

Defences of Laud: Reformed episcopacy

In the light of criticisms of this nature, it is possible to reconstruct Laud's scrupulous attention to the reform of the Church and his efforts to align himself and his Church with the earlier reforms and reformers of the sixteenth century. Beyond this ambition was his intention to orient the English episcopate towards the intentions of the earliest English reformers and to stress the episcopate's reformed identity. Laud's supposed collusion with the Roman Church and his putative temptation by a cardinal's hat existed in association with a further contemporary condemnation of this Archbishop: his supposed efforts to undo the work of the Tudor reformers.[69] Laud himself is the source for this point. His account of his arrest and trial recorded one significant allegation of his work against the Protestant reforms of the sixteenth century: his order to remove the copies of John Foxe's *Acts and Monuments* from English parish churches.[70] The *Acts and Monuments* had been set up in most churches and cathedrals since the reign of Elizabeth.[71] Together with the King James Bible (and before that the

Bishops' Bible), Foxe's text and its descriptions of the godly dying at the hands of Roman Catholics was widely available.⁷² Laud was alleged to have ordered the removal of a text strongly associated with the reform of the English Church. In his defence, Laud stressed his allegiance to the liturgy and doctrines of the 'first reformation', and said he saw upholding its principles as his task as the English primate.⁷³

Laud's argument can be placed in a broader set of meanings. At a time when the episcopate was under exceptional and ultimately destructive pressure, polemical defences appeared at a time of dramatic change. During the 1641 debates in the Long Parliament, points were raised for the reformed identity of bishops, an identity located in the English episcopate's capacity to uphold the intentions of the reformers. A petition from gentlemen in Cheshire argued to Parliament that bishops 'have beene so great asserters of our Religion against its common enemy of Rome.' Similarly a petition from the University of Oxford stressed that English bishops had 'most strongly asserted the truth of that Religion We professe, against the many fierce oppositions of our Adversaries of *Rome*'.⁷⁴ Laud also gave early voice to this idea; speaking in the 1640s against his persistent enemy Bishop Williams of Lincoln, Laud lamented disunity among bishops as being something that 'the Romanists will take advantage of'.⁷⁵

At Williams's trial, Laud again stressed that 'this day's work opens a way for the Romanists to take advantage by it, to see so eminent a Bishop as he, to become thus censurable'.⁷⁶ In the circumstances this was special pleading by Laud, not least as other Protestant nations managed without bishops. In making these claims, Laud and the petitioners to Parliament pointed out that the safety of the work of the reformers lay with English bishops, a point also raised in an anonymous tract of 1645, which argued for the dangers in disturbances to the settled religious order in England.⁷⁷ These works argued for the existence of an order of bishops who were different from the Roman bishops and who were distinguishable by the protection which they offered to reformed religion.

Laud on trial

Allegations of Laud's actions against the reformed English Church were most fully outlined at his trial for treason, held in 1644, which culminated in his execution in 1645. This was also the event which allowed Laud to most vigourously and extensively expound the reformed basis of his authority.

The points raised by Laud at his trial can be located among other polemical arguments, in which Laud expressed his reformist credentials. He expressed his adherence to the Tudor reformers and also that his attackers were the true innovators against reformed religion. Laud inverted claims of his own innovation, instead aligning his policies with the work of Tudor reformers. This strategy predated his trial. Speaking in 1637, Laud had derided Calvinism as 'new fangled', thus identifying innovation as originating elsewhere besides the episcopate.[78] Turning his opponents' arguments against themselves became a feature of Laud's defence at his trial. They also influenced the works of clergy associated with Laud and anxious to defend him. Peter Heylyn augmented Laud's emphasis on the religious innovation of his opponents, including Henry Burton (1578–1648), formerly Clerk of the Closet to Henry Prince of Wales but latterly the Rector of St Matthew's Friday Street. Prynne directly echoed Laud's inversion of the usual argument about the innovation of bishops, instead referring to the 'new fashions of Geneva'.[79] In *A Briefe Answer to the Challenges of H.B.* [Henry Burton], Heylyn saw the intended punishment of Archbishop Laud as evidence of his opponents' innovation and novelty. Writing from Oxford a year after Laud's execution in 1645, Heylyn reflected on some of the fates that could have befallen the Archbishop after he had been found guilty of treason.[80] Fixing on what was a fate worse than death, Heylyn informed his readers that the elderly Laud, instead of execution, could have been shipped to New England where he would have been imprisoned by 'two Schismatics'.[81] Heylyn showed his displeasure at the very notion of Laud's penal transportation, recording his belief that Laud 'had done nothing deserving of either death or bonds'.[82] Yet he was also concerned to emphasize the schismatic character of the gaolers and in doing so echoed his master's insistence on the religious innovation of his opponents.

Laud the protestant bishop

Transportation and gaol were potential consequences of Laud's trial. Coming after the trial of Strafford and before the King's own trial and execution, Laud's trial is familiar to scholars and so too are basic outlines of the charges and his subsequent vigorous defence. This defence is a dense record of his entire public career in the Church. Even though he was denied even an adequate supply of writing paper when imprisoned in the Tower of London, Laud managed to develop a detailed and precise defence against the charges.[83] For instance, on the issue of kneeling during services, Laud painstakingly recorded that it was one Dr Brown who was seen kneeling, not the Archbishop himself.[84] Similarly, when accused of deviation from the *Book of Common Prayer* for deleting a Collect from a service, Laud turned to meteorological records to point out that the weather had been unseasonal and the prayer for rain had been unnecessary.[85] When accused of using a credential, or side table, to hold the elements at Communion, Laud protested that the communion table at that particular service had been too small and a side table was necessary to hold everything.[86]

In resorting to this detailed justification, Laud used a widely established practice. When Prebendary Smart had earlier complained of the apparent innovations in the worship at Durham Cathedral, John Cosin had pointed out that what Smart beheld 'were no other than what have been usually and anciently practised in other cathedral churches of England'.[87] Referring to specific claims of introducing popish innovations to the cathedral in the shape of decorations and statues, Cosin argued that he had done nothing unusual, for 'the pictures of cherubims over the choir stalls and a tomb . . . have been there nigh 300 years'.[88] What Cosin did, as had Laud, was to defend himself against charges of innovation. Cosin did so by appealing to earlier ages of church history and to established practice. Laud turned to a more immediate defence, the Protestant reforms, to identify justifications not only for his conduct but also for the continuing existence of bishops within the English Church.

The sheer level of detail in Laud's defence at his trial can obscure the coherent structure of his writings, a structure derived from the history of the reformed English Church. It is the organization of this defence which directs attention to its value for this analysis. Beginning with his immediate predecessor, George Abbot, Laud moved further back in time to his Elizabethan and finally early-Tudor predecessors as archbishop. In defending himself, Laud drew upon the precedents created by earlier English bishops and Laud indicated how his actions and sacramental functions adhered to reformist principles. He cited textual evidence from the reigns of Edward VI and Elizabeth I to dispel accusations that he had altered coronation oaths.[89] Accused of popish practices at the coronation of Charles I (over which Archbishop Abbot had presided) Laud insisted that the service used was that 'established by law in the Common-Prayer book of this Church'.[90] Laud's defence moved further back in time as his arguments progressed; offending aspects of Charles I's coronation were also 'my predecessor's fault', as 'my predecessor executed at that time'.[91] Thus Archbishop Abbot became responsible for any un-Protestant lapses in ritual or doctrine.

Kenneth Fincham and Nicholas Tyacke establish a reason for Laud's approach to Abbot, arguing that Laud belonged to an anti-Calvinist faction of bishops which sidelined Abbot. Laud's trial defence certainly indicates one archbishop comparing himself favourably with his predecessor.[92] Laud's recourse to Abbot was therefore essentially negative, citing him as the cause of anything later found offensive.

Cranmer for the defence

Laud's use of Abbot stands in contrast to his citation of earlier bishops. While Abbot was a convenient scapegoat in Laud's trial defence, Laud used an earlier primate, Thomas Cranmer, in a more dynamic fashion, to underpin and justify practices which Laud sought to defend and which his opponents viewed as evidence of anti-Protestantism. In doing so, he drew together the strands of a particular identity for English episcopacy, in which bishops could be seen as godly agents of reform. The depth and detail of Laud's trial defence and also the detail of the evidence brought against him, made the actions and reputation of the Tudor primate central to the eleventh day of the trial. Physical artefacts from Laud's residences formed the basis of many accusations made against him, for example books removed from his study or vestments from his chapel. For instance, Laud's apparently illegal alteration to coronation oaths was a point made against him from evidence in books removed from his study.[93] As such, this issue turned on a matter which was explicitly episcopal and which in turn prompted Laud's interpretation of the reformed identity of the episcopacy. It is important to examine in some detail the situation over which Laud and his prosecutors argued. The issue turned upon the decoration of Laud's private chapels and the Tudor precedents which he cited for these decorations.[94]

A witness called against Laud at the trial was a glazier, Mr Brown, whose evidence at the trial led to discussion of the significance of Cranmer in shaping and justifying Laud's actions. Brown had come to testify that Laud had introduced popish images to his chapels. He testified that 'there was no picture of God the Father in the windows at Lambeth'. But more worryingly, Brown had found 'a picture of God the Father in a window at Croydon', an episcopal palace.[95] The issue was sufficiently important in the eyes of Laud's opponents that before Brown came to Westminster to offer this testimony, William Prynne had been to Lambeth Palace, by that time no longer occupied by Laud, to personally take 'a survey of the windows at Lambeth'.⁹⁶ According to Prynne's survey, the windows he encountered in Laud's private chapels were popish in their emphasis, for 'the pictures of these stories [in the stained glass windows] are in the Massbook'. It was this latter argument of Prynne's which allowed Laud to resort to the reputation of Tudor bishops to explain his conduct as bishop. Laud disclaimed responsibility for the popish windows at Lambeth, as 'Archbishop Morton did that work, as appears by his device in the windows.' Here Laud referred to the archbishop under King Henry VII in the late-fifteenth century.⁹⁷

The window at Croydon allowed Laud to be more specific in his defence. The testimony of Mr Brown had included the observation that the arms of Archbishop Cranmer were in the window depicting God the Father. While Laud had simply displaced the responsibility for the popish windows at Lambeth by referring to Morton, a pre-Reformation prelate, Cranmer's work during the Reformation meant that Laud drew a more active point in defence of himself and the window at Croydon. According to Laud 'it appears this picture was there before my time; and continued there in so zealous an Archbishop's time as Cranmer was well known to be'.⁹⁸ Laud countered the accusation he was responsible for a popish window and pointed out that its presence in the chapel during Laud's archiepiscopate could be defended by reference to a conspicuously Protestant archbishop. The reference to a window and its history under a long-dead archbishop is not comprehensive evidence for Laud's reformist identity. However, Laud asserted what appeared to be a commonly held reputation of Cranmer for zealousness. While Morton's part in glazing Lambeth Palace chapel passed without commentary, Laud was at pains to stress that a zealous Tudor bishop had approved of the practices of which he stood accused. In this aspect of his defence, Laud echoed other characteristics of his public career which he stressed during his trial, including converting recusants back to the Church of England and defending the Church of England in public dispute with Catholics.⁹⁹

Laud's defence understood reformed bishops in terms of their differences from popish bishops. To this end, the Reformation occupied a prominent place in Laud's thinking beyond simply the windows in his chapels. Accused by Burton of innovation in placing holy tables behind rails and against the east walls of chancels, Laud responded that he was following a practice in place 'ever since the Reformation'.¹⁰⁰ Another alleged innovation was reverencing the holy table by bowing, yet according to Laud this was 'retained at the Reformation'.¹⁰¹

One stained glass window does not necessarily underpin an entire order of reformed bishops and it is instead possible to identify a further and more intricate strand to Laud's thought. Laud's defence found reformed precedents for each of his acts which seemed to have been an innovation from the Reformation. Yet it would be to misinterpret his defence and his strategy to see him resorting only to fixed precedents. His defence pointed to the mutability and changeability of precedents, challenging the logic of his prosecutors who saw him deviating from precedents and pointing out where reformers, statutes and practices all differed. He pointed out that the 'Articles of Edw. VI. and those made under Q. Elizabeth differ very much. And those of Edw. VI. are not now binding.' As a consequence, Laud argued that the textual evidence used against him was inconsistent and '[s]o whether the clause be in or out them [the Articles], 'tis not much material'.[102]

Part of this mutability was the change in the reputations of bishops from the sixteenth century into the seventeenth. Laud argued that the bishops of Edward's reign differed from those of Elizabeth's, identifying the text and use of the Litany as a prominent point of distinction between them. He noted that 'in the Litany in Henry VIII. his time, and also under Edward Vi., there was this clause: "From the tyranny of the Bishop of Rome . . . Good Lord, deliver us"'.[103] Laud did more than point out that the intentions and actions of reformers could differ. As he argued, the bishops of Elizabeth's reign deleted the popish clause from the Litany, 'and yet the prelates for that, not accounted innovators, or introducers of Popery'.[104] In this way claims of mutability and immutability converged. Laud pointed out that the Reformation was not a fixed point, for the intentions of its participants shifted over time. But he also used the reputations and actions of earlier bishops to bolster his case, on the basis that there was an enduring reformed identity among bishops past and present.

Laud saw both similarities and differences between himself and sixteenth-century bishops. The difference was that earlier bishops were not accused of popishness, whereas Laud and his colleagues were. The similarity was that Laud could appeal to bishops acting no differently from him and introducing no greater innovation than Laud himself. The significance of this point is what it reveals of the substance and form of reformed episcopacy.

Conclusion

Of course, a verdict against Laud was a foregone conclusion but this is perhaps only obvious in hindsight. Laud certainly showed no sign of dejection; indeed his prosecutors seemed positively taken aback at the vigour of his defence. Laud tried to show how the reputation of a dead archbishop exonerated him from allegations of being a popish bishop. During his trial defence, Laud pointed out that manifestations of reformed religiosity from the sixteenth century were in fact the foundation of what his prosecutors alleged were popish actions. He prefigured the preoccupations of Restoration divines, who argued about the circumstances when religious dissent could be either legal or illegal.[105]

According to Laud, the reforms which had made him and Cranmer reformed archbishops had been a process permitted by precise historical circumstances. Dissenting writers of the later-seventeenth century, when they examined the bishops of the sixteenth century, identified prelates in the act of rebelling from a higher religious authority. Religious disputes in the Church after Laud's trial and execution revisited the preoccupations manifested in his trial. Conforming divines and bishops after Laud again explained the circumstances under which the episcopate could seem to be reformed. Laud argued that the national English Church could and had reformed itself. His thought reverberated during the Commonwealth, where a number of churchmen attempted to salvage something from the wreckage. For many this meant the compromise of Reduction, or curtailing the episcopate by having bishops govern with elders or presbyters over much reduced geographic areas. Bishops who promoted reduction schemes did so in an attempt to preserve something of episcopal structures, but not all clergy sympathetic to episcopacy agreed with this approach and one in particular, John Gauden, writing in the wilderness years of the Commonwealth but hoping for the restoration of crown and state, suggested a series of benchmarks which showed that the episcopate was already reformed. He was not alone in these actions and other writers sympathetic to bishops found evidence of their reformed religiosity in the unlikeliest of places, including the Middle Ages.

5

The Uncertain Path to Restoration

Introduction

Demands for the total abolition of episcopacy gained momentum across the early- to mid-seventeenth century. The English Parliament achieved this aim by 1646. Abolishing bishops led to drastic institutional and disciplinary changes to the English Church, but these changes were also tangible and visible. People on Tower Green could see Laud's head come off. In the wake of his execution, iconoclasts vandalized cathedrals (the splendid black and white marble font that Laud had given to Canterbury Cathedral was, however, dismantled and hidden for safety) and Laud's own residence, Lambeth Palace, became a prison. Great harm was done to the palace's fabric and to Laud's other residences, including the stained glass windows that both Laud and his prosecutors had so earnestly discussed. Following Laud's execution and the abolition of episcopacy, we find the order in abeyance and individual bishops in exile or prison.

Trenchant criticisms of the unreformed character of episcopacy also brought forth other responses besides executions and artistic vandalism. One was the schemes for its reduction, ideas exemplified by John Gauden's (1605–62) writings and those of his associate, Archbishop James Ussher of Armagh (d.1656). Another was the attempted integration of the longer history of the episcopate, including its medieval personnel, into the reformed church. Arthur Duck's (1580–1648) biography of Archbishop Chichele, a late-medieval bishop, reflects this strategy. Duck and Gauden share experience of active participation in Church life during the disturbances of the 1640s, and the works of both allow the episcopate to be seen in a broader world of episcopal circles as both writers were in the intellectual orbit of bishops. Duck's career as a church official spans the earlier- to mid-seventeenth century; he was the chancellor of Laud's diocese of Bath and Wells and a civil lawyer based at Doctor's Commons, and his reputation for upholding high views of episcopacy created many enemies for him among the episcopate's opponents for his exalted views on the powers of bishops.[1] Gauden received a bishopric in 1660, but in both cases their writings are from earlier in the seventeenth century. Both emerge from a period where attacks against bishops culminated in the abolition of episcopal government by Parliament by 1646, where episcopacy was under exceptional pressure and in which the royal supremacy had been dissolved. But with Gauden especially, we find an episcopal sympathizer and future bishop at work articulating a defence of episcopacy. Of course, Gauden could not have known at the time he was writing that 1660 would bring the Restoration of monarchy and episcopacy. However, like the exiled king, his court and many loyalist clergy and gentry, he hoped that this would happen, and intellectually he worked to make the episcopate ready for Restoration, should such a happy event occur.

Duck and Gauden bring together a complex interplay of ideas concerning the need to reduce the episcopate and to vitiate impressions that it was a popish remnant, ideas coming from writers sympathetic to the episcopate and who suffered their own privations when it collapsed. Their works shed light on the controversial debates about episcopacy and on how reformed writers defined episcopacy as an appropriate form of government for a reformed church rather than as a popish relic. These works raise an issue which emerged in the sixteenth century and which remained actively under discussion in the late seventeenth century: the reduction in the powers of the episcopacy. Tudor reformers pursued a scheme to reduce the size of dioceses and to increase the number of bishops while simultaneously reducing the range and extent of their authority.[2] During the Commonwealth, this work continued, in Ussher's case as a means to hopefully rescue something of the episcopate from the wreckage and to make a case for the retention of bishops, even if their powers were to be shared with presbyters or elders. A number of churchmen including Joseph Hall and Ussher, both bishops, developed these ideas in the seventeenth century. Hall came round to accepting the idea of an episcopate cooperating with synodical government, while Ussher returned to the early Church to promote a purified scheme of episcopal rule where bishops would be 'reduced into that same state where they continued many hundred yeares after Christ'.[3] The central purpose of the scheme to reduce episcopacy was to reform further the episcopate and to integrate it into more apparently godly forms of church government by abolishing or diminishing episcopal functions and responsibilities and by curtailing the individual authority of bishops in their dioceses.

Gauden in particular was associated with the Ussherian circle, a group of clergy linked with the Irish prelate Archbishop James Ussher, who proposed schemes to align episcopacy with the religious authorities of the Commonwealth. Yet Gauden's own writings advanced a vision of episcopacy which was already sufficiently reformed. Gauden stands forth distinctively from his intellectual surroundings in this regard; likewise his writings posited that elements of episcopacy which some urged be reduced were in fact appropriate instruments of reformed authority.

Gauden and Duck merit analysis together in terms of how both writers argued for the reformed basis of episcopal authority while drawing this point out of strikingly different sources.[4] They both engaged with their immediate intellectual and political environment; their works acknowledged the episcopate's reputation as a remnant of papal rule in England but recast it so that the episcopate's past did not conflict with its latter-day incarnation. For Gauden, reduction of the episcopate was unnecessary. Those features of episcopal rule which some wished to see removed, Gauden claimed as characteristics of reformed office, locating in reformed confessions approval for the order of bishops and justification for its retention.

Heralds of reform: Medieval protestants

Highlighting the reformed character of episcopal authority necessarily draws attention to a complex dialogue between the episcopate's past and present. For a moment let us move back from the Commonwealth to slightly earlier in the seventeenth century to see to what extent Gauden's ideas are prefigured or react against earlier thinking. Sir Arthur Duck, a loyal servant of Church and crown, died in 1648 and was thus spared the trauma of seeing Charles I lose his head in 1649. He was, however, alive to know of Laud's execution and the abolition of episcopacy. Duck was a civil lawyer and in this capacity served as a diocesan chancellor. He also wrote on Church history, including the episcopate, and a major work is his 1617 biography of Archbishop Henry Chichele (1364–1443), who lived during the reign of King Henry VI. Duck reflects the priorities of other writers of their period, who looked backwards in time to discern the origins of episcopacy and to trace continuities between (for them) the present and the early Church.

Many works of this nature (such as Thomas Bedford's *Luthers Predecessors*) were intended to answer the question 'where was your church before Luther?', one posed repeatedly across the sixteenth and seventeenth centuries by Roman

Catholic controversialists and answers spanned both Duck's lifetime and the publishing afterlife of his text. Bedford answered the question in 1624, Edward Boughen in 1653 and in 1685 Gregory Hascard, the Dean of Windsor, was still providing evidence for the answer.[5] Henry Cave's *History of the Papacy* and Humphrey Prideaux's writings developed lengthy pre-histories for the reformers of the sixteenth century. Prideaux for instance traced the Tudor reformers back to the Lollards in his 1688 text *The Validity of the Orders of the Church of England*.[6] On one level, these writers accounted for continuities between what modern historians recognize as the pre-Reformation and post-Reformation epochs. These works intended to show that the Protestant Church was there before Luther. But on another level such works served to historicize reform by contrasting it with a larger body of unreformed corruption. According to writers such as Cave and Prideaux, proto-Protestants were discernible in the pre-Reformation period, establishing continuities with later generations of reformers, but were also discernible because they reacted against prevailing aspects of the Church of their period, thus marking out the pre-Reformation Church as an institution distinct from the godly Church of later days. Mostly this meant looking for the victims of history, especially Tyndale or Wycliffe, whose lives and actions testified to an active strain of godliness in a period of doctrinal error and darkness.

Duck pursued a different path, not looking to early sufferers for reform or to conspicuous rebels, but he went to the top and recruited a long dead archbishop as a harbinger of the reformed episcopate. By bringing Chichele into the Protestant fold, he showed that the English episcopate, while derided as popish, had long shown its reformed hallmarks. His model was not a victim of medieval episcopal malice, such as a Wycliffe or a Tyndale, but a representative of the episcopate from the high point of the medieval Church. As Levack points out, the biography of Chichele was a clearly anti-papal work and followed in a similar vein to Francis Mason's *Vindiciae Ecclesiae Anglicanae*, another work that set out to show Romanists just exactly where the Church of England had been before Luther.[7] But Duck went further than simply showing that the godly were present at any age of Christian history and demonstrated that reformed episcopacy had an established history.

Duck's actual authorship of the ideas on reformed episcopacy is difficult to establish as they are in a text attributed to Duck, but translated and augmented over forty years after his death in 1648.[8] A Latin version of this work is known from the Jacobean period and the work thereafter pursued a complex trajectory through the seventeenth century, and its textual transmission is responsive to the crisis of abolition and the triumph of restoration. While the English version is from the end of the seventeenth century, this English text and its fresh dedication to Archbishop Tenison drew its meaning from Duck's earlier seventeenth-century material. In his own lifetime, pamphlets and polemic associated Duck with William Laud, Matthew Wren, John Lambe, and other churchmen condemned by the Parliamentary opponents of episcopacy. Duck's career and controversial reputation indicate that points on episcopacy that appeared in the late seventeenth century emerged from earlier decades of religious controversy.[9] Duck's work, in different textual incarnations, traced the characteristics of the reformed episcopate back to the fifteenth century and to the archiepiscopate of Henry Chichele. Duck considered Chichele to be a fully formed reformed bishop in an unreformed Church. His means of elucidating Chichele's reformed character was through a comparative analysis of the man and his origins.

We should note that other English churchmen stressed not only the singular significance of bishops but also some continuity between pre- and post-Reformation episcopacy. Before the English schism from Rome, Dean John Colet of St Paul's (1467–1519) argued for the special status and responsibilities of bishops, as they were the agents on earth of the celestial bishop, Christ.[10] Colet claimed that 'the Bishop is a veritable sacrament'.[11] Colet's arguments survived the processes of reformation. For example, in the late sixteenth century, Richard Hooker argued in *Of the Laws of Ecclesiastical Polity* that high rank and powers of oversight characterized in episcopal office. Hooker also argued that bishops held special powers of ordination, a point which stressed the continuities in office which Parker's consecration both acknowledged and justified.[12]

Tudor and Stuart ecclesiastical polity acknowledged the special significance of episcopacy by the particular tasks and responsibilities of the episcopate. Bishops and archbishops had the right to issue licences to preach through the archiepiscopal Court of Faculties.[13] Archbishops of Canterbury from Whitgift under Elizabeth to Gilbert Sheldon during the Restoration concurred in insisting that entry to the offices of priest and deacon was through episcopal ordination.[14] Other sacramental functions remained explicitly episcopal; new churches or chapels in the seventeenth century could only be consecrated by bishops, indicating the episcopate's specific functions and responsibilities.[15] These special responsibilities contrasted with arguments from the later sixteenth century, especially those by the reformer Martin Bucer, that there was nothing to distinguish between bishops and other clergy.[16] They also contrast with the marginalized status of confirmation in the post-Reformation Church, whereby a rite exclusively reserved for administration by bishops was inconsistently enforced, even if theoretically the laying on of episcopal hands meant that bishops came face-to-face with their flocks at least once in the lifetimes of each.[17]

Two important traditional roles of bishops in the pre-Reformation Church were to ordain clergy and consecrate churches; this was equally a responsibility of bishops after the Reformation. Consecrating churches and ordaining clergy formed as much the work of Roman Catholic bishops in contemporary continental Europe, and the medieval predecessors of the reformed bishops, as it did English bishops, and these responsibilities of bishops fuelled polemical confusion between popish and English bishops. The Combination Lectures of the Elizabethan period suggested that the Church of England was but 'halfly reformed', because of 'popish remnants'.[18] It was this confusion to which Duck responded when he disentangled Chichele from a Romanist environment and transposed him into a prematurely reformed Church.

According to Duck's biography of Chichele, the Archbishop could have been a Protestant bishop and his exercise of office in the fifteenth century gave meaning and substance to the reformed episcopate of the seventeenth century. As a diocesan chancellor, Duck wrote with insights into diocesan organization and worked closely with the bishops of Bath and Wells. Duck's work therefore rested on the episcopal organization of the Church of England and he discerned in Chichele a reformed bishop more than a century before the Tudor reforms.[19] His *Life of Henry Chichele* in either its earlier or later manifestation was one of the few explorations of this medieval prelate's life to be produced in the seventeenth century.[20] The tract, specifically its preface, eschewed analysis or interpretation of Chichele's life and instead transmitted biographical data. It is of value here because of the comments that Duck offered in the dedicatory epistle. In this preface, Duck expressed his conception of a reformed Chichele, one who could have offered his allegiance to the reformed Church of England. Archbishop Chichele simply had the misfortune to be born in the fourteenth century and to serve as an archbishop in the fifteenth century, rather than in the sixteenth or seventeenth century. Except for this impediment, he would have belonged to the reformed Church of England. Duck wrote: 'If this Prelate had lived in happier Times, he would probably have exerted those great Talents which he carried far in so dark an Age, in Services of a high nature.'[21]

Duck's most singular claim about Chichele concerned his metropolitical relations with the papacy.[22] In Duck's assessment, Chichele was an early exponent of reformed episcopacy, for the Archbishop 'asserted the Rights of the Crown, and the Liberties of this Church against Papal Usurpations'.[23] According to Duck, Chichele's archiepiscopate was strikingly anachronistic for the fifteenth century, for he possessed 'great Qualities, and so much the greater, because the Corruptions of the Clergy from the Papacy down to the Begging Orders, were then to an insupportable degree'.[24] In the midst of this corruption, Chichele stood out as an early advocate of reform. This biography of Chichele shows the re-writing of Church history and the re-orienting of the outlook and actions of the medieval episcopate in order to present the episcopacy as reformed.

Earlier appeals to the unreformed Church as a harbinger of the Reformation contextualize Duck's resort to a medieval churchman as a herald of reformed religion. In 1608, Thomas James's *An Apologie for Iohn Wicliffe, shewing his conformitie with the now Church of England* depicted Wycliffe as congruent with the post-Reformation Church.[25] Yet by the seventeenth century, Wycliffe had long stood within the ranks of the reformed tradition, in a way a medieval archbishop did not. The distinctiveness of Duck's work lies in his choice of subject matter on which to rest arguments for the early manifestations of reformed episcopacy. Duck's political origin makes sense of these decisions. Identified in popular polemic with Archbishop Laud and serving as a diocesan chancellor, Duck emerges from a Church preoccupied with the claims of bishops to govern their dioceses, and his exploration of the early-medieval Church rested upon the qualities that made a bishop reformed.

This complexity in connecting past with present is shown in another way: the arguments for the reduction of episcopacy. Reductionists such as Archbishop Ussher of Armagh reached the conclusion that the episcopate needed further alteration to bring it out of its unreformed, medieval condition. At this point, reduction meant reducing the geographic reach of diocesan authority and stripping the episcopate of its more extravagant trappings and its singular functions and privileges. The new model of episcopacy could be woven together from a range of sources, including Ussherian publications and writings of anti-episcopal scholars such as Richard Baxter. Their substance was an assertion that episcopacy was unreformed and should be further reformed. These arguments emerge from a period when opponents of episcopacy argued that there was little to distinguish between popish and English bishops. The reformation of the Church became an immediately compelling argument for the authority of restored bishops and for neutralizing arguments that episcopacy was a popish relic.

Duck's work stands in tension with John Gauden's assessment of the basis of episcopal rule. Gauden's work identified the distinguishing features of reformed bishops and filled in characteristics of reformed episcopacy by drawing comparative points from European Reformations. Duck's attempt to delineate reformed episcopacy differed from Gauden's. Duck's argument complicated the approach that Gauden had taken, that was to distinguish between medieval and reformed episcopacy. Duck blurred what were for Gauden separate ecclesiastical realities, bringing a member of the medieval prelacy into the orbit of reformed episcopacy.

Gauden and the scope of episcopacy

Gauden was elevated to the episcopate in 1660, serving only briefly until his death in 1662. However, during the Civil Wars and Commonwealth, and during the suppression of the episcopate, of deans and chapters, and of the Prayer Book, Gauden developed a fully thought-out explication of the reformed episcopate's origins and unique powers and character. Gauden's work emerged from the exceptional circumstances of the failure of the Commonwealth in the 1650s and the restoration of King and Church and the necessity, in his view, to justify the episcopal authority which he then hoped would be restored. Many churchmen, and for a time Gauden himself, devoted thought and energy to the reduction of episcopacy, meaning that the diocesan oversight and temporal responsibilities of bishops would be reduced and simplified, in an effort to make bishops seem reformed. Gauden later changed his mind, arguing that bishops were already reformed and therefore not in need of reduction or reformation. As Spurr points out, the Commonwealth produced a younger generation of clergy who had collaborated with the Cromwellian forces yet who also emerged as conforming members of the restored episcopal Church after 1660. Among these were Gauden and other members of the Ussherian circle, whose major preoccupations had been to defend episcopal rule according to the standards of Presbyterian ecclesiology.[26]

Gauden's origins were informed by both political and intellectual forces. In the lead up to 1660, bishops faced a range of choices in asserting and defending their authority. Edward Hyde, the Earl of Clarendon, recorded that bishops were by no means 'all of one mind', and surviving and newly appointed bishops in 1660 reached different conclusions about the extent and basis of their authority, including the possibility of its reduction and the collaboration between episcopacy and presbytery.²⁷ One of Gauden's works on episcopal government, *Analysis: The Loosing of St Peters Bands*, referred in its title to the Solemn League and Covenant and Gauden's immediate background was the ecclesiastical settlement of the Commonwealth, which had found bishops an unacceptable source of authority. The work, a 13-page pamphlet printed in 1660, was the result of several years of deliberation on the question of the government of the Church by episcopacy. By 1653 Gauden was associated with a group intellectually allied to Archbishop Ussher of Armagh, the Primate of Ireland, and was promoting Ussher's scheme for a reduced episcopacy.²⁸ Ussher's scheme met with approval in anti-episcopal circles. The anti-episcopal scholar and Huguenot Pierre du Moulin called James Ussher 'a rare ornament', but one bishop's rarity merely stressed that all other reformed prelates were a 'multitude of Romanizing bishops' while Ussher was working constructively to reconfigure episcopacy as a reformed institution.²⁹ Du Moulin was a foreign, reformed observer of English episcopacy, and several English bishops like Gauden and Bishop Henry Compton of London (d.1713) attempted to claim that reformed churchmen from non-episcopal churches admired English episcopacy. Milton's *Of Reformation in England and the Causes that have hitherto hindered it* from 1641 noted this strategy but pointed to the same issue that Moulin had stressed: that some bishops may be personally agreeable, but that episcopacy in general was unreformed. Milton acknowledged that 'they add that some of the learnedest of the reformed abroad admire our Episcopacy' but that they admire 'not Episcopacy'.³⁰

Milton was alert to a well-established strategy of placing English episcopacy in a setting which emphasized its reformed identity. One of Gauden's works on episcopal identity, *Hieraspistes*, argued for the preservation of the episcopate on the terms of its experience of reform. Gauden stressed that the 'ancient and Catholick Government of Godly Bishops' conformed to ancient presbyterial standards of church government.³¹ Gauden's emphasis here was on the apostolic linkages of the episcopacy, although this emphasis reveals the different import of his other works, which stressed the acceptably reformed characteristics of English bishops. In *St Peters Bands*, he described the conditions of the Solemn League and Covenant, which required the '*abjuring or extirpating of all Episcopacy*'. Gauden found this requirement inexplicable, for the episcopate thus suppressed was 'reformed and regulated as it ought to be'.³² According to Gauden, English bishops were acceptably reformed.

While a part of Ussher's circle and an intellectual contributor to the Archbishop's scheme, Gauden's contribution to defending and outlining episcopal power ultimately stood out markedly from contemporary ideas. His appeal to reformed precedents, in Scotland and Europe, carried a different emphasis to Ussher's plans to reduce episcopacy, ideas which paralleled associated schemes to revise and reduce the *Book of Common Prayer* to a model suitable for wider acceptance.[33] In *St Peters Bands*, bishops appeared as already reformed and as having earned the approval of reformed confessions. His text offered a precise understanding of reformed episcopal authority. He placed the English episcopate in a wider, reformed world of European confessions, including Calvinists, and therefore acknowledged that reformist principles were often inimical to the government of bishops. Gauden excused the anti-episcopal impulses coming from other Protestant communities and inverted them. As he explained 'a few *reformed Churches*' did not have bishops but yet '*want* not *contempt* of *Bishops*', and instead 'the necessity of times' resulted in such feelings becoming manifest. While foreign Protestants disapproved of their bishops, 'they approve and venerate *Episcopacy* in others.' Gauden looked to churches beyond England to find stated approval for English bishops.

Significantly he did not examine the reformed churches in Denmark, Norway and Sweden which had preserved both bishops and cathedrals during processes of Lutheran reform conducted by princes and where all non-Lutheran bishops had been deposed by 1537.[34] Elizabeth I had enthusiastically endorsed the fruits of the Danish Reformation and expressed her admiration for the model of ecclesiastical administration which prevailed in Denmark, indicating the emphasis on both royal and episcopal discipline which had characterized some aspects of Scandinavian reform.[35] Instead, Gauden looked at places where there were not bishops to be found, as it was important to his purpose to show that apparent opponents of episcopacy could be brought within the episcopal fold. Gauden argued that continental foreign confessions had no objections to bishops but particular circumstances meant that they were unable to have any. His ideas reflected the earlier writings of Richard Hooker, whose *Ecclesiastical Polity* had both defended episcopacy as the ideal form of ecclesiastical government and acknowledged, without disapproval, that some reformed churches had altered or even abandoned episcopal government.[36] Gauden argued that anti-episcopal impulses in other Protestant churches could reveal approval for English bishops, a paradoxical argument which Gauden achieved through an historical survey of different reformed communities.

Gauden was not the only English episcopal writer to bring European reformed authorities into his work, as Bancroft had earlier cited Calvin as supporting episcopacy when preaching at Paul's Cross in 1589 (or 1588 in the original calendar), and John Whitgift also drew Calvin into the orbit of reformed episcopacy and its relations with magisterial authority.[37] Bancroft became Archbishop of Canterbury in 1604 and throughout his public career at university, court and parliament defended the episcopate's singular significance. His sermon from Paul's Cross was republished in the seventeenth century, and so too was Bancroft's point that 'S. Ierom saith, and *M. Calvin* seemeth . . . to confesse that Bishops have had the said superiority ever since the time of S. *Mark* the Evangelist'.[38] In this sermon, Apostolic, Patristic and Reformed (in this case Genevan) authorities all combined to acknowledge the authority of the episcopate and Bancroft set episcopal authority in both ancient and reformed environments.[39]

Nor was the publication of *St Peters Bands* the last time Gauden's views would appear. The complexity of ascribing *jure divino* origins to the episcopate was also made clear in the opinions of foreign Protestant theologians which English bishops solicited during the Restoration. These opinions were originally gathered by Henry Compton, the Bishop of London (in office 1676–1713), and disseminated by Edward Stillingfleet (1635–1699), his colleague on the episcopal bench. One of the foreign theologians to whom the English bishops appealed, the Huguenot Monsieur Claude, argued that fate determined whether an ecclesial community was governed by a bishop or a presbyter.[40] According to Claude, bishops were as acceptable to reformed religion as a Calvinist presbyter, but their office owed more to contingency than to an apostolic origin. Similarly, the conforming divine Herbert Thorndike noted that Presbyterians regarded English episcopal government as a compromise, for the Tudor reformers had been influenced by Phillip Melancthon rather than Calvin. Thorndike noted that 'Some of our Scottifh Presbyterians have observed that the Church of *England* was reformed by those, that had more esteem of *Melancthon* than of Calvin'.[41] Stillingfleet used and reflected upon foreign Protestant opinions; importantly, he acknowledged the absence of episcopal oversight among European Protestants, but could use this absence to justify English episcopacy as a reformed institution.

While Stillingfleet accepted that not all Protestant Reformations had valued episcopacy, he argued that the absence of the episcopate in European reformed confessions could endorse reformed episcopacy. Stillingfleet did argue that the English Reformation proceeded differently from other Protestant reforms, for '*Calvin* and some other found, that their Counsel was not like to be followed in our *Reformation*.' Nonetheless, the Church of England could demonstrate its 'consent with other Protestant Churches, which did allow and practise the same, or more ceremonies, as the *Lutheran churches* generally did'.[42] Likewise an early and anonymous biographer of Archbishop Tillotson recorded that the Presbyterian divine, Edward Calamy, was offered a bishopric by Charles II and that his response revealed a Presbyterian conceding the superiority of episcopal rule. That 'good old man deliberated about it some Considerable time, professing to see the great inconvenience of the Presbyterian parity of Ministers'.[43]

Gauden drew evidence from different Protestant communities. According to him, the Church of Scotland 'once enjoyed the best *constitutions* of *Episcopacy* in the world'.[44] Gauden was disappointed at the evolution of the hostility to Scottish bishops. By the time Gauden came to survey episcopacy not just in England but in Scotland, Scottish episcopacy had endured several decades of controversial activity following its revival by James VI.[45] Scottish bishops had functioned as an agent of royal authority for Charles I, notably in the appointment of Archbishop Spottiswoode of St Andrews as Chancellor, but by 1638 many bishops had also fled Scotland for England.[46] Scottish bishops experienced their own period of abeyance and the collapse of their authority. The Kirk in Scotland functioned in Gauden's text as an illustration of exemplary Protestant episcopacy. Appeals to the Kirk as a model of conservative church government had earlier been made in sermons by Lancelot Andrewes (bishop of Winchester 1619–26) and Richard Bancroft. Both appropriated words from the Scottish reformer John Knox and precedents in church government from the Scottish presbytery as showing English episcopacy as a positive model for English church government.[47] Gauden's text, written in June 1660 for the benefit of the returning King and government-in-exile, looked to a temporarily un-episcopal church to argue that a cleric could be both reformed and a bishop.

Conclusion

Bishops' detractors (and often their victims) traced a largely negative continuity in episcopal rule, rhetorically failing to find divergent conduct between unreformed and reformed bishops. But neither Duck nor Gauden summoned up in writing an episcopate which had dropped from the sky fully reformed. Rather, the reformed episcopacy was a matter of emphasis, a point made by Duck's delineation of a medieval prelate who stood out markedly from his brethren. Seventeenth-century writers identified the reformed basis of their power and offered statements reconciling their office and the reformation of the English Church. Gauden wished to convince first the religious authorities of the Commonwealth and then the returning royal court that reformed approval could be found for the exercise of episcopal authority. The ambiguous circumstances of the translation and publishing of Duck's work make questions of actual authorship as uncertain as questions of audience, but in casting Chichele as a harbinger of reform, his point on the distinction between reformed and unreformed bishops was clear. However, his making these points does not mean that these perspectives prevailed. The reputation of the episcopate and of individual members of the bench of bishops for being popish remnants persisted throughout the seventeenth century. But this reputation merely gave added significance to episcopal assertions of reformed authority, as bishops stressed not merely their power but their purpose, one which they insisted could cohere with the imperatives of reform.

Duck died in time to avoid the Commonwealth but Gauden lived through it. The abolition of the episcopate did not mean that churchmen ceased to think about it, and neither did surviving bishops nor their sympathetic clergy give up on the idea of its restoration. Gauden worked assiduously to prepare the episcopate intellectually for Restoration, suggesting that, should it come back, it would do so as a reformed entity not in need of reduction. Gauden's ideas are not novel. Other churchmen like Ussher attempted to make the episcopate inoffensive by suggesting its reduction, but in repudiating this idea and proposing it was already quite satisfactory, Gauden has more in accord with Duck's estimation of history and his location of impeccably reformed bishops where one would least expect to find one. Gauden lived to see the Restoration and to claim a bishopric. Restoration did not, however, mean that the bishops' problems were over. After 1660 attacks against the order continued, and we now turn to consider one of the most persistent complaints against bishops: what they looked like.

6

The Restoration, Episcopal Self-representation and the Defence of Vestments

Introduction

As we have seen, from the sixteenth century onwards English dissenting laity and clergy disputed a wide spectrum of episcopal duties and powers, including the necessity or even the validity of episcopal ordinations, the scope of the episcopate's temporal jurisdiction, including its role in the House of Lords, and the right of bishops to conduct visitations and to demand conformity to their authority. At the core of most anti-episcopal writing and legislation was the belief that the English Church was insufficiently reformed and that the existence of bishops was the chief defect among other diverse remnants of popery such as the surplice, the signing of the cross and kneeling to receive the sacrament at Communion. But bishops as a group, identified with symbolic items of dress, were a major issue. A key element of many discourses against episcopacy was an attack on the appearance of bishops, notably the continuing use of the rochet and chimere as the identifying raiment of the episcopate. This had come to a head during Laud's archiepiscopate, where as was seen, Laud and other bishops stood accused of overtly popish practices. But complaints about what bishops looked like did not originate during Laud's period of influence, nor did they go away after the fall and then rise of the episcopate during and after the Commonwealth. The vestments themselves have long since crumbled to dust, but they have left vivid after traces in the literature.

The purpose of this chapter is to show that episcopal vestments, while a core aspect of anti-episcopal writings, also were central to strategies to defend episcopacy. In particular, the idea that vestments were 'matters indifferent', an approach familiar from many modern sources,[1] is an inadequate intellectual model to explain defences of episcopal choir dress.[2] By following arguments about episcopal choir dress through seventeenth-century controversial writings,

I will show that defenders of episcopacy argued that English bishops and Roman bishops differed from each other and that these distinctions were revealed by external trappings which stood as positive evidence of reformed religion, rather than a matter indifferent. A study of vestiarian controversies in the Restoration contributes important insights about how power was negotiated and legitimated and about the wider historical meanings attached to the intentions of Tudor reformers in the seventeenth century. The decision to retain episcopal choir dress, meaning the white robe with lawn sleeves called the rochet and the black or red sleeveless silk gown called the chimere, featured in defences of episcopacy as evidence of the discernment of reformers and the godly prudence of their decisions. Every bishop I have hitherto looked at in this book would have appeared in public dressed in this raiment: Bancroft in High Commission, Laud in the dock and so on. Doing so often attracted adverse comment on their popish appearance. Accordingly, while we will focus here on the Restoration, consideration of what bishops wore also provides a chance in this final chapter to bring together a number of the points made by and about bishops from the Tudor period into the later seventeenth century and so see what ideas on the episcopate's functions and roles had come about by the Restoration.

So far the use of episcopal choir dress as a means of neutralizing anti-episcopal polemic has not been addressed in modern scholarship, and the argument that vestments were positive evidence of reformed religiosity is underexplored. While scholars are alert to the rhetorical and political import of early modern symbolism, costume and ritual, assessments of this import are often addressed to the appearance of Renaissance kingship rather than episcopal polity.[3] Helen Pierce's important survey of graphic satire in mid-seventeenth century England points to the place of episcopal vestments in polemical debates, but overall Pierce illuminates the negative connotations of episcopal garb.[4] Writings surveyed here permit an alternative interpretation, and defenders of episcopacy aimed to demonstrate how English bishops were distinct from their Roman counterparts, and how the very aspects of the Church condemned by polemicists in fact showed that episcopacy set a benchmark of reformed ecclesiology.

To reach these insights, this chapter focuses largely on debates about episcopacy which took place in the Restoration period (c.1660–1689). The Restoration merits particular scrutiny and provides a source of meaningful analysis as during this period episcopacy received renewed visual emphasis after years of upheaval. To develop these ideas, I examine in detail the works of George Hooper (1640–1727), locating in his work markedly original ideas in defence of the office of bishop and the external trappings which marked out the office as significant. Hooper, an orientalist, Arabist, mathematician, classicist and Bishop of Bath and Wells, entered the polemical fray in defence of bishops at the height of Restoration political crises in the 1680s, including the aftermath of the Popish Plot and the Exclusion Crisis.[5] Prominent as a royal chaplain, as a notably combative prolocutor of the lower house of Convocation, and finally as a bishop, Hooper's career as a restoration polemicist for episcopacy is noteworthy for the attention he gave to the vestments worn by clergy. Particular attention will be paid to his text *The Church of England Free from Imputation of Popery*, published first in 1683.[6] In this work, Hooper discussed at length what he called the 'First Reformation', attempting to justify the intentions of the Tudor reformers in maintaining some vestments and in discarding others. In this text, episcopal vestments were not Hooper's only concern, but the chief animating feature of this tract was the need to defend episcopal authority by showing that it was not popish. In Hooper's mind, the issue of church government and the maintenance of traditional vestments were united, and Hooper chose to defend not only the vestments, but also the episcopal authority which they signified.

Episcopal choir dress and vestiarian disputes

George Hooper wrote against the background of the long-standing vestiarian controversies of the post-Reformation period and a number of political crises of the Restoration age, including the Popish Plot and the Exclusion Crisis. These crises served to intensify general paranoia about popery.[7] More broadly his work is also defined by a period when clothing, sacred or secular, had been controversial, and where fashions could provoke biblically inspired discourses against 'soft raiment'[8] or sermons condemning excess in dress in times of national stringency.[9] Reformed English religion also promoted the *Homily Against Excess of Apparel*, which remained in print in the seventeenth century.[10] Its themes found common acceptance in other Protestant communities, such as the eschewal by Dutch merchants of the 'Golden Age' of elaborate clothing or expensive fabrics.[11] The controversy aroused by raiment points to the wider cultural and historical parameters of arguments about rochets and chimeres. Indeed it is important to qualify the statement that Hooper was writing at a time when clothing could be controversial, as this statement in true of many periods of history. Clothing in fact carries an enduring capacity to cause controversy in different societies, as contemporary controversies over, for example, the burqua demonstrate. But rochets and chimeres did not offend because they were particularly sumptuous items of clothing, or the 'excess apparel' of the homily. Indeed, at court and at major public events, bishops may even have seemed underdressed. John Stow, for example, refers to a civic occasion when 'the Lord Mayor of London, with his brethren and aldermen all in scarlet, besides citizens in coats of velvets and chains of gold' appeared at St Paul's.[12] Compared to such civic and secular finery, black rochets and white chimeres would have paled in comparison. However, scarlet aldermanic robes were markers of civic office, and luxury dress on the laity may have shocked some churchmen, but they were not markers of inadequate religious reform. Bishops caused offence to some churchmen and laity precisely because they were bishops who looked like bishops. In other words, their robes marked out their office, and directed attention to an aspect of church government many English churchmen would gladly have seen abolished.

We should consider for a moment what had happened to the episcopate in the years since Laud's execution. While the Civil Wars present themselves as a period of disturbance and destruction, the historian John Morrill conversely has argued that the 1640s and 1650s were relatively stable ecclesiastically. Morrill's investigation of parish registers and churchwardens' accounts reveals the continuing use of *The Book of Common Prayer* in many churches even after the abolition of bishops, the execution of Archbishop Laud in 1645 and the publication of the Directory for Public Worship, which replaced the prayer book. He reconstructs from this same evidence the continued celebration of communion at Easter and Christmas and the continuity in Church personnel, as many vicars and rectors remained in office from the 1640s into the 1650s.[13] Morrill argues that 'popular Anglicanism' survived.[14] But the parochial continuities uncovered by Morrill contrast with upheaval at the highest ecclesiastical levels. While many clergy continued to function in their parishes and used the prayer book, these clergy were no longer licensed or supervised by bishops. Instead, political and religious forces in the 1640s violently threw down bishops and broke continuities in episcopal government and cathedral worship. By 1660, the ranks of the bishops had been severely depleted. Manuscript sources left by Thomas Birch, biographer of Archbishop John Tillotson, indicate the parlous state of the episcopate by 1660. For example, Birch recorded that 'Tillotson took orders (as he hath told me) from the Old Scottish Bp of Galloway, who at that time had recourse made to him on that account'.[15] Birch recounted an episcopate on the verge of extinction. Some bishops had survived through to

1660, including William Juxon, bishop of London before the Commonwealth, who by 1660 was old and sick.[16] Many other elderly bishops had died before the Restoration. The depletion of numbers was not so much from suffering imposed by the government (although Laud and Matthew Wren were both imprisoned) but through old age and the reluctance of deprived bishops to perform more consecrations.

The events of 1660 gave the new Archbishop of Canterbury, William Juxon, the freedom and capacity (if hardly the bodily strength and mental faculties) to openly consecrate new bishops to vacant sees. Events moved swiftly and even in 1660, the year of the Restoration, clergy gathered in Westminster Abbey to be consecrated to the vacant bishoprics.[17] One of them, Gilbert Sheldon (appointed Bishop of London in 1660) acclaimed the triumph and providence of the episcopate's resurrection.[18] On one level, he was correct to see it this way: regardless of the points Charles II made in the Declaration of Breda before his restoration, promising relief to those of tender consciences, in reality by 1662 a mostly rigid Anglican conformity was imposed.[19] However, these new bishops were appointed to superintend bishoprics with depleted resources and were enthroned in cathedrals which had often been severely vandalized.[20] Accordingly, Hooper's work also was informed by the renewed visual assertion during the Restoration of the splendour and authority of episcopacy. Following the political as much as the architectural and artistic upheavals of the Civil Wars and the Great Fire of London, episcopal patronage allowed for the reconstruction and beautification of churches and cathedrals. This same patronage allowed for the strong visual assertion of episcopal power as mitres, crests and monuments added to the visual impression already created by the rochet and chimere. During the Restoration, a number of bishops emerged as patrons of the arts, especially John Cosin at Durham, John Hacket at Lichfield, Henry Compton in London (to whose energies as dean and then bishop the rebuilding of St Paul's owes much[21]) and several archbishops at Canterbury Cathedral.

Hooper's work is also explained by his combative career in the Church. While he had been a star pupil of Dr Busby at Westminster School and was a renowned linguist and mathematician at university, Hooper's relationship with the episcopal hierarchy was complex. Although he later rose to the episcopal bench, in the 1680s Hooper's reputation was as a sometimes controversial opponent of ecclesiastical hierarchies. This reputation was consolidated in the 1690s when his exercise of his office of prolocutor of the lower house of Convocation both defied and enraged Archbishop Tillotson.[22] While he was not an episcopal sycophant, he was generally loyal to the episcopate. However, the independence he showed as prolocutor may go some way to explaining the imaginative cast of mind he shows in *The Church of England Free from the Imputation of Popery*. Hooper's response to many decades of familiar and repetitive invective against bishops and their vestments is strikingly original. By turns pedantic and sarcastic, Hooper reviewed arguments about vestments (which he assessed within a broader range of condemnations of other rites, ceremonies and trappings of the Church of England) in order to show that the English episcopate stood forth distinctively from Roman episcopacy. He further urged that maligned vestments in fact provided positive evidence of the reformed credentials of the episcopate.

Hooper's writing contributed to disputes over permissible and impermissible items of clerical apparel which resounded throughout controversial tracts written over the sixteenth and seventeenth centuries. While many ceremonies, rituals and items of church decoration served as highly visible sources of tension in post-Reformation England, episcopal vestments attracted particular attention because they raised issues in polemical literature specific to the exercise of religious authority and because they demarcated the episcopate as a singular and authoritative order of the ministry.[23] The three layers of clergy – bishops, priests, deacons – all wore vestments, and to an extent all and any vestments raised the ire of polemicists, such as Sampson and Humphrey's sermons at Paul's Cross against vestments.[24] Thus, the 1572 *First Admonition to Parliament*, a tract which emerged from the Admonition Controversy and the disputation between Thomas Cartwright and John Whitgift, during which episcopacy was systematically challenged, attacked 'copes, caps, surplesses, tippets and such like baggage'.[25] However the use of any vestment was enforced on the order of diocesan bishops, who regulated apparel through their visitations and punished backsliders in their courts. Indeed, the *First Admonition* was alert to this point, arguing that it was bishops who were 'consuming the greatest part of their time' in the use and maintenance of vestments.[26] Throughout the sixteenth and seventeenth centuries, bishops had maintained the use of the rochet and chimere both as their customary apparel in church and as everyday dress, as tracts poured from underground presses decrying bishops as popish for the clothes they wore.[27] Episcopal vestments were sharply provocative, and specific episodes have left vivid traces of their capacity to offend. A notable case was in 1630 when Archbishop Laud appeared in the doorway of St Katherine Cree Church in London attired in episcopal raiment, an act which was deemed such an affront to godly propriety that it featured prominently in his treason trial alongside criticism of the glazing of his chapel and led to his appearance being violently mocked in William Prynne's *Canterburies Doom*.[28] The Cree Church consecration was nothing short of an episcopal takeover of a church whose living was held by a puritan minister, Stephen Denison, whom we encountered in Chapter 3.[29] Laud, attired in his episcopal vestments, marked out the church building as a sacred space. Although English reformed theology allowed for a church building to be regarded as a sacred space and Bishop Lancelot Andrewes had devised a liturgy for consecrations, Laud took this further, as he was also insisting that the church could not be used until a bishop had consecrated the building.[30] At this consecration, Laud marked out not only the significance of the building, but also the significance of episcopal order as a distinctive and distinctive-looking layer of the orders of the ministry.[31]

Hooper and other controversialists who wrote about ceremonies and vestments were shaping their discourse in a society acutely conscious of the semiotic significance of external signs and symbols, or what Kevin Sharpe refers to as the 'aesthetics and psychology of power'.[32] The catechism from the *Book of Common Prayer*, used by curates throughout England to instruct the youth in their care, expressed the capacity for outward symbols to be a sign of inward grace. Following the revision to the prayer book catechism and the publication of a larger catechism by Dean Alexander Nowell of St Paul's, children learning the catechism were taught to say that sacraments were 'an outward and visible sign of an inward and spiritual grace'.[33] Likewise the prayer book's preface 'Concerning Ceremonies' argued that outward things were edificatory because of their capacity to make clear internal spiritual processes.[34] The theology of the Prayer Book concurred with reformed theology in Europe which viewed external signs as signifiers of internal grace.[35] The theology of the sacraments shows that the Church of England did not treat external signs as trivialities and neither were disputes about external trappings trivial arguments. Although the vestments worn by the clergy were not themselves sacraments, they were intrinsic to the administration of the sacraments of the Eucharist and Baptism; they were also potent symbols of authority to observers in a society which accepted that external signs carried deeper meaning. In this regard, the vestments of bishops stand out as especially significant, as the different design between the rochet and chimere of a bishop and the surplice and tippet of an ordinary clergyman marked out the singular significance and authority of the entire episcopal order.[36] Disputes over vestments therefore present themselves as significant contests; arguments over external signs penetrated directly into profound arguments over the exercise of authority in post-Reformation England.

The rochet and chimere in historical perspective

The vigour of the anti-vestiarian attacks were prompted not only by the significance of the outward signs conveyed by vestments but also by the consistency and distinctiveness of episcopal dress in both pre-Reformation and post-Reformation England. Barring minor shifts in details (such as the gradual adoption of periwigs by bishops in the seventeenth century and the general avoidance of mitres by most post-Reformation bishops[37]), during and after the English Reformation bishops continued to wear the raiment which their opponents found so provocative. If anything the rochet and chimere became even more prominent after the Reformation, as the range of options open to bishops in terms of vestments contracted; the chasuble vanished from English use, as did most other eucharistic vestments, leaving English bishops with no other options for raiment except the rochet and chimere.[38] The Italian traveller Count Magalotti (1637–1712), attending Divine Service in Exeter Cathedral in the 1660s, commented that the bishop (Dr Anthony Sparrow) was 'dressed in the habit which was used by the Catholic bishops of the kingdom before the apostacy'.[39] Magalotti's references to dress and vestments make clear the national distinctiveness of English episcopal raiment (for his reference was to the kingdom of England) and the continuities in dress from the pre-Reformation to the post-Reformation period.

The insistence of bishops on wearing their vestments created a major site of tension in the seventeenth-century Church. A range of textual and visual sources take us from the Jacobean period to the Restoration, enunciating a constant theme of criticism of episcopal vestments and making clear the limitations of efforts to contain vestiarian disputes. English vernacular art, such as the carvings on bench ends, gave pigs' faces to figures dressed in episcopal robes.[40] The subversive potential of this imagery was also played out at the Hampton Court Conference of 1604 in the reign of James I, when the controversialist Andrew Melville manhandled Bishop Richard Bancroft, tugging on his lawn sleeves and commenting that they were 'Romishragis'. The fact of wearing them made Bancroft 'the capitall enemie of all the reformed kirks in Europ'.[41] Such attitudes endured. The letters of the controversialist William Prynne to Archbishop William Laud from the Tower of London in the

1630s facetiously observed of Laud's 'unfaithfull dealing' that 'it became your Lordship's rochet'.[42] An anonymous writer at the time of Laud's arrest in the early 1640s referred disparagingly to 'wearing the white Surplice, Lawn Sleeves, Tippet, foure corner cap etc'.[43] John Milton found episcopal choir dress not only popish but inherently ridiculous, commenting that 'we would burst our *midriffes* rather than laugh to see them under Sayl in all their Lawn, and Sarcenet, their shrouds, and tackle, with a *geometricall rhomboid* upon their heads'.[44] These references to episcopal choir dress indicate the importance given to symbolic and ceremonial forms. They were also in part inspired by sumptuary disapproval.[45] As the reference to the whiteness of the vestments suggests, white linen was an expensive commodity, expensive to produce and to keep clean and was thus a statement of reasonable wealth and status.[46] But as Pierce's survey of mid-seventeenth-century graphic satire has demonstrated, the episcopal robes were convenient tropes for condemning episcopacy in general by the 1640s.[47] One contemporary writer ironically observed of 'the pluming of some Bishops' that anti-episcopal writers are 'so acquainted with every feather of them', such was the level of detail about episcopal vestments in polemical literature.[48]

Significantly, the association which polemical writers drew between the vestments and the office of bishop is not confined to anti-episcopal tracts, but is also found in the productions of elite culture. Studying Anthony van Dyck's portrait of Archbishop Laud (painted c.1635), art historian Michael Jaffé points out that van Dyck 'did not need to lumber the image with armorials or inscriptions, or even with the apparatus of the Primacy'. Instead, the white rochet and the black chimere which Laud is shown wearing in the portrait were sufficient to mark his office and status.[49] Jaffe argues that van Dyck's work set a standard for episcopal portraits. But in many ways it merely repeated earlier representations of bishops, in which the rochet and chimere were used as a short hand for depicting episcopal office. Most obviously, the episcopal portrait which Thomas Cranmer (1489–1556) commissioned from Gerlach Fliche (Figure 1) imitated that of his predecessor William Warham (1450–1532) by Hans Holbein (Figure 2).[50] Cranmer's portrait emulated the symbolism of episcopal authority celebrated in the Holbein work, but the processional cross and the be-jewelled mitre of the Holbein work have gone. Instead Cranmer's rochet and chimere were sufficient visual cues of episcopacy. Cranmer's contemporary, Bishop Hugh Latimer, similarly suggested that his episcopal robes were signifiers of his office and its authority. Recalling how disgruntled he was when he arrived at a village to conduct a visitation to find the villagers were all away celebrating Robin Hood's

Figure 1 Thomas Cranmer by Gerlach Flicke oil on panel, 1545, © National Portrait Gallery.

Day, Latimer said 'I thought my rochet should have been regarded, though I were not'.[51] Latimer's comment is especially significant, suggesting that the robes and what they stood for transcended the individual wearer.

In these paintings and comments the vestments, even if they were signifiers of office and rank, were intended to be polemically neutral. But polemicists found in visual representations of episcopacy evidence of the popishness of the order, revealed externally by the bishops' 'Romish rags'. Works near-contemporary with van Dyck's painting used the rochet and chimere as means of condemning episcopacy in general. The title page of Alexander Leighton's 1641 tract *A Decade of Grievances* depicted a metaphorical vision of the downfall of popish bishops, showing them tumbling out of a tree.[52] All are attired in rochets and chimeres. Similarly Archbishop Laud, clad in rochet and chimere, appeared on the title page of *Canterburie[s] Pilgrimage: or the Testimony of an accused Conscience*, a polemical tract against episcopacy.[53] In images such as these, the nexus of episcopacy, episcopal vestments and popery were all strongly asserted.

Figure 2 William Warham after Hans Holbein the Younger oil on panel, early Seventeenth century (1527), © National Portrait Gallery.

Criticisms of the popish character of episcopacy moved beyond appearance to challenge the authority of episcopal office and to stress its popish corruption. The often satirical comments on episcopal vestments by Prynne, Milton and others were less concerned with the vestments as physical items and more with how they revealed prelatical deceit and manipulation of power. These points went to the core of many arguments against the retentions of vestments and trappings. Thomas Cranmer's preface to the prayer book had stressed the need for outward forms to be clearly understandable and not to create confusion. However, later critics of episcopal dress argued that the rochet and chimere tended only to confusion, making English bishops seem popish and suggesting their authority was unreformed.[54] Milton's *Of Reformation* (1641) employed vestments as a means of condemning episcopacy in its entirety, using its visual manifestation as the most direct and compelling means of doing so.[55] Hooper's *The Church of England Free from the Imputation of Popery* also makes clear that attacks against bishops for what they wore were signifiers of deeper contests about the negotiation and exercise of authority.

Visual assertions of episcopacy

Bishops and the clergy who conformed to and supported episcopal authority responded to these pejorative comments. Out of these criticisms emerged a range of tracts intended to defend the Church of England and more narrowly, the episcopate, from allegations of popery. These included George Hooper's text. The background of his work comprises a large number of polemical writings by conforming divines intended to show that although the Church of England retained bishops and their customary garb, English bishops were not the same as Roman Catholic bishops. These works include Edward Fowler's *The Case of the Church of England symbolizing so far as it doth with the Church of Rome, makes communion with them unlawful*, as well as writings by notable preachers and controversialists William Sherlock, Gregory Hascard, Thomas Tenison and John Tillotson.[56] More specifically, Hooper undertook the writing and publishing of *The Church of England Free from the Imputation of Popery* at the direct behest of Bishop Henry Compton of London, who was in frequent correspondence with continental Protestant divines to adduce evidence that English episcopacy was reformed.[57]

Hooper's writing was surrounded not only by a wide range of writings about vestments and ritual, but by the emphatic visual assertion of episcopal power. During the time Hooper planned, published and revised his work, the visual splendour of episcopacy was enhanced; added to the already provocative rochet and chimere were further visual symbols of episcopacy. A brief survey of the monuments which commemorated seventeenth-century bishops is instructive for what it reveals of their splendid appearance during the Restoration. Archbishop Matthew Hutton (d.1606) lies on his monument in York Minster in rochet and chimere, but wearing a foursquare geometrical cap, a visible symbol of his Calvinist religiosity (Figure 3).[58] Nearby are Archbishops Toby Matthew (d.1628) and Accepted Frewen (d. 1664), whose sculptural monuments convey a similarly austere sense of Calvinist religion to Hutton's.[59] Bishops were commemorated in effigies showing them, as was Hutton, in their rochets and chimeres and many bishops left these permanent visual records of their office and appearance.[60] But in the same aisle of York Minster are commemorated Archbishops Richard Sterne (d.1683) (Figure 4), John Dolben (d.1686) (Figure 5) and Thomas Lamplugh (d.1691) (Figure 6), Restoration prelates whose elaborate Baroque monuments display not only a different visual aesthetic to Hutton's awkward Jacobean monument, but also a different conception of episcopal appearance.[61] Gone is Hutton's austere Calvinist square cap. Sterne, Dolben and Lamplugh are shown in the full visual splendour of Restoration

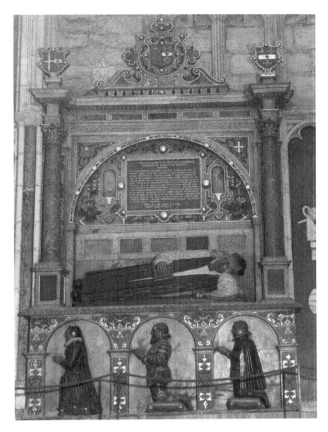

Figure 3 Effigy of Matthew Hutton c.1606 South Choir Aisle, York Minster, © Dean and Chapter of York: Reproduced by kind permission.

episcopacy, most spectacularly Dolben, whose effigy reclines languidly gazing into the distance as ornate Baroque putti fly above him.[62] Other monuments erected during the Restoration to bishops suggest that this impression of the enhanced splendour of episcopacy was to be found throughout England. Archbishop Gilbert Sheldon's tomb in Croydon Minster has atop it a marble effigy showing the prelate in a flowing chimere, grasping a crozier and wearing a mitre.[63] The tomb by Grinling Gibbons of Narcissus Marsh, Archbishop of Dublin, in St Patrick's Cathedral reduces the symbols down to a mitre placed on a cushion, both carved from marble.[64] The solitary mitre is, however, potently evocative of his office and authority.

Certain factors gave impetus to this increasing emphasis on episcopal appearance including the necessity to restore many cathedrals which had been left ruined and ransacked by the fighting in the Civil Wars. After

Figure 4 Effigy of Richard Sterne South Choir Aisle, York Minster, © Dean and Chapter of York: Reproduced by kind permission.

1660, considerable restoration work was begun on cathedrals including Canterbury, Durham, Exeter and most of all Lichfield, which had been severely damaged during a siege.[65] A further impetus in the metropolis was the Great Fire of London in 1666, which destroyed St Paul's Cathedral and most parish churches in London, and after which there was a concerted effort to renew the fabric of English churches.[66] Yet a further impetus was the enduring attacks against episcopacy, suggesting that the visual assertion of episcopacy was in part the assertion of episcopal power against forces which sought to undermine it. Restoration of damaged or destroyed churches and cathedrals most often proceeded under the patronage of bishops, including not just their consent to restore, but also their promotion of restoration and their willingness to pay for it. Seventeenth-century English bishops publicly exhibited their authority and gave it physical form through this patronage, and this is the cultural background to Hooper's work, much as the vestiarian

The Restoration, Episcopal Self-representation and the Defence of Vestments 107

Figure 5 Effigy of John Dolben South Choir Aisle, York Minster, © Dean and Chapter of York: Reproduced by kind permission.

disputes provided the polemical background. The repairs made to the art and architecture of Durham Cathedral by Bishop John Cosin (d.1672) after the Civil Wars did not merely replace or repair what had been destroyed or vandalized by Scottish soldiers. Instead, the canopies of the choir stalls and the organ case placed in the cathedral by Cosin sprouted a sequence of ornamental mitres, an artistic redevelopment expected of a bishop known to be an enthusiastic patron of art and music, but a decoration which also attested to the re-established episcopal authority in the Palatinate.[67] Cosin's expense accounts attest to his personal contribution to the restoration of the Cathedral and the decorations were a strongly personal communication of the symbolism of costume and appearance which displayed episcopal authority.[68] Durham was not the only cathedral to benefit from episcopal patronage in the Restoration. Canterbury Cathedral received a handsome archiepiscopal

Figure 6 Effigy of Thomas Lamplugh By Grinling Gibbons, c.1691 South Choir Aisle, York Minster © Dean and Chapter of York: Reproduced by kind permission.

throne carved by the master craftsman Grinling Gibbons, and donated by Archbishop Thomas Tenison.[69] Other cathedrals damaged in the Civil Wars such as Lichfield were repaired under episcopal patronage and resources such as organs and choirs of boys and men brought back.[70] At Lichfield, Bishop Hacket commissioned Christopher Wren to rebuild the central spire shattered by Cromwellian cannon.[71] This patronage shows that the traditional garb of bishops, while remaining an affront to many Protestants, participated in the developing visual assertion of episcopacy. Restoration art and the religious culture surrounding episcopacy gave additional impetus to attacks against prelacy and also meant there was more need than ever to defend episcopacy and its raiment.

Defending episcopal dress: George Hooper

Writing against this background, Hooper constructed a broad defence of both vestments and the clergy who wore them, and developed an argument based upon appeals to both antiquity and modernity. Episcopacy, according to Hooper, was a valid form of church government because of its apostolic lineage, but Hooper did not rest content with the antiquity of episcopacy, instead looking to more contemporary historical events to proclaim that the Church of England was 'the greatest and best Church of the Reformation'.[72] In drawing these conclusions, both bishops and vestments were his yardsticks of measurement, as both were tangible evidence of the godly prudence of English reformers, and both were a means of comparing the excellence of the English Reformation against the benchmark of continental reforms. The Church of England, urged Hooper, had this pre-eminent place among contemporary reformed churches because of the discerning and prudent judgments which reformers had made, including the retention of both episcopacy and the vestments which were the external signifiers of their office. Hooper's text also reveals the comparisons between reformed English bishops and unreformed Catholic bishops. While many episcopal opponents believed there was no distinction, Hooper's acknowledgement that there were 'Popish Bishops' in Europe draws attention to his intention to undermine the polemical assertions that it was impossible to distinguish popish bishops from reformed English bishops.[73]

Hooper recognized that attacks on the appearance of bishops pointed the way to a much deeper level of animus, outward garb being identified as a visible symbol of imperfect reform. In the eyes of non-conformists, the government of the Church by bishops and the authority they held was the most troublesome of the many popish imperfections that remained in the late sixteenth and seventeenth centuries. During the reign of Charles II, Hooper listed 'Government by Bishops, a Liturgy of some Ancient Prayers, Kneeling at the Communion, the Cross at Baptism, the Surplice, and the Observation of some Christian Fasts and Feasts' as enduring causes of controversy and breaches in discipline, indicating the lengthy currency of these complaints.[74]

Hooper, albeit mockingly, recounted the long history of controversial writing on both vestments and church government, recalling in 1683 that: 'To prove the Rites of our Church unlawful step by step, had been a troublesome Task [for anti-episcopal polemicists]'.[75] While Hooper would clearly have preferred that the opponents of the Church had not bothered to take the trouble, he also referred to the 'length of their Discourse', indicating the great age and voluminous quantity of the writings on vestments.⁷⁶ Over the seventeenth century, the rubric of the *Book of Common Prayer* and the Church of England's vestiarian legislation had both incurred polemical attack for the rituals and ornaments they permitted. Tracts such as *A Dispute vpon the Qvestion of Kneeling in the Acte of Receiving the Sacramental bread and wine, proving it to be unlawfull* and *The Protestation Of the Two and Twenty Divines, For the Setling of the Church: And the Particulars by them excepted against in the Liturgie: Not that the Book of Common Prayer of the Church of England should be utterly abolished, but purged of all Innovations and Absurdities* are typical of the literature condemning the rituals of the Church.⁷⁷ Importantly, Hooper was also aware that disputes over external garments were intrinsic to much deeper controversies about how religious power was negotiated and exercised, and that episcopal authority could be weakened by the claim it was popish in origin and expression. Part of this lengthy discourse advocated that English Protestants should 'pluck up Episcopacy Root and Branch as Popish, and . . . Establish Presbytery, the Form of Gods own appointment',⁷⁸ language still current in the Restoration but derived from the Root and Branch Petition of decades earlier. As Hooper understood it, conflict over the external trappings of the Church of England were a prelude to attacks against its episcopal hierarchy.

Hooper also understood that attacks against bishops' vestments were contestations over religious identity in post-Reformation England. Studies of imagery and symbolism in the early modern world point out that the meanings of images and objects carried an often negotiated meaning relating to the ritual performance of power rituals.⁷⁹ In the case of episcopal vestments, it was a meaning negotiated between bishops, polemicists, politicians and subordinates.⁸⁰ At stake in these polemical exchanges was the identity of faith communities and institutions as being Protestant and reformed; this was an identity which bishops claimed and their opponents contested. As Sharpe points out, images and visual appearance were part of the arts of persuasion, or were a means of branding something with a particular identity.⁸¹ For Hooper, the vestments were tools of persuasion, visual evidence of the processes of reform and the godliness of bishops. To Hooper, it mattered that bishops should not be denied the title Protestant. Complaining of invective circulating in England that the episcopate was popish, Hooper located the source of this invective in the conventicles and meeting houses of Protestant dissenters: 'Do they not find there Popery and our Church in a breath? the Rites of that Church so mention'd, as to include ours? and themselves flattered with the Title of True Protestants, to our Exclusion?'⁸² Hooper reiterated this point, suggesting that dissenters claimed the title of 'True Protestants on the one side, by the same reason we are Papists on the other'.[83]

In claiming a reformed identity for episcopacy, Hooper's work stands forth distinctively in his treatment of vestments and Church authority. Much of the evidence collected or sponsored by other defenders of episcopacy, such as Bishop Compton, intended to render bishops inoffensive and uncontroversial by suggesting that indifferent fate had created the current form of the Church of England.[84] Hooper's work indicates a different approach to the question of defending Church authority. He showed that the vestments worn by bishops could in fact provide positive evidence of how the bishops of the Church of England differed from the Roman Church, arguing that the maintenance of vestments was a thoughtful and godly decision by reformers. Similarly, government of the Church by bishops was far from indifferent; had it been so, 'our Church might have taken leave to have chosen a sort of Aristocracy, as others have been pleas'd with a kind of Democracy.' However, Hooper rejected this assessment of random historical development, instead insisting upon episcopacy as being an intrinsic aspect of reformed religion and a marker of the excellence of the English Reformation.[85]

Throughout his tract, Hooper makes clear the significance of this understanding of Church authority, and its chief purpose was to undermine objections to the retention, by the 'first Reformers', of some institutions and vestments. Hooper ridiculed the idea that English vestments could disconcert and horrify dissenters, suggesting that dissenters reacted to vestments as if clergy wearing vestments 'were an apparition'.[86] Through his mocking comments, he sought to undermine the horror which puritans felt towards vestments which were only 'innocent linen'.[87] Although his work is shot through with sarcasm, Hooper was in no doubt that the issues he dealt with were serious rather than 'matters indifferent' and had as their objective the destruction of the episcopal hierarchy. His tone may have been mocking, but Hooper argued that the polemic against vestments was the foundation of arguments which tended to the abolition of much else besides the rochet and chimere: 'And then we were to have no Bishops, because the Pope was one.'[88]

Hooper's work reveals an imaginative reconfiguring of old arguments against episcopacy into arguments in its favour. Close reading of Hooper's text shows that over the course of the tract he advanced a set of consistent arguments in favour of episcopacy. His ideas used the terminology of matters indifferent, or '[i]ndifferent circumstantial things' but overturned this idea.[89] His text suggests that the retention of vestments did not occur because they were simply an unimportant or indifferent matter. In this point, he diverged from many decades of conforming writing, which had decried dissent as unreasonable agitation over matters indifferent.[90] His work can be read as proposing a novel interpretation, suggesting that Tudor reformers had made a positive choice to retain vestments. Hooper argued that the 'Spiritual Governours' of the Reformation had decided on what to retain and what to reject 'as they should see cause'.[91] Accordingly, Hooper suggested that deliberate choices had been made, a strand of argument removing him from the more familiar trajectory of 'matters indifferent' and making clear the originality of this text.

Later in the tract, Hooper sharply clarified this point. Acknowledging that not all choices concerning retention or discarding ceremonies related to matters indifferent, Hooper argued that some choices about the retention of both episcopacy and its external trappings were for the good of Protestantism. According to Hooper: 'All the Innocent Ceremonies indeed we did not keep; because their Number was Excessively great'.[92] Thus, according to his assessment of sixteenth-century history, the 'First Reformers' had made deliberate decisions about what aspects of the pre-Reformation Church should be retained or discarded. 'The first Governours of our Reform'd Church did not only use their Liberty, and impose them as things Indifferent; but as things expedient, and to which they were oblig'd in all Godly Prudence'.[93] Hooper therefore diverged from a centuries-old strategy of suggesting that the wearing of vestments, as well as kneeling at communion or making the sign of the cross, were harmless matters. Hooper argued that the preservation of vestments, and of the order of bishops who wore them, were positive evidence of reformation, and the external sign provided by the vestments was a necessity for the consolidation of reformed religion. Deliberate choices, made after godly deliberation, had preserved these items. Hooper proposed a vision of the Reformation in which the reformers had carefully discriminated and deliberate choices had been made about the retention of pre-Reformation trappings.

Although vestments were but 'an Innocent Habit made of Linnen', in Hooper's text they were also positive evidence of the reformed character of the English Church.[94] Importantly, in a text devoted to defending not only episcopal power but also the external signs of that power, Hooper was preoccupied with visual evidence and what eyes could see. As he wrote of course there was more and more to see of episcopacy, as cathedrals were restored and beautified. A survey of his complete text shows that Hooper formulated a particular strategy of contrasting reformed with popish episcopacy, based on what external markers could be seen. He argued that this was a contrast many misunderstood, for there were those 'who know so little the constitution of the Protestant Religion, as to not see it in our Church'.⁹⁵ Yet according to Hooper, the distinctions were clear, even if many eyes were blind to it, and his account of the process of the Reformation, and the choices made by bishops in this time, provided evidence of both the necessity and the godliness of episcopal government and its external signs.

We should consider further the idea encountered in Hooper's text that bishops and vestments were part of a godly reformation. For Hooper, bishops set an unimpeachable and clearly visible standard of reformed ecclesiology. Not least, bishops including Cranmer and Ridley had inaugurated the Reformation, but retaining episcopacy was also a form of resistance against popery, and clad in their rochets and chimeres, English bishops were for Hooper a visible force of authority differentiating godly English religion from popish error. Hooper asked 'Shall we allow the Pope so much power as to make that unlawful by his Use, which the Apostles and their Disciples have recommended to us, by theirs'.⁹⁶ Again, antiquity and modernity converge in Hooper's thinking, episcopacy not only justified by its apostolic origins, but in the contemporary distinctions between popish and reformed bishops which Hooper asserts, and the benchmark which bishops set as a force in opposition to papacy.

To reach this interpretation, Hooper placed the English episcopate and its trappings of office within a broader world of both continental reforms and continental Catholicism. In doing so, he was not unusual in his period; one need only think of Bishop Compton searching for evidence for the acceptability of episcopacy among continental Protestants. But a competitive emphasis, as well as an assertion of the evidence which the eyes could see, defines Hooper's work as distinctive within its period. He suggested that the external trappings of the Church of England and its episcopal hierarchy were intrinsic to the progression of the reformation and to the reformed identity of the English Church. In part, a reading of Hooper's text shows that he considered this reformed reputation was based on restoring the ancient and primitive face of the Church. Thus, the 'first reformers' had made choices about government and ritual which returned the English Church to 'the Standard of the *Primitive Church*'.⁹⁷ Some of his contemporaries also pursued this path; a year after Hooper's 1683 work, the text *The Case of the Cross in Baptism Considered* argued signing the cross manually was 'much more ancient than the first Corruption and Depravation of the Church of Rome'.⁹⁸ Two years after Hooper's tract appeared, an anonymous work defended kneeling to receive the sacrament at Communion as it was a practice according with the '*first and purest Ages*'.⁹⁹

But Hooper's text cannot be read as inhabiting a world which believed the Early Church alone set benchmarks of ecclesiology and doctrine. His eyes were fixed on his immediate world and the churches – Roman Catholic and evangelical – in Europe. In this world, Hooper suggested that the bishops of his church and their external trappings provided benchmarks of moderation. Radically, his text inhabits a markedly different world to many contemporary works, as he proposed that continental Catholicism and the evangelical churches in Europe almost converged in their lack of moderation: 'Geneva itself, was not far from *Italy*'.[100] Hooper urged that reform itself could warp too far, and could end up popish in its lack of restraint: 'every Man was to be Pope himself'.[101] In contrast to this possibility, the Church of England presented a positive model of reform. Hooper's text shows that the decisions made by English reformers were not indebted to more extreme continental reforms, nor were the fruits of English reform popish in nature.

Hooper responded to attacks on the Church of England, its episcopacy and its vestments. His text demonstrates how he used and inverted those attacks to show the church's bishops as suitably reformed and their external appearance showed decisions had been made to encourage godly reform. Attacks against the church's bishops were taken by Hooper to show that Protestantism itself was harmed by criticism of episcopacy: 'when the measure of a thorough Reformation shall be the utmost Opposition to *Rome*, and a Protestant Church quarrelled and reputed Popish for some common innocent Usages; then it is they the *Romish* Advocates may triumph well.'[102] He emphasized the harm which Protestantism in general would incur from attacks on episcopacy: 'we have seen what occasion of Obloquy and Reproach it brings on the Cause of the Reformation.'[103] Here, Hooper inverted common arguments that the bishops of the Church were popish: instead, his survey of the controversies which the institution and trappings of episcopacy provoked revealed bishops as a benchmark of positive reform, and that attacks against them weakened Protestantism. Hooper in fact went on the attack, discarding arguments concerning 'matters indifferent' and instead suggesting that English bishops could be viewed as sharply competitive in the standard they set, godly in comparison to Catholic bishops, but moderate in comparison with other reformed religious authorities. His text proposed a nexus of appearance and power, one to be expected in a work which had had as its background the mature visual assertion of Restoration episcopacy, but which suggested that the appearance of bishops derived from judicious reforms that had preserved both the order and its vestments.

Conclusion

Taking advantage of the artistic opportunities provided by the architectural disasters associated with the Civil Wars and the Great Fire, Restoration episcopal patronage allowed for the public display in churches and cathedrals of the signs of episcopal authority. However, the visual manifestation of episcopacy had long attracted adverse comment. Episcopal vestments – the rochet and chimere – had been the focus of many anti-episcopal tracts written since the sixteenth century. However, they could also provide the means of defence. George Hooper's *The Church of England Free from the Imputation of Popery* argued that vestments were more than 'matters indifferent', as many preceding churchmen had viewed them. Instead, Hooper proposed a noteworthy interpretation of both the progression of reform and the exercise of episcopal authority.

Hooper's work is significant for his notable divergence from well-trod arguments that vestments were a 'matter indifferent'. His work is further important for what it reveals of the ongoing attempts during the Restoration to legitimate and defend episcopacy. His work was paralleled by the ever more assertive visual display of episcopal authority in cathedrals. But even as this authority was enshrined, it needed ongoing defence, as Hooper's text shows. The visual assertion of episcopal power did not signify episcopal security, but was a sign of enduring insecurity, as much as the continued controversy over the appearance of the rochet and chimere remained an enduring threat. Hooper's work makes clear that he contributed to a polemical environment in which the reformed character of the episcopate required ongoing and ever more extensive defence, even as the display of this power became ever more obvious.

Conclusion: Identifying Reformed Authority

In a world where polemicists contested the necessity and usefulness of bishops, and where polemical exchanges were intensely sharpened by decades of debate, bishops invoked a reformed identity that was complex in nature and subject to shifts in meaning and emphasis. Contests over the meaning of reformed episcopacy and the extent and necessity of their powers took place in a variety of ways, including the transmission of spoken insights, debate at court and in parliament, during which bishops appeared in raiment that provoked both fear and suspicion, and through the exchange of polemical texts. For parts of the seventeenth century it was actually dangerous to be a bishop. During the Restoration, with bishops once again safe in their episcopal palaces, contestation took the form of ever more frequent exchanges of both short and long tracts, which poured from printing presses. Contestation about bishops could therefore take a variety of forms, but so could the identity invoked and contested. The identity which bishops claimed, or which writers sympathetic to bishops claimed on their behalf, was intended to neutralize polemical arguments that bishops were a visible sign of imperfect and incomplete reform. So too was the broader terminology of these polemical exchanges in a state of flux. What it meant to be godly, or to be a dissenter or a puritan were contested identities and charged terms. Opponents of episcopacy claimed for themselves the identity of godly victims of episcopal authority and perceived themselves as dissenters from illegitimate episcopal identity. Upholders of episcopal identity used the term 'puritan' to suggest egregious rebellion from lawful authority. In the midst of this contestation over not only the source and basis of Church authority, but also the appropriate terms with which to express this authority, the necessity of bishops and the validity of their authority remained the principal source of contention.

English monarchs preserved and used the English episcopate during the Reformation, but religious reform confused and complicated the purpose and necessity of bishops in a reformed Church. Bishops, including originally Ridley of London, Latimer of Worcester, Hooper of Gloucester, Farrar of St David's and Cranmer of Canterbury, wielded reformed ecclesiastical authority.

Diocesan structures, as well as the metropolitical provinces presided over by archbishops, survived reforms under both Henry VIII and Edward VI. While early Tudor bishops were not always in doctrinal or even personal accord with each other, they superintended religious reform during the reigns of Henry VIII and Edward VI. Churchmen had long accepted the confluence of princely patronage and religious reform. Early in James I's reign Dr Richard Eedes, the Dean of Worcester, interpreted the responsibility of princes to advance reform.[1] According to Eedes, the superintendence of Church discipline and doctrine lay with princes, as he urged that 'the *Church* [is] in all dutie more than bound to *Princes*, because shee hath her peace in their favour'.[2] A later churchman, Thomas Tenison pointed to the importance of episcopacy in this polity. He stressed that '*Episcopal Government*' was 'agreeable to the Scheme of Monarchy', stressing that episcopacy would be supported by and in turn support monarchical rule.[3]

While underpinned by monarchy and by constitutional theories that argued that kingship was ideally supported by episcopacy, members of the episcopate were often silent on defining the doctrinal cohesion of their office, order or powers.[4] Yet it is clear that individual bishops were anxious to consolidate their authority and justify their order. This authority could be and was breached, and bishops lost status and revenues from 1646 to 1660 and faced several generations of polemical attack disputing their functional and sacramental necessity. Most ominously for bishops, their status, power and even appearance seemed unacceptably popish in the opinion of a large body of Protestant polemicists. What made episcopacy especially alarming, in the eyes of its detractors, was the manner in which individual bishops appeared to mimic the disciplinary capacity of Roman Catholicism. The ability of these apparently unreformed prelates to rule the English Church was often disputed by their lower clergy and their place in the Church seemed unclear and ambiguous.

The apparent popishness of the English episcopate continued to pose a problem for the reputations of bishops up to the end of the seventeenth century. By that point many years of polemical writings as well as the parliamentary agitations of the 1640s had linked episcopacy with popishness and then ineluctably with persecution inflicted by bishops. By 1646, when Parliament abolished episcopacy, many Protestant polemicists were sufficiently convinced of the episcopate's actively harmful influence and sufficiently outraged by the conduct of individual bishops like Laud and Wren to have pressed urgently for the episcopate's abolition.

Polemical attack and eventually parliamentary abolition provoked sustained defences of episcopacy, and I have examined the strategies for both tearing down and sustaining episcopacy. Throughout the seventeenth century, a range of writers who were themselves bishops or else clergy sympathetic to bishops asserted that episcopate could claim the identity of the active continuators of the Tudor reformers and protectors of English Protestantism. Clergy more commonly thought of as 'Arminian' pursued a similar trajectory of thought, stressing that episcopal identity could be identified by episcopal activities which developed and protected the work of original reformers.

In the period I have surveyed, bishops interacted not only with a broader landscape of political demands (notably their role in the House of Lords) but with a much broader world of continental reforms, where non-episcopal and episcopal reformed churches provided the substance of both attack against and defence of bishops. The progress of reformation elsewhere in Europe could be raised as an argument against episcopacy, showing that reforms had tended to dispense with bishops. By contrast, bishops remained in England and continued as the third and highest tier of the orders of the spirituality. While episcopal revenues were often reduced because of religious change, offices such as the Court of Faculties and High Commission ensured the continued institutional and legal strength of English bishops.[5]

According to contemporary (and mostly critical) observers, English reforms seemed to have wrought little effect on the status, responsibilities or powers of bishops. Garbed in their rochets and chimeres and still to be found in palaces and cathedrals, the bishops of the reforming and reformed English Church looked like the unreformed bishops of medieval English and contemporary Roman Catholicism. Yet the analysis of primary sources offered in this book reveals that members of the episcopate tried to neutralize such allegations.

Thomas Cranmer was enthroned in Canterbury Cathedral in 1533 wearing the papal pallium; by the time of his trial and execution he was a heretic bishop. Matthew Parker's consecration in 1559 consolidated the institutional distinction between Romanist and reformed bishops. Parker, a keen antiquarian and devotee of the Anglo-Saxon Church, found his consecration confusing and he was compelled to argue through to his own satisfaction the possibility that early Christianity and a reformed primate could be connected.[6]

For the deprived minister Josias Nichols, reformed bishops sheltered and encouraged churchmen such as himself who were alleged (so he said) to be Puritans. In the eyes of their opponents, bishops were the persecutors of the godly, but definitions and understandings of reformed authority could come from the deprived and dispossessed ministers who looked back to a (recent) golden age of episcopal patronage. Texts by bishops themselves and clergy sympathetic to bishops also pursued this identity, showing the enduring and continuing usefulness of bishops to reformed religion through their patronage of godly clergy.

Nichols's works reveal a clear rhetorical strategy: as a deprived minister he protested against his suspension and pointed to the existence of bishops whose functions and priorities validated his own churchmanship, which bishops now punished as dissent. Nichols's surveys of bishops in *Plea of the Innocent* and *Abrahams Faith* were intended to show him conforming to the Church, even though he was a dissenter. Nichols drew on the episcopate of an earlier generation to justify himself as a loyal member of the Church. So too did Archbishop William Laud, who compared himself with the bishops of Henry VIII's reign, notably Thomas Cranmer, in order to demonstrate that the episcopate he led was reformed. Laud's resort to the example of Cranmer was one aspect of a complex and enormously detailed defence of episcopacy in the 1640s. Although Laud and the clergy closely associated with him, including John Cosin and Archbishop Richard Neile of York, appeared to their critics to be taking the Church of England towards Rome, bishops also seemed (to these critics) ipso facto popish, as they were an element of the English Church that required further reform. Laud attempted to vitiate such criticisms by drawing a comparison between earlier bishops who seemed to endorse the reformed identity and their later brethren, himself included.

Arthur Duck and John Gauden both responded to one of the chief themes of the seventeenth century, in which advocates as diverse as Archbishop Ussher and anonymous dissenting pamphleteers urged the reduction of episcopacy, meaning that the size of dioceses and sacramental and jurisdictional powers of bishops would be reduced and the lordliness of bishops cut down to Presbyterian standards. I also showed these calls for reduction emerging from a longer history of sixteenth-century reforms of episcopacy. Writings by Duck and Gauden make sense as a subject for joint study in the light of this setting and the demands it prompted for the reduction of episcopacy. Duck, looking to medieval harbingers of reform, argued that evidence indicated that bishops were sufficiently reformed; Gauden, looking to the immediate world of European reform, argued against the reduction of episcopacy.

Gauden's *St Peters Bands* had been written with the hope in mind that monarchy and the episcopate would both revive. Gauden experienced the felicity of the Restoration, but as we have seen from arguments about episcopal raiment, criticisms of episcopacy were not silenced by the apparent triumph of

1660. George Hooper's writings make a natural place to end analysis of both the attack and the defence of episcopacy as he looked back over 100 years of religious debate on Church authority and rested his case on what he believed had been the intentions of reformers during the Tudor period. The issue he focused on – clerical raiment – was approached in the same way that orthodox religious thought understood the sacraments. External signs betoken inner realities. This could go both ways and for episcopal detractors, the rochet and chimere were outward signs of inner popishness. In surveying the catalogue of criticisms of episcopal wealth, duties, actions and even dress, it can seem that bishops were expected by their contemporaries to be and do too much. Hooper's text thus goes to the heart of much of the criticism of bishops, and through both scholarship and sarcasm he wanted to show that vestments were harmless and bishops were necessary.

The prayers from the order of consecration of bishops in the Edwardine *Book of Common Prayer* placed high expectations on bishops. They needed an extensive array of qualities and held a range of responsibilities, to 'use the authoritie geuen unto him, not to destroie, but to saue, not hurt, but to helpe'. A bishop also needed to be a 'wise and faithful seruant', as well as 'dilygente, sobre, discrete'.[7] Out of a variety of roles and expectations, it was enough for many bishops that they should chiefly be known as reformed and godly, an identity that large volumes of polemical writings sought to deny them. The episcopate was only seriously threatened by the Long Parliament's actions of the 1640s. Otherwise the institution of the episcopate withstood more than a century of controversy from the burning of most of the Edwardian episcopate in 1555–56, the Admonition Controversy of the 1570s and the Marprelate tracts of the next decade, the Root and Branch Petition of the 1640s through to the personal animosity of James II towards his bishops. But to the end of the seventeenth century, episcopal identity remained shifting and uncertain. Bishops were required to be different things, to be victims, champions and defenders, as well as apostolic and contemporary, and the history of the first one and a half centuries of reformed English episcopacy suggests nothing so much as dogged survival in the pursuit of an intensely desired identity.

Notes

Introduction

1 Alan Haynes, *Robert Cecil 1st Earl of Salisbury: Servant of Two Sovereigns* (London: Peter Owen, 1989), p. 144.
2 Thomas Macaulay, *History of England from the Accession of James the Second* (London: Everyman Edition, 1913–15), vol. II, p. 103.
3 The bishops in Scotland could be just as militant, however. In 1637 when the Bishop of Brechin used the controversial and much hated Prayer Book for the first time, he took the precaution of taking two loaded pistols into the cathedral with him; John Miller, *The Stuarts* (London: Hambledon Continuum, 2004), p. 80.
4 Joseph Hall, *Works* (ed. Philip Wynter), (Oxford: Oxford University Press, 1843), vol. I, p. lvii. The work of Parliament against bishops was also given mocking reference in 'a good Admonition to Protestants', affixed to the forged letter from Lord John Finch to John Cosin; Anon., *The Coppy of a Letter Sent from Iohn Lord Finch, late Lord Keeper, to his Friend Dr. Cozens: With A Commemoration of the Favours Dr. Cozens Shewed him in his Vice-Chancellorship. Unto VVhich is Annexed a Good Admonition to Protestants (1641)*, pp. 5–6.
5 Anon., *Prelatique Preachers None of Christ's Teachers* (London, 1662), p. 2.
6 See Chapter 4 below.
7 See Chapter 6 below.
8 [Edward Stillingfleet], *A Vindication of their Majesties Authority to fill the Sees of the Deprived Bishops: In a Letter out of the Country. Occasioned by Dr. B—'s Refusal of the Bishoprick of Bath and Wells* (London: for Ric. Chiswell, 1691), p. 6. See also Hugh A. L. Rice, *Thomas Ken: Bishop and Non-Juror* (London: SPCK, 1958); William Sancroft, *A Vindication of the Arch-Bishop and several other Bishops from the Imputations and Calumnies Cast upon them by the Author of the Modest Enquiry* (London, 1690).
9 See Chapter 6 below. A rochet is a white linen robe with gathered sleeves; a chimere is a red or black silk sleeveless gown worn over it. Both were the habitual dress of bishops.
10 Kenneth Fincham, 'Episcopal government, 1603–1640', in Kenneth Fincham (ed.), *The Early Stuart Church, 1603–1642* (London: Macmillan, 1993), pp. 71–91; Lacey

Baldwin Smith, *Tudor Prelates and Politics, 1536–1558* (Princeton: Princeton University Press, 1953); R. B. Manning, 'The crisis of episcopal authority during the Reign of Elizabeth I', *Journal of British Studies* (vol. 11, no. 1, 1971), pp. 1–25; William Sheils, 'Some problems of government in a new diocese: the bishop and the Puritans in the diocese of Peterborough, 1560–1630', in Rosemary O'Day and Felcity Heal (eds), *Continuity and Change: Personnel and Administration of the Church of England 1500–1642* (Leicester: Leicester University Press, 1976), p. 176; D. E. Kennedy, 'The Jacobean episcopate', *Historical Journal* (vol. 5, no. 2, 1962), pp. 175–81; Andrew A. Chibi, 'The social and regional origins of the Henrician episcopacy', *Sixteenth Century Journal* (vol. 29, no. 4, 1998), pp. 955–73.

11 Works on individual bishops include the following: Diarmaid MacCulloch, *Thomas Cranmer: A Life* (New Haven: Yale University Press, 1996); Jasper Ridley, *Thomas Cranmer* (Oxford: Clarendon Press, 1962); H. R. Trevor-Roper, *Archbishop Laud* 2nd edn (London: Phoenix, 2000); S. J. Gunn and P. G. Lindley (eds), *Cardinal Wolsey: Church, State and Art* (Cambridge: Cambridge University Press, 1991); Glyn Redworth, *In Defence of the Church Catholic: The Life of Stephen Gardiner* (Oxford: Oxford University Press, 1990); Peter Lake, 'Matthew Hutton – a puritan bishop?', *History* (vol. 64, no. 211, 1979), pp. 182–204; Caroline Litzenberger, 'Richard Cheyney, Bishop of Gloucester: an infidel in religion?', *Sixteenth Century Journal* (vol. 25, no. 3, 1994), pp. 567–84; Patrick Collinson, *Archbishop Grindal 1519–1583: The Struggle for a Reformed Church* (Berkeley: University of California Press, 1979); Victor Sutch, *Gilbert Sheldon: Architect of Anglican Survival 1640–1676* (The Hague: M. Nijholl, 1973); Edward Carpenter, *The Protestant Bishop: Being the Life of Henry Compton, 1632–1713 Bishop of London* (London: Longmans, Green and Co., 1956).

12 Hugh Trevor-Roper, *Historical Essays* (London: Macmillan, 1957); Walter G. Simon, *The Restoration Episcopate* (New York: Bookmen Associates, 1965).

13 Norman Sykes, *Old Priest and New Presbyter: Episcopacy and Presbyterianism since the Reformation with especial relation to the Churches of England and Scotland* (Cambridge: Cambridge University Press, 1957), p. 205.

14 Sykes, *Old Priest and New Presbyter*, p. 20.

15 See J. P. Somerville, 'The Royal Supremacy and episcopacy 'Jure Divino', 1603–1640', *Journal of Ecclesiastical History* (vol. 34, no. 4, 1983), pp. 548–58.

16 This acceptance was by no means universal and Richard Montagu, Bishop of Chichester and then Norwich, 'unchurched' those Protestant confessions that did not have bishops; W. J. Tighe, 'William Laud and the reunion of the Churches: some evidence from 1637 and 1638', *Historical Journal* (vol. 30, no. 3, 1987), p. 718.

17 Ralph Houlbrooke, 'The Protestant episcopate, 1547–1603: The pastoral contribution', in Felicity Heal and Rosemary O'Day (eds), *Church and Society in England: Henry*

VIII to James I (London: Macmillan, 1977), pp. 78–98; Barrett L. Beer, 'Episcopacy and reform in Mid-Tudor England', *Albion* (vol. 23, no. 2, 1991), pp. 231–52.

18 Felicity Heal, *Of Prelates and Princes: A Study of the Economic and Social Position of the Tudor Episcopate* (Cambridge: Cambridge University Press, 1980), pp. 163, 165, 170, 321.

19 John Foxe, *Book of Martyrs: Being a History of the Persecution of the Protestants* (London: Ward, Lock, Bowden and Co., 1888), p. 422.

20 Heal, *Of Prelates and Princes*, p. 216.

21 Diarmaid MacCulloch, *The Boy King: Edward VI and the Protestant Reformation* (New York: Palgrave, 1999), pp. 199–200.

22 Patrick Collinson, 'Episcopacy and reform in England in the later sixteenth century', in *Godly People: Essays on English Protestantism and Puritanism* (London: The Hambledon Press, 1983), pp. 157–8. On scholarly assessments of the episcopate, see Collinson, *The Religion of Protestants* (Oxford: Oxford University Press, 1982), pp. 43–4; Patrick Collinson, 'Episcopacy and reform', p. 157. See also Patrick Collinson, John Craig, and Brett Usher (eds), *Conferences and Combination Lectures in the Elizabethan Church* (Dedham and Bury St Edmunds: Boydell Press/Church of England Record Society, 2003).

Chapter 1

1 S. R. Gardiner (ed.), 'Notes on the Debates in the House of Lords, officially taken by Henry Elsing, Clerk of the Parliaments, A.D. 1621', (*Camden Society*, first series, vol. 103, 1870), p. 40.

2 For which view, see Stanley Archer, 'Hooker on Apostolic Succession: the two voices', *Sixteenth Century Journal* (vol. 24, no. 1, 1993), p. 68.

3 On the revenues of the reformed episcopate, see: Felicity Heal, *Of Prelates and Princes: A Study of the Economic and Social Position of the Tudor Episcopate* (Cambridge: Cambridge University Press, 1980).

4 On the Swiss suspicion of bishops, see Patrick Collinson, *The Elizabethan Puritan Movement* (London: Cape, 1967), pp. 104–5.

5 Apart from the Scandinavian Lutheran bishops and the English episcopate, episcopacy also survived in the reformed Church of Transylvania. I am grateful to Diarmaid MacCulloch for this point.

6 On Scottish fears of bishops, see Alan. R. MacDonald, 'James VI and I, the Church of Scotland, and British ecclesiastical convergence', *Historical Journal* (vol. 48, no. 4, 2005), p. 889.

7 The Act of Parliament for the new bishoprics is BL MS Cotton. Cleo. E. iv. fol. 182.

8 Some dioceses such as Bristol were traditionally poor; they began as such under Henry VIII and remained so into the seventeenth century. The anxious manoeuvrings among bishops for placement on the deaths of their brethren reveal the poverty of post-Reformation bishoprics as John Chamberlain reported in the early seventeenth century that Bristol, then vacant through the death of the incumbent bishop, was so poor that 'we heare not yet of any suitors or pretendants for yt.' Norman McClure (ed.), *The Letters of John Chamberlain* (Philadelphia: American Philosophical Society, 1939), vol. II, p. 375.

9 Westminster's elevation was only temporary; see C. S. Knighton, 'Westminster Abbey restored', in Eamon Duffy and David Loades (eds), *The Church of Mary Tudor* (Aldershot: Ashgate, 2006), p. 79.

10 Joseph Ketley (ed.), *The Two Liturgies, AD. 1549 and AD. 1552: With Other Documents Set Forth by Authority in the Reign of King Edward VI* (Cambridge: Cambridge University Press, 1844), pp. 181-6. The significance of Queen Mary's actions in preserving episcopal infrastructure is discussed in David Loades, *Politics, Censorship and the English Reformation* (London: Pinter Publishers, 1991), p. 197.

11 *The First and Second Prayer Books of Edward VI* (London: Everyman Edition, 1910), p. 461. The Ordinal was printed in 1550 but backdated to 1549 and appended to the Prayer Book of that year.

12 Ketley (ed.), *The Two Liturgies*, pp. 182-4. On early reformed thinking on discipline see C. M. F. Davies and J. Facey, 'A Reformation dilemma: John Foxe and the problem of discipline', *Journal of Ecclesiastical History* (vol. 39, no. 1, 1988), pp. 37-65.

13 Michael A. R. Graves, *The House of Lords in the Parliaments of Edward VI and Mary I* (Cambridge: Cambridge University Press, 1981).

14 See Andrew Foster, 'The clerical estate revitalized' in Kenneth Fincham (ed.), *The Early Stuart Church, 1603-1642* (London: Macmillan, 1993).

15 The actions of Bishop Henry Compton (d.1713) are representative here, and he left written records of his discussions with clergy; Henry Compton, *The Lord Bishop of London's Fourth Letter to the Clergy of his Dioceses* (London, 1683); *The Bishop of London's Eighth Letter to his Clergy, upon a Conference How they Ought to Behave Themselves under the Toleration* (London: Benj. Motte, 1692); *The Bishop of London's Ninth Conference with his Clergy upon the Fifth and Tenth Injunctions Given by the King* (London: Benj. Motte, 1699).

16 Robert Kingdon, 'A new view of Calvin in the light if the registers of the Geneva Consistory', in Wilhelm H. Neuser and Brian G. Armstrong (eds), *Calvinus Sincerioris Religionis Vindex: Calvin as Protector of the Purer Religion*, Sixteenth Century Essays and Studies, 1977, vol. XXXVI, pp. 21-34.

17 Mary Prior, '"Reviled and crucified marriages": the position of Tudor bishops' wives', in Mary Prior (ed.), *Women in English Society, 1500-1800* (London: Methuen, 1985), pp. 118-48.

18 W. G. Hoskins, *The Age of Plunder: The England of Henry VIII 1500–1547* (London: Longman, 1976), p. 144.
19 Archbishops had worn this since at least the eighth century; Wilhelm Levison, *England and the Continent in the Eighth Century* (Oxford: Clarendon Press, 1946), pp. 19–21.
20 Alice Hunt, *The Drama of Coronation: Medieval Ceremony in Early Modern England* (Cambridge: Cambridge University Press, 2008), p. 77.
21 Hunt, *Drama of Coronation*, p. 77.
22 On Edward's accession see Chris Skidmore, *Edward VI The Lost King of England: The Struggle for the Soul of England After the Death of Henry VIII* (London: Phoenix, 2008), p. 55.
23 Thomas Cranmer, *Works* (ed. G. E. Duffield), (Appleford: Sutton Courtney Press, 1964), pp. 20–1.
24 Judith Richards addresses the constitutional significance of this sermon in 'English allegiance in a British context: political problems and legal resolutions', *Parergon* (vol. 18, no. 2, 2001), p. 108. The changing significance of English coronations is discussed in Leopold G. Wickham Legg, *English Coronation Records* (Westminster: Archibald Constable, 1901). For the significance of the archiepiscopal actions in coronations before Edward's see H. G. Richardson, 'The coronation in medieval England', *Traditio* (vol. 16, 1960), pp. 111–75.
25 Diarmaid MacCulloch, *Thomas Cranmer: A Life* (New Haven: Yale University Press, 1996), p. 117. On the earlier history of the administrative infrastructure of the archbishopric, see Sybil M. Jack, 'The conflict of Common Law and Canon Law in early sixteenth-century England: Richard Hunne revisited', *Parergon* (New Series, no. 3, 1985), p. 136.
26 MacCulloch, *Thomas Cranmer*, p. 116; Stanford Lehmberg, *The Reformation Parliament 1529–1536* (Cambridge: Cambridge University Press, 1970), pp. 191.
27 Paul Ayris, 'Continuity and change in diocese and province: the role of a Tudor bishop', *Historical Journal* (vol. 39, no. 2, 1996), p. 292; see further Ayris, 'The rule of Thomas Cranmer in diocese and province', *Reformation and Renaissance Review* (vol. 7, no. 1, 2005), pp. 69–110.
28 J. E. Cox (ed.), *Miscellaneous Writings and Letters of Thomas Cranmer, Archbishop of Canterbury, Martyr, 1556* (Cambridge: Cambridge University Press, 1844), p. 305.
29 Hugh Latimer, *Sermons* (London: Everyman, 1906), p. 33; Hooper's views are in H. Robinson (ed.), *Zurich Letters* (Cambridge: Cambridge University Press, 1842), p. 51.
30 See Norman Sykes, *Old Priest and New Presbyter: Episcopacy and Presbyterianism Since the Reformation with Especial Relation to the Churches of England and Scotland* (Cambridge: Cambridge University Press, 1957), p. 205.
31 Kenneth Fincham, 'Ramifications of the Hampton Court Conference in the dioceses, 1603–1609', *Journal of Ecclesiastical History* (vol. 36, no. 2, 1985), p. 210. A contrasting account of Heton is in Heal, *Of Prelates and Princes*, pp. 227–8.

32 York Minster Library Additional Manuscripts 18: *The Diary and Journal of his Grace Toby Matthew, Lord Archbishop of York from the 3rd Sept. MDLXXXIII to the 23rd Sunday after Trinity MDCXXII.*

33 Ralph Houlbrooke, 'The Protestant Episcopate, 1547–1603: the pastoral contribution', in Felicity Heal and Rosemary O'Day (eds), *Church and Society in England: Henry VIII to James I* (London: Macmillan, 1977), pp. 78–98.

34 The relation between these bishops is spelt out in Paul Ayris, 'Continuity and change', pp. 291–313 and J. J. Scarisbrick, *Henry VIII* (Berkeley and Los Angeles: University of California Press, 1968), p. 377.

35 On the Great Bible see Daniel Eppley, *Defending Royal Supremacy and Discerning God's Will in Tudor England* (Aldershot: Ashgate, 2007). The image is reproduced and discussed in John N. King, 'The royal image', in Dale Hoak (ed.), *Tudor Political Culture* (Cambridge: Cambridge University Press, 2002), pp. 108–9.

36 For example see Craig D'Alton on the role of bishops under Warham in tracking down late Lollards and early Lutherans in the 1520s; D'Alton, 'Cuthbert Tunstal and heresy in Essex and London', *Albion* (vol. 35, no. 2, 2003), pp. 218–19.

37 The conservative bishops of Henry VIII's Church are discussed in Fiona Kisby, '"When the King Goeth a Procession": chapel ceremonies and services, the ritual year, and religious reforms at the early Tudor court, 1485–1547', *Journal of British Studies* (vol. 40, no. 1, 2001), p. 70.

38 William Tyndale, 'W. T. to the Reader', in David Daniell (ed.), *Tyndale's Old Testament* (New Haven: Yale University Press, 1992), p. 5.

39 Samuel Clarke, *The Marrow of Ecclesiastical History: Divided into Two Parts: the First, Containing the Life of Our Blessed Lord & Saviour Jesus Christ, With The Lives of the Ancient Fathers, School-Men, First Reformers, and Modern Divines: The Second, Containing the Lives of Christian Emperors, Kings and Sovereign Princes: Whereunto are added the Lives of Inferiour Christians, Who Have Lived in These Latter centuries: and Lastly, are Subjoyned the Lives of Many of Those, Who by their Vertue and Valor Obtained the Sir-Name of Great, Divers of Which, Give Much Light to Sundry Places of Scripture, Especially to the Prophecies Concerning the Four Monarchies: Together with Lively Effigies of the Most Eminent of them Cut in Copper* (London: for W. B. [William Birch], 1675), p. 166.

40 Anon., 'An Epitaph, or rather a short discourse made vpon the life and death of Dr. Bonner', in *The Harleian Miscellany; or, a Collection of Scarce, Curious and Entertaining Pamphlets and Tracts*, vol. I (London: for Robert Dutton, 1808), p. 388. Criticisms of Bonner are noted and interpreted in Frederick S. Boas, *University Drama in the Tudor Age* (Oxford: Clarendon Press, 1914), pp. 382–85.

41 These views are recorded in Pauline Croft, 'The reputation of Robert Cecil: libels, political opinion and popular awareness in the early seventeenth century', *Transactions of the Royal Historical Society* (sixth series, vol. 1, 1991), p. 46.

42 Mark E. VanderSchaaf, 'Archbishop Parker's efforts towards a Bucerian discipline in the Church of England', *Sixteenth Century Journal* (vol. 8, no. 1, 1977), p. 101.
43 *The Correspondence of Matthew Parker D.D., Archbishop of Canterbury* (eds John Bruce and Thomas Thomason Perowne), (Cambridge: Cambridge University Press, 1853), p. 125.
44 Patrick Collinson, 'The Reformer and the Archbishop: Martin Bucer and an English Bucerian', *Journal of Religious History* (vol. 6, no. 4, 1971), p. 313.
45 Details on the clergy present at this event are to be found in Joyce M. Horn (ed.) *Fasti Ecclesiae Anglicana 1541–1857 vol. III: Canterbury, Rochester and Winchester Dioceses* (London: The Athlone Press, 1974), p. 8. Pole's appointment as legate and then primate is discussed in Judith Richards, *Mary Tudor* (Oxford: Routledge, 2008) p. 173.
46 J. A. I. Champion, *The Pillars of Priestcraft Shaken: The Church of England and its Enemies, 1660–1730* (Cambridge: Cambridge University Press, 1992), p. 61.
47 Parker's contradictory assessments of Augustine of Canterbury are in his *Correspondence*, p. 425.
48 Foxe's earliest editors and sources of information were Elizabethan bishops. Foxe was a correspondent of Archbishop Parker and his successor, Edmund Grindal, both of whom provided him with information about English martyrs, and an early Latin draft of *Actes and Monuments* was edited by John Aylmer, the bishop of London. William Nicholson (ed.), *Remains of Edmund Grindal* (Cambridge: Cambridge University Press, 1843), p. 231.
49 John Foxe, *Martyrologia, or, Records of Religious Persecution: Being a New and Comprehensive Book of Martyrs, of Ancient and Modern Times, Compiled Partly from the Acts and monuments of John Foxe, and Partly from other Genuine and Authentic Documents, Printed and in Manuscript* (London: J. Mason, 1848–51), pp. 4–9.
50 H. G. Owen, 'The Episcopal Visitation: its limits and limitations in Elizabethan London', *Journal of Ecclesiastical History* (vol. 11, no. 2, 1960), pp. 179–85.
51 John Whitgift, *Works* (ed. John Ayre), (Cambridge: Cambridge University Press, 1851–53) vol. II, p. 290.
52 On the extensive literature on episcopal resources see: Felicity Heal, 'The bishops and the Act of Exchange of 1559', *Historical Journal* (vol. 17, no. 2, 1974), pp. 227–46; Heal, 'The Tudors and the Church lands: economic problems of the Bishopric of Ely during the sixteenth century', *Economic History Review* (2nd series, vol. 26, 1973), pp. 198–217; Heal, 'The Archbishops of Canterbury and the practice of hospitality', *Journal of Ecclesiastical History* (vol. 33, no. 4, 1982), p. 544–63; and Sybil M. Jack, 'English bishops as tax collectors in the sixteenth century', *Parergon* (vol. 14, no. 1, 1996), p. 129–63.
53 With the exception of the Isle of Man, which was part of the diocese of York but not part of the Kingdom of England and Wales.

54 P. Tudor-Craig, 'Henry VIII and King David', in D. Williams (ed.), *Early Tudor England* (Woodbridge: Boydell Press, 1989), pp. 183–206; C. Bradshaw, 'David or Josiah? Old Testament kings as exemplars in Edwardian religious polemic', in B. Gordon (ed.), *Protestant History and Identity in Sixteenth Century Europe* (Aldershot: St Andrew's Studies in Reformation History, 1996), vol. 1, pp. 79–90.

55 Jeffrey R. Collins, 'The Restoration bishops and the Royal Supremacy', *Church History* (vol. 68, no. 3, 1999) p. 551.

56 On this interpretation of the *Zurich Letters*, see Patrick Collinson, 'Episcopacy and reform in England in the later sixteenth century', in *Godly People: Essays on English Protestantism and Puritanism* (London: Hambledon Press, 1983), p. 167.

57 A. S. McGrade, 'Episcopacy', in Torrance Kirby (ed.), *A Companion to Richard Hooker* (Leiden: Brill, 2008), p. 484.

58 Claire Cross, 'Churchmen and the Royal Supremacy', in Felicity Heal and Rosemary O'Day (eds), *Church and Society in England: Henry VIII to James I* (London: Macmillan, 1977), p. 30.

59 Whitgift's thought is analysed by Sykes in *Old Priest and New Presbyter*, p. 3.

60 Richard Eedes, *Six Learned and Godly Sermons: Preached Some of Them before the Kings Maiestie, some before Queen Elizabeth* (London: Adam Islip, for Edward Bishop, 1604), p. 62. For Whitgift see his *Works*, vol. 1, p. 6.

61 House of Lords Braye MSS I.fol. 88 (30 December 1629).

62 O. U. Kalu, 'Continuity in change: Bishops of London and religious dissent in early Stuart England', *Journal of British Studies* (vol. 18, no. 1, 1978), p. 41.

63 Susan Holland, 'George Abbot: "the wanted Archbishop"', *Church History* (vol. 56, no. 2, 1987), p. 178.

64 See Kenneth Fincham, *Visitation Articles and Injunctions of the Early Stuart Church* (Woodbridge: Boydell Press/Church of England Record Society, 1998) for a full discussion of this topic.

65 BL Tanner MSS. 68, fo.92, 2 May 1636; cited in Peter King, 'Bishop Wren and the suppression of the Norwich Lecturers', *Historical Journal* (vol. 11, no. 2, 1968), p. 242.

66 Kenneth Fincham, *Prelate as Pastor: the Episcopate of James I* (Oxford: Clarendon Press, 1990), p. 205.

67 [John Fieldes], *First Admonition to Parliament* ([Hemel Hempsted?], 1572).

68 Peter Milward (ed.), *Religious Controversies of the Jacobean Age: A Survey of Printed Sources* (London: The Scolar Press, 1978).

69 Patrick Collinson, *The Religion of Protestants* (Oxford: Oxford University Press, 1982), p. 40. On the Root and Branch Petition, see J. P. Kenyon (ed.), *The Stuart Constitution: Documents and Commentary 1603–1688* (Cambridge: Cambridge University Press, 1966), pp. 171–5.

70 Say and Seale instead urged judicious pruning, shedding some superfluous branches but keeping a form of episcopacy; William Lord Viscount Say and Seale,

Tvvo Speeches in Parliament of the Right Honourable William, Lord Vicount Say and Seale Mr. of his Majesties Court of Wards and Liveries, and one of his Majesties Most Honourable Privie Councell, the First upon the Bill against Bishops Power in Civill Affaires and Courts of Judicature. The Other a Declaration of Himself Touching the Liturgie, and Separation (London: Thomas Underhill, 1641), pp. 1, 4.

71   The root and branch petitions are extensively studied in Lorraine Gallant, 'Apocalyptic and non-apocalyptic anti-episcopalianism in early modern England, 1558–1646' (Dalhousie University MA, 1999).

72   Robert Sanderson, *Episcopacy Not Prejudicial to Royal Power* (London: Robert Pawlet [1661], 1678), p. 14.

73   Richard Field, *Of the Church: Fiue Bookes* (London: Imprinted by Humfrey Lownes, for Simon Waterson, 1606), vol. I, p. 323.

74   John Davenant, *Determinationes Quaestionum Quarundam Theologicarum* (1634), quoted in G. K. A. Bell, *Christian Unity: The Anglican Position* (London: Hodder and Stoughton, 1948), p. 25.

Chapter 2

1   On the meaning of conforming puritanism see especially Daniel W. Doerksen, *Conforming to the Word: Herbert, Donne and the English Church before Laud* (London: Associated University Presses, 1997), chapter one.

2   H. M. Curtis, 'Hampton Court Conference and its aftermath', *History* (vol. 46, no. 156, 1961), pp. 1–16.

3   The fullest contemporary account is William Barlow's *The Summe and Substance of the Conference, which, it pleased his Excellent Maiestie to haue with the Lords, Bishops, and other of his Clergie* (London: John Windet, 1604).

4   On Nichols' life before the Hampton Court Conference see Peter Jensen, 'The catechisms of Elizabethan England', *Reformed Theological Review* (vol. 39, no. 1, 1980), pp. 1–9.

5   BL Royal MS 17. B.XXII is the presentation copy.

6   John Harington, *Supplie or Addicion to the Catalogue of Bishops to the Yeere 1608* (ed. R. H. Miller), (Potomac, Maryland: Jose Porrua Turanzas S.A., 1979); Josias Nichols, *The Plea of the Innocent Wherein is Auerred; that the Ministers & People Falslie Termed Puritanes, are Iniuriouslie Slaundered for Enemies of Troublers of the State. Published for the Common Good of the Church and Common Wealth of this Realme of England as a Countermure against all Sycophantising Papsts, Statising Priestes, Neutralising Atheistes, and Satanising Scorners of all Godlinesse, Trueth and Honestie. Written: by Iosias Nichols, a faithfull minister of the Ghospell of Christ: and an humble seruant, of the English Church* ([R. Schilders](?), 1602). Nichols's

Plea was published but no publisher or printer was identified on the title page and nor was there any indication given as to where the tract could be purchased; *Abrahams Faith: That is, The Olde Religion. Wherein is Tavght, that the Religion Now Publikely Taught and Defended by Order in the Church of England, is the Onely True Catholike, Auncient, and Vnchangeable Faith of Gods Elect* (London: Thomas Wight, 1602).

7 On the longer history of moderate non-conformity and its reactions to the English Church, see Warren Johnstone, 'Apocalypticism in Restoration England', (University of Cambridge PhD, 2000), Chapter 4 and Johnstone 'The Anglican Apocalypse in Restoration England', *Journal of Ecclesiastical History* (vol. 53, no. 3, 2004), pp. 467–501.

8 Christopher Hill, *Society and Puritanism in Pre-Revolutionary England* (London: Mercury Books, 1966), pp. 28–9.

9 See especially Collinson, *The Religion of Protestants* (Oxford: Oxford University Press, 1982) and 'A comment: concerning the name Puritan', *Journal of Ecclesiastical History* (vol. 31, no. 4, 1980), pp. 483–88. See also Glyn J. R. Parry, 'The creation and recreation of Puritanism', *Parergon* (vol. 14, no. 1, 1996), pp. 31–55.

10 Peter Lake, 'The dilemma of the establishment Puritan: the case of Francis Johnson and Cuthbert Bainbrigg', *Journal of Ecclesiastical History* (vol. 29, no. 1, 1978), pp. 22–35; Alastair Bellany,' A poem on the Archbishop's Hearse: Puritanism, libel and sedition after the Hampton Court Conference', *Journal of British Studies* (vol. 34, no. 1, 1995), pp. 137–64.

11 E. T. Davies, *Episcopacy and the Royal Supremacy in the Church of England in the Sixteenth Century* (Oxford: Basil Blackwell, 1950), p. 100.

12 Michael A. R. Graves, 'Elizabethan men of business reconsidered', *Parergon* (vol. 14, no. 1, 1996), pp. 120–1. On the work of the 'men of business' see also Barry Shaw, 'The Elizabethan men of business and the implementation of domestic policy 1569–1584', (University of Queensland PhD, 1987).

13 See Patrick Collinson, *The Elizabethan Puritan Movement* (London: Cape, 1967), pp. 497–8.

14 For an important revision of Cecil's influence on the episcopate see Brett Usher, *William Cecil and Episcopacy 1559–1577* (Aldershot: Ashgate, 2003).

15 William Sheils, 'Some problems of government in a new diocese: the bishop and the Puritans in the diocese of Peterborough, 1560–1630', in Rosemary O'Day and Felicity Heal (eds), *Continuity and Change: Personnel and Administration of the Church of England 1500–1642* (Leicester: Leicester University Press, 1976), pp. 182–3.

16 Sheils, 'Some problems of government', p. 176.

17 Asking why no wide-scale persecution of Catholic laity or religious followed the 1605 Gunpowder Plot, Okines finds his answer in the work of Fincham and Lake,

and builds upon their picture of a religiously conciliating monarch; A. W. R. E. Okines, 'Why was there so little government reaction to the Gunpowder Plot?', *Journal of Ecclesiastical History* (vol. 55, no. 2, 2004), pp. 275–92.

18 Stephen A. Bondos Greene, 'The end of an era: Cambridge Puritanism and the Christ's College election of 1609', *Historical Journal* (vol. 25, no. 1, 1982), pp. 197–208.

19 Bondos-Greene, 'The end of an era', p. 197.

20 Kenneth Fincham and Peter Lake, 'The ecclesiastical policy of King James I', *Journal of British Studies* (vol. 24, no. 2, 1985), pp. 169–207. Fincham and Lake have expanded upon their points in other publications. See especially Kenneth Fincham, *The Prelate as Pastor: The Episcopate of James I* (Oxford: Clarendon Press, 1990) and chapters in Kenneth Fincham (ed.), *The Early Stuart Church, 1603–1642* (London: Macmillan, 1993).

21 These ideas have subsequently been expanded into a chronologically lengthier work which encompasses the reign of James's son, Fincham and Lake, 'The ecclesiastical policies of James I and Charles I', in Fincham (ed.), *The Early Stuart Church, 1603–1642* (London: Macmillan, 1993).

22 Michael Questier, 'Loyalty, religion and state power in early modern England: English Romanism and the Jacobean Oath of Allegiance', *Historical Journal* (vol. 40, no. 2, 1997), pp. 311–18 and 'The politics of religious conformity and the accession of James I', *Historical Research* (vol. 71, no. 174, 1998), p. 25.

23 Harington referred throughout the *Supplie or Addicion* to 'my Author', meaning Bishop Godwin. Francis Godwin, *A Catalogue of the Bishops of England, Since the First Planting of Christian Religion in this Island* (London: Thomas Adams, 2nd edn., 1615).

24 On the availability of both Parker and Godwin's catalogues in seventeenth-century book collections see Wilfred Prest, 'Law, learning and religion: gifts to Gray's Inn library in the 1630s', *Parergon* (vol. 14, no. 1, 1996), pp. 211–12.

25 Chris Given-Wilson, *Chronicles: The Writing of History in Medieval England* (London: Hambledon and London, 2004), pp. 84–5. The chroniclers of medieval abbeys and priories were not writing episcopal catalogues in the manner of Parker, Godwin or Harington, but often structured narrative histories of foundations through abbatial biographies.

26 Peter Sherlock, *Monuments and Memory in Early Modern England* (Aldershot: Ashgate, 2008), pp. 230–48.

27 William Dugdale, *The History of St Paul's Cathedral in London, From its Foundation Untill These Times* (London: Longman, Hurst, Rees, Orme and Brown, 1818); *Monasticon Anglicanum* (London: Sam Keble, 1693).

28 Not until William Temple became Archbishop of Canterbury in 1942 did a son succeed his father at Canterbury; Temple's father Frederick was Archbishop in the late-nineteenth century.

29 Matthew Parker, *De Antiquitate Britannicae Ecclesiae & Priuilegiis Ecclesiae Cantuariensis cum Archiepiscopis eiusdem 70.*, (London, 1572).
30 Harington, *Supplie or Addicion*, p. 59.
31 Ibid., pp, 44, 55.
32 Lambeth Palace Library CM XVI/14, 'A roll containing the names and dates of consecration and translation of the Archbishops of Canterbury from Pecham to Abbot'.
33 Anon., *Catalogue of All the Bishops which have Governed in the Church of England and Wales, Since the Conversion of the Saxons. Together with the Honourary Offices Which They or Any of Them Have Enjoyed in the Civil Government* (London, 1674), pp. 91, 149.
34 Edward Carpenter, *Cantuar: The Archbishops in their Office* (London: Cassell, 1971), p. 150.
35 The Welsh dioceses were under the supervision of the archbishopric of Canterbury.
36 Ralph Morice, 'Cranmer and Canterbury School' [1579], in J. G Nichols (ed.), 'Narratives of the Days of the Reformation', (*Camden Society*, first series, no. 77 1859), p. 273.
37 Nichols, *The Plea of the Innocent*, title page.
38 Thomas Fuller, *Worthies of England* (London: Allen and Unwin, 1952), p. 500. John Strype was even more damning, accusing Harington's work of being boring and useless as well as too critical of the bishops, complaining that while Harington 'undertakes to give some strictures' of the Elizabethan bishops, his material was 'but light rumours of the court, and often idle and trifling.' Strype, *The History of the Life and Acts of the Most Reverend Father in God, Edmund Grindal* (New York: Burt Franklin Reprints, 1974), p. 454. These references are cited in the 1979 edition of the *Supplie or Addicion* and are gathered together by R. H. Miller.
39 Harington, *Nugae Antiquae* (London: Vennor and Hood, 1804), vol. II, p. 238.
40 For these aspects of the text see Marcus K. Harmes and Gillian Colclough, 'Henry Prince of Wales, Proverbs and the English Episcopate', *Explorations in Renaissance Culture* (vol. 37, no. 2, 2011), p. 108.
41 Phyllis Hembry, *The Bishops of Bath and Wells 1540–1640: Social and Economic Problems* (London: Athlone Press, 1967), p. 102.
42 The *Supplie or Addicion* was originally transmitted in a manuscript form, and the edition published in the 1650s appears to be lifted from B. L. Add. MS. 46370 (the 'A' manuscript), which does not include 'The occasion why'; see Miller, introduction to *Supplie or Addicion*, p. 11.
43 Roy Strong, *Holbein and Henry VIII* (London: Routledge, 1967), p. 23. The Protestant themes in Tudor and Jacobean portraiture are further discussed in Margaret Aston, *The King's Bedpost: Reformation and Iconography in a Tudor Group Portrait* (Cambridge: Cambridge University Press, 1993).

44 Kevin Sharpe '"So hard a text"? Images of Charles I, 1612–1700', *Historical Journal* (vol. 43, no. 2, 2000), p. 385. See also Curtis Perry, 'The citizen politics of nostalgia: Elizabeth in early Jacobean London', *Journal of Medieval and Renaissance Studies* (vol. 23, no. 1, 1993), pp. 89–111.

45 See the commentary on Harington in the introduction to the 1979 edition of the *Supplie or Addicion* which is one of the few twentieth-century works to devote extended attention to Harington's supplement in its own right rather than as a source of information for episcopal history. King James's instructions to Prince Henry on the respect owed to bishops are in *CSP Dom 1619–1623*, (ed. Mary Anne Everett Green) (London: Longmans, Brown, Green, Longmans and Roberts, 1858), CVII, p. 35.

46 These words are cited in G. P. V. Akrigg, *Jacobean Pageant, or the Court of James I* (London: Hamish Hamilton, 1962), p. 135.

47 Harington, *Supplie or Addicion*, p. 92.

48 Ibid., p. 192.

49 Ibid., p. 42.

50 Anon., *Catalogue of All the Bishops*, pp. 68–9.

51 Harington, *Supplie or Addicion*, p. 33.

52 Harington, *Supplie or Addicion*, pp. 33–4. As well as Thomas Cranmer and Nicholas Ridley, Harington here refers to Hugh Latimer, martyred in 1555, Thomas Rogers and John Hooper, who also perished during the reign of Queen Mary, and Miles Coverdale, who, as recounted in chapter one, went into exile during the reign of Mary and returned to England, although not to the episcopal bench, upon Elizabeth's accession.

53 Harington, *Supplie or Addicion*, pp. 34–5.

54 Ibid., p. 34.

55 Peter Clark, 'Josias Nichols and religious radicalism, 1555–1639', *Journal of Ecclesiastical History* (vol. 28, no. 2, 1977), p. 145.

56 The King's intentions to enforce conformity are outlined in a minute in the hand of Robert Cecil, his minister; BL Add.MS 287571, f. 199.

57 C. W. Foster (ed.), *The State of the Church in the Reigns of Elizabeth and James I, as Illustrated by Documents Relating to the Diocese of Lincoln* (Lincoln: Lincoln Record Society, 1926), p. 368.

58 Foster (ed.), *The State of the Church*, p. 368.

59 Kenneth Fincham sees Abbot as a continuator of policies which had been marginalized since Grindal's downfall; Fincham, 'Prelacy and politics: Archbishop Abbot's defence of Protestant orthodoxy', *Historical Research* (vol. 61, 1988), p. 37.

60 See R. M. Fisher, 'The Reformation of clergy at the Inns of Court 1530–1580', *Sixteenth Century Journal* (vol. 12, no. 1, 1981), pp. 88.

61 Patrick Collinson, 'The Reformer and the Archbishop: Martin Bucer and an English Bucerian', *Journal of Religious History* (vol. 6, no. 4, 1971), p. 319.
62 Lake, 'The dilemma of the establishment Puritan', pp. 23–35.
63 Bellany, 'A poem on the Archbishop's Hearse', pp. 137–64.
64 Ibid., pp. 137–64.
65 Nichols, *Plea of the Innocent*, p. 3.
66 Ibid., p. 5.
67 Ibid., pp. 31–2. For the Marprelate Tracts see Joseph Black, 'The rhetoric of reaction: the Martin Marprelate tracts (1588–89), anti-Martinism, and the uses of print in early modern England', *Sixteenth Century Journal* (vol. 28, 1997), pp. 707–28 and his edition of the original tracts, *The Martin Marprelate Tracts* (Cambridge: Cambridge University Press, 2008).
68 An observation cited in Peter Sherlock, *Monuments and Memory in Early Modern England*, p. 171.
69 Fincham, *Prelate as Pastor*, p. 237.
70 On Nichols's local context and the definitions of Puritanism which he will have encountered see Anthony Fletcher, 'National and local awareness in the county communities', in Howard Tomlinson (ed.), *Before the English Civil War: Essays in Early Stuart Politics and Government* (London: Macmillan, 1983), p. 164.
71 Seventeenth-century responses to the label Puritan are brought together in Christopher Hill's *Society and Puritanism*, Chapter 1. See also Jonathan M. Atkins, who stresses that Puritans were known through their rejection of episcopacy; Atkins, 'Calvinist bishops, church unity and the rise of Arminianism', *Albion* (vol. 18, no. 3, 1986), p. 411.
72 Cited in Hill, *Society and Puritanism*, p. 15.
73 Hill, *Society and Puritanism*, p. 17.
74 Patrick Collinson, 'John Field and Elizabethan Puritanism', in *Godly People: Essays on English Protestantism and Puritanism* (London: Hambledon Press, 1983), p. 336.
75 Nichols, *Abrahams Faith*, sig.B2.
76 Ibid., sig. B2.
77 Collinson, *Elizabethan Puritan Movement*, pp. 159–90.
78 For an account of these authors see Collinson, 'Episcopacy and reform in England in the later sixteenth century', in *Godly People*, p. 160. Contemporary observers sought to distinguish between good and bad bishops; see A. S. McGrade, 'Richard Hooker on episcopacy and bishops, good and bad', *International Journal for the Study of the Christian Church* (vol. 2, no. 2, 2002), pp. 28–43. In Marshal's 1536 tract, there were allegorical figures of good and bad episcopal rule.
79 Nichols, *Plea of the Innocent*, p. 61.
80 In his major biography of Grindal, Collinson clarified the place of the prophesyings in the downfall of Grindal. Collinson, *Archbishop Grindal 1519–1583: The Struggle*

for a Reformed Church (Berkeley: University of California Press, 1979). On this issue see also Stanford Lehmberg, 'Archbishop Grindal and the Prophesyings', *Historical Magazine of the Protestant Episcopal Church* (vol. 34, 1965), pp. 87–145. Grindal's complaint to Queen Elizabeth is printed in *Remains of Edmund Grindal* (ed. William Nicolson), (Cambridge: Cambridge University Press, 1843), p. 378.

81 Nichols, *Plea of the Innocent*, p. 9. Later writers echoed this estimate including John Milton and William Prynne; see Collinson, 'The Reformer and the Archbishop', p. 319.

82 Nichols, *Plea of the Innocent*, p. 9.

83 Ibid., p. 17.

84 Tom Webster and Kenneth Shipps (eds), *The Diary of Samuel Rogers, 1634–1638* (Woodbridge: Boydell Press/Church of England Record Society vol. 11, 2004), p. xvii.

85 Kenneth Fincham (ed.), *Visitation Articles and Injunctions of the Early Stuart Church* (Boydell Press/Church of England Record Society vol. 1, 1994), vol. I, p. xix.

86 Peter Lake, 'Matthew Hutton – a puritan bishop?' *History* (vol. 64, no. 211, 1979), pp. 182–204.

87 Kenneth Fincham, 'Ramifications of the Hampton Court Conference in the dioceses, 1603–1609', *Journal of Ecclesiastical History* (vol. 36, no. 2, 1985), p. 211.

88 John Bruce and Thomas Thomason Perowne (eds), *The Correspondence of Matthew Parker D. D., Archbishop of Canterbury* (Cambridge: Cambridge University Press, 1853), p. 240.

89 On Whitgift see John Guy, 'The Elizabethan establishment and the ecclesiastical polity', in Guy (ed.), *The Reign of Elizabeth I: Court and Culture in the Last Decade* (Cambridge: Cambridge University Press, 1995), p. 126; Patrick Collinson, 'The "nott conformytye" of the young John Whitgift', *Journal of Ecclesiastical History* (vol. 15, no. 2, 1964), p. 195. The Lambeth Articles are transcribed in John Strype, *The Life and Acts of John Whitgift, D. D* (Oxford: Clarendon Press, 1829), vol. 1, p. 111 and in Edward Cardwell (ed.), *Documentary Annals of the Reformed Church of England* (Oxford: Oxford University Press, 1844), p. 50.

90 The proceedings and outcomes of this event have been examined in Nicholas Tyacke, 'The "rise of Puritanism" and the legalizing of dissent, 1571–1719', in Ole Peter Grell, Jonathan I Israel and Nicholas Tyacke (eds), *From Persecution to Toleration: The Glorious Revolution and Religion in England* (Oxford: Clarendon Press, 1991), pp. 17–49.

91 See Colin Buchanan (ed.), *The Savoy Conference Revisited* (Cambridge: Grove, 2002), p. 33.

92 Oliver Ormerod, *The Picture of a Puritaine* (London, 1605), p. 68; King James I, *The Workes of the Most High and Mighty Prince, James, by the Grace of God Kinge of Greate Brittaine, France & Ireland Defender of ye Faith etc* (London: by

James [Montague] Bishop of Winton & Deane of His Majesties Chappell Royall, 1616), p. 144. See also C. H. George, 'Puritanism as history and historiography', *Past and Present* (vol. 41, no. 1, 1968), pp. 79, 81.

93 Anthony Arthur, *The Tailor-King: The Rise and Fall of the Anabaptist Kingdom of Münster* (New York: St Martin's Press, 1999), pp. 168–9.

94 Thomas Rogers, *Catholic Doctrine of the Church of England: An Exposition of the Thirty-Nine Articles of the Church of England* [1621] (ed. J. J. S.Perowne), (Cambridge: Cambridge University Press, 1854), pp. 339–31.

95 John Whitgift, *Works* (ed. John Ayre), (Cambridge: Cambridge University Press, 1851), vol. I, p. 394.

96 Samuel Clarke, *A General Martyrologie: Containing a Collection of all the Greatest Persecutions which have Befallen the Church of Christ, from the Creation to our Present Times. Whereunto are added, The Lives of Thirty-Two Divines, Famous in their Generations for Learning and Piety, and Most of them Great Sufferers in the Cause of Christ* (London: for William Birch, 1677), p. 36.

97 Pauline Croft, 'Wardship in the parliament of 1604', *Parliamentary History* (vol. II, 1983), pp. 40–2 and Croft, 'The religion of Robert Cecil', *Historical Journal* (vol. 34, no. 4, 1991), p. 775.

98 William Covell, *A Modest and Reasonable Examination of some things in use in the Church of England* (London: Clement Knight, 1603), p. 3.

99 On the controversies see Walter Phillips, 'Henry Bullinger and the Elizabethan Vestiarian Controversy: an analysis of influence', *Journal of Religious History* (vol. 11, no. 3, 1981), pp. 363–84.

100 [Dudley Fenner], *A Briefe and Plaine Declaration, Concerning the Desires of all Those Faithfull Ministers, That Haue and do Seeke for the Discipline and Reformation of the Church of Englande: Which May Serve for a Iust Apologie, Against the False Accusations and Slanders of their Aduersaries* (London: Robert Walde-graue, 1584).

101 Cited in Conrad Russell, 'The Reformation and the creation of the Church of England', in J. S. Morrill (ed.), *The Oxford Illustrated History of Tudor and Stuart Britain* (Oxford: Oxford University Press, 2000), p. 287.

102 Richard Montagu, *A Gagg for the new Gospell? No: A Nevv Gagg for an Old Goose Who Would Needes Vndertake to Stop all Protestants Mouths for Euer, with 276. Places out of their owne English Bibles. Or an Answere to a Late Abridger of Controuersies, and Belyar of the Protestants Doctrine. By Richard Mountagu. Published by authoritie* (London: William Barret, 1624), pp. 323–4.

103 See Kenneth Fincham and Nicholas Tyacke, *Altars Restored: The Changing Face of English Religious Worship, 1547-c.1700* (Oxford: Oxford University Press, 2008), p. 127. See also John Spurr, *The Post-Reformation: Religion, Politics and Society in Britain 1603–1714* (London: Pearson, 2006), p. 57.

104 Clarke, *A General Martyrologie*, p. 156.

105 Ibid., p. 156.

106 Although Bishop Goodman thought that some, even many of his brother bishops were Puritans, other evidence reveals the efforts of Bishop Laud and the Duke of Buckingham, to distinguish between the Orthodox and Puritan candidates for the episcopate; William Laud, *Works* (Oxford: John Henry Parker, 1847–60), vol. III, p. 159.

107 These comments by John Howson, a prebendary of Christ Church Oxford, are cited in Susan M. Holland, 'George Abbot: "the wanted Archbishop"', *Church History* (vol. 56, no. 2, 1987), p. 178.

108 Collinson, 'The Jacobean Religious Settlement: The Hampton Court Conference', in Howard Tomlinson (ed.), *Before the English Civil War* (London: Macmillan, 1983), pp. 27–51.

109 Alan Ford, *James Ussher: Theology, History and Politics in Early-Modern Ireland and England* (Oxford: Oxford University Press, 2007), p. 172.

110 Baxter also drew other bishops into his fold, including Hall and Ussher; Richard Baxter, *Five Disputations of Church-Government and Worship* (London: R.W. for Neville Simmons, 1659), pp. 339, 344.

111 William M. Lamont, 'The rise and rall of Bishop Bilson', *Journal of British Studies* (vol. 5, no. 2, 1966), p. 23.

112 Kenneth Fincham, 'Clerical conformity from Whitgift to Laud', in Peter Lake and Michael Questier (eds), *Conformity and Orthodoxy in the English Church c.1560–1660* (Woodbridge: The Boydell Press, 2000), pp. 125–58.

113 Fincham reiterates this interpretation in an article devoted to George Abbot; 'Prelacy and politics: Archbishop Abbot's defence of Protestant Orthodoxy', *Historical Research* (vol. 61, no. 144, 1988), pp. 140–4.

114 [John Williams], *The Holy Table, & and Thing more Anciently, Properly, and Literally used under the New Testament, then that of an Altar: Written Long ago by a Minister in Lincolnshire, in answer to D. Coal; a Judicious Divine of Q. Maries dayes* ([London]: Printed [by Nicholas Okes] for the Diocese of Lincoln, 1637).

115 S. R. Gardiner (ed.), 'Documents relating to the proceedings against William Prynne, in 1634 and 1637', (*Camden Society*, new series, no. 18, 1877), p. 45.

116 See especially Peter Lake, *Moderate Puritans and the Elizabethan Church* (Cambridge: Cambridge University Press, 1982).

117 Nicholas Tyacke, 'Puritanism, Arminianism and Counter-Revolution', in Conrad Russell (ed.), *The Origins of the English Civil War* (London: Macmillan, 1973), p. 130.

118 Maurice Lee Jr, *Great Britain's Solomon: James VI and I in His Three Kingdoms* (Urbana: University of Illinois Press, 1990), pp. 188–9.

119 Peter Lake, *The Boxmaker's Revenge: 'Orthodoxy', 'Heterodoxy' and the Politics of the Parish in Early Stuart London* (Stanford: Stanford University Press, 2001), p. 2.

120 Lake, *Moderate Puritans and the Elizabethan Church*, pp. 169–200.

121 Clark, 'Josias Nichols and religious radicalism', p. 133. Susan Brigden, *New Worlds, Lost Worlds: The Rule of the Tudors 1485–1603* (London: Viking, 2000), p. 328.

122 N. F., *Vnparalled Reasons for Abollishing Episcopacy* (London: for S. S. 1642), p. 7.

123 Even while criticism of bishops continued unabated. William Prynne especially objected to Bishop Cosin urging prayers for the dead, although this is a specific instance of a wider criticism of apparently popish practices; Prynne, *A Briefe Suruay and Censure of Mr Cozens his Couzening Deuotions Prouing both the Forme and Matter of Mr Cozens his Booke of Priuate Deuotions, or the Hours of Prayer, Lately Published, to be Meerely Popish: to differ from the Priuate Prayers authorized by Queene Elizabeth 1560. to be Transcribed out of Popish Authors, with which they are here Paralleled: and to be Scandalous and Preiudiciall to our Church, and Aduantagious onely to the Church of Rome. By William Prynne Gent. Hospitij Lincolniensis* (London: [By Thomas Cotes], 1628), pp. 25–6.

124 William Prynne, *A Looking-glasse for all Lordly Prelates Wherein they may cleerely behold the True Divine Originall and Laudable Pedigree, whence they are Descended; Together with their Holy Lives and Actions Laid Open in a Double Parallel, the First, betweene the Divell; the Second, betweene the Iewish High-Priests, and Lordly Prelates; and by their double dissimilitude from Christ, and his Apostles* ([London?], 1636), p. 97.

125 Anon., *Englands Reioycing at the Prelats Downfall* (1641), pp. 7–8.

126 Williams' intention is quoted in Kenneth Fincham and Nicholas Tyacke, *Altars Restored*, p. 178.

127 On the provision of lecturers and lectureships see Paul S. Seaver, *The Puritan Lectureships, 1560–1662* (Stanford: Stanford University Press, 1970) and R. M. Fisher, 'The origins of divinity lectureships at the Inns of Court, 1569–1585', *Journal of Ecclesiastical History* (vol. 29, no. 2, 1978), p. 147.

128 Cited in Croft, 'The religion of Robert Cecil', p. 777.

129 Croft, 'The religion of Robert Cecil', p. 777.

Chapter 3

1 See for example Robin Briggs, *Witches and Neighbours: The Social and Cultural Context of European Witchcraft*, 2nd edn (Oxford: Blackwell, 2002), p. 204.

2 Philip C. Almond, *Demonic Possession and Exorcism in Early Modern England: Contemporary Texts and their Cultural Contexts* (Cambridge: Cambridge University Press, 2004), pp. 331–57.

3 George Clark, *A History of the Royal College of Physicians of London* (Oxford: Clarendon Press for The Royal College of Physicians, 1964), p. 198.

4 Frank Walsh Brownlow, *Shakespeare, Harsnett and the Devils of Denham* (Toronto: Toronto University Press, 1993), p. 65.
5 On Harsnet's regulation of books see Brian Cummings (ed.), *The Book of Common Prayer: The Texts of 1549, 1559, and 1662* (Oxford: Oxford University Press, 2011), p. lxxii.
6 Brownlow, *Shakespeare, Harsnett and the Devils of Denham*, p. 46. Harsnet died in office in 1631.
7 J. Venn and J. A.Venn (eds). 'Darrell, John' in *Alumni Cantabrigienses* (10 vols), (1922–1958), (online ed.). Cambridge University Press, http://venn.lib.cam.ac.uk/cgi-bin/search.pl?sur=&suro=c&fir=&firo=c&cit=&cito=c&c=all&tex=DRL575J&sye=&eye=&col=all&maxcount=50, accessed 6 March, 2012.
8 Keith Thomas, *Religion and the Decline of Magic* (New York: Scribner, 1971), p. 478.
9 Brownlow, *Shakespeare, Harsnett and the Devils of Denham*, p. 56.
10 Tracts by, about and against Darrel include Anon., *The Triall of Maist. Dorrell, or A Collection of Defences Against Allegations Not Yet Suffered to Receiue Convenient Answere Tending to Cleare Him From the Imputation of Teaching Sommers and Others to Counterfeit Possession of Divells. That the Mist of Pretended Counterfetting being Dispelled, the Glory of Christ his Royall Power in Casting out Divels (at the Prayer and Fasting of his People) may Evidently Appeare* ([Middelburg: R. Schilders], 1599); John Deacon and John Walker, *A Summarie Ansvvere to al the Material Points in any of Master Darel his Bookes More Especiallie to that One Booke of his, Intituled, the Doctrine of the Possession and Dispossession of Demoniaks out of the Word of God. By Iohn Deacon. Iohn Walker. Preachers* (Londini: Impensis Geor. Bishop, 1601); John Deacon, *A Breife Narration of the Possession, Dispossession, and, Repossession of William Sommers and of Some Proceedings against Mr Iohn Dorrell Preacher, with Aunsweres to Such Obiections as are Made to Prove the Pretended Counterfeiting of the Said Sommers. Together with Certaine Depositions taken at Nottingham concerning the said matter* ([Amsterdam?: S.n.], Anno M. D. XCVIII [1598]); Samuel Harsnet, *A Discouery of the Fraudulent Practises of Iohn Darrel Bacheler of Artes in his Proceedings Concerning the Pretended Possession and Dispossession of William Somers at Nottingham: of Thomas Darling, the boy of Burton at Caldwall: and of Katherine Wright at Mansfield, & Whittington: and of his Dealings with one Mary Couper at Nottingham, Detecting in Some Sort the Deceitfull Trade in These Latter Dayes of Casting out Deuils* (London: Imprinted by [John Windet for] Iohn Wolfe, 1599). Tracts about Darrel continued to appear as late as 1641.
11 Thomas, *Religion and the Decline of Magic*, p. 481.
12 On Protestant forms of exorcism, see Lizanne Henderson, 'The survival of witchcraft prosecutions and witch belief in South-West Scotland', *Scottish Historical Review* (vol. 85, no. 1, 2006), p. 63.

13 See Stuart Barton Babbage, *Puritanism and Richard Bancroft* (London: SPCK, 1962), although the idea goes back to the Earl of Clarendon in the seventeenth century.
14 CUL, EDR, A/5/1. Fol.4v, cited in Scott Wenig, 'The Reformation in the diocese of Ely during the episcopate of Richard Cox, 1559–77', *Sixteenth Century Journal* (vol. 33, no. 1 2002), p. 173.
15 Joseph Black, 'The rhetoric of reaction: the Martin Marprelate tracts (1588–89), anti-Martinism, and the uses of print in early modern England', *Sixteenth Century Journal* (vol. 28, 1997), pp. 707–28. On Bancroft and Hacket, see Alexandra Walsham, '"Fanatick Hacket": prophecy, sorcery, insanity, and the Elizabethan Puritan Movement', *Historical Journal* (vol. 41, no. 1, 1998), p. 30.
16 Leland H. Carlson, 'The Court of High Commission: a newly discovered Elizabethan Letters Patent, 20 June 1589', *Huntingdon Library Quarterly* (vol. 45, no. 4, 1982), p. 298. Bancroft's sermon was printed as *A Sermon Preached at Pavls Crosse* (London, 1634).
17 Edward Carpenter, *Cantuar: The Archbishops in their Office* (London: Cassell, 1971), p. 176.
18 Kenneth Fincham, 'Ramifications of the Hampton Court Conference in the dioceses 1603–1609', *Journal of Ecclesiastical History* (vol. 36, no. 2, 1985), pp. 208–27.
19 Alan Macfarlane, *Witchcraft in Tudor and Stuart England*, 2nd edn, (London: Routledge, 1999), p. 88.
20 Almond (ed.), *Demonic Possession and Exorcism*, p. 1.
21 Christina Larner, 'Crimen Exceptum?: The crime of Witchcraft in Europe', in Brian P. Levack (ed.), *Witch-hunting in Early Modern Europe: General Studies* (New York and London: Garland Publishing Inc., 1992), p. 91.
22 On the procedure of the Star Chamber, see Thomas G. Barnes, 'Due process and slow process in the late Elizabethan-early Stuart Star Chamber', *The American Journal of Legal History* (vol. 6, no. 3, 1962), p. 227.
23 The cases are usefully summarized by James Sharpe, *Witchcraft in Early Modern England* (Harlow: Pearson, 2001), pp. 28–9.
24 Brian P. Levack, 'Possession, Witchcraft and the law in Jacobean England', *Washington and Lee Legal Review* (vol. 52, 1995), p. 1628.
25 Philip C. Almond, *The Witches of Warboys: An Extraordinary Story of Sorcery, Sadism and Satanic Possession* (London: I.B. Tauris, 2007), p. 28.
26 Larner, 'Crimen Exceptum?', p. 91.
27 *The Triall of Maist. Dorrell*, p. 24.
28 Benjamin J. Kaplan, 'Possessed by the Devil?: A very public dispute in Utrecht', *Renaissance Quarterly* (vol. 49, no. 4, 1996), p. 738.
29 Anita M. Walker and Edmund H. Dickerman, 'A woman under the influence: a case of alleged possession in sixteenth-century France', *Sixteenth Century Journal* (vol. 22, no. 3, 1991), p. 535.

30 Moshe Sluhovsky, 'A divine apparition or demonic possession? Female agency and church authority in demonic possession in sixteenth-century France', *Sixteenth Century Journal* (vol. 27, no. 4, 1996), p. 1041.
31 Moshe Sluhovsky, 'The Devil in the convent', *The American Historical Review* (vol. 107, no. 5, 2002), pp. 1379–411.
32 Hans Peter Broedel, 'To preserve the manly form from so vile a crime: Ecclesiastical anti-sodomitic rhetoric and the gendering of Witchcraft in the *Malleus Maleficarum*', *Essays in Medieval Studies* (vol. 19, 2002), p. 142.
33 Darren Oldridge, 'Protestant conceptions of the Devil in early Stuart England', *History* (vol. 85, no. 278, 2000), p. 241.
34 Oldridge, 'Protestant conceptions', p. 241.
35 Ben Jonson, *The Devil is an Ass* (ed. Peter Happé), (Manchester: Manchester University Press, 1996), Act V, scene iii.
36 Kaplan, 'Possessed by the Devil?', p. 743.
37 *The Triall of Maist. Dorrell*, p. 6.
38 Ibid., p. 66.
39 Abraham Hartwell, translation of Michel Marescot, *A True Discourse, Upon the Matter of Martha Brossier of Romorantin, Pretended to be Possessed by a Devill* (London, 1599).
40 Briggs, *Witches and Neighbours*, p. 214.
41 Michael MacDonald (ed.), *Witchcraft and Hysteria in Elizabethan London* (London: Tavistock/Routledge, 1991), p. li.
42 Harsnet, *Discovery*, p. 298.
43 Ibid., p. 310.
44 Ibid., sig.D1.
45 Broedel, 'To preserve the manly form', p. 136.
46 Carson I. A. Ritchie, 'Sir Richard Grenville and the Puritans', *English Historical Review* (vol. 77, no. 304, 1972), 522.
47 Peter Lake, *Anglicans and Puritans?: Presbyterianism and English Conformist Thought from Whitgift to Hooker* (London: Allen and Unwin, 1988), p. 13.
48 Diarmaid MacCulloch, *Thomas Cranmer: A Life* (New Haven: Yale University Press, 1996), pp. 212–3.
49 The behaviour of the children at Warboys was extensively described in a contemporary tract *The Most Strange and Admirable Discoverie of the Three Witches of Warboys, Convicted, and Executed at the Last Assizes at Huntington, for the Bewitching of the Five Daughters of Robert Throckmorton Esquire* (London: the Widow Orwin, for Thomas Man and John Winnington, 1593).
50 *A Briefe Narration*, sig.C1.
51 *Letters of John Chamberlain* (ed. Norman McClure), (Philadelphia: American Philosophical Society, 1939), pp. 186–7.

52 *The Triall of Maist. Dorrell*, p. 4.
53 *A Briefe Narration*, sig. C2.
54 D. P. Walker, *Unclean Spirits: Possession and Exorcism in France and England in the Late-Sixteenth and Early-Seventeenth Centuries* (London: The Scolar Press, 1981), p. 65.
55 Samuel Clarke, *Lives of Sundry Eminent Persons in this Later Age in Two Parts: I. of Divines, II. of Nobility and Gentry of both sexes/by Samuel Clark; Printed and Reviewed by himself just before his Death; to Which is Added His Own Life and the Lives of the Countess of Suffolk, Sir Nathaniel Barnardiston, Mr. Richard Blackerby and Mr. Samuel Fairclough, drawn up by other hands* (London: for Thomas Simmons, 1682), pp. 5–6.
56 Clarke, *Sundry Eminent Persons*, pp. 5–6.
57 John Darrel, *A Brief Apologie Prouing the Possession of William Sommers. Written by Iohn Dorrell, a Faithful Minister of the Gospell: but Published without his Knowledge, with a Dedicatorie Epistle Disclosing Some Disordered Procedings against the Saide Iohn Dorrell* ([Middleburg: R.Schilders], 1599), p. 7.
58 Darrel, *A Brief Apologie*, p. 28.
59 *The Triall of Maist. Dorrell*, p. 20.
60 Darrel, *A Brief Apologie*, p. 5.
61 Ibid., p. 7.
62 *A Briefe Narration*, sig.B2.
63 Darrel, *A Brief Apologie*, p. 7.
64 Ibid., p. 26.
65 The godly community there included the earls of Huntingdon, who were patrons of godly lecturers and preachers; see Christopher Haigh, 'The troubles of Thomas Pestell: parish squabbles and ecclesiastical politics in Caroline England', *Journal of British Studies* (vol. 41, no. 4, 2002), p. 404.
66 Brownlow, *Shakespeare, Harsnett and the Devils of Denham*, p. 57.
67 Darrel, *A Brief Apologie*, epistle dedicatory.
68 John Darrel, *A Detection of that Sinnful Shameful, Lying, and Ridiculous Discours of Samuel Harshnet* (1600), sigs. A1, A4.
69 See Marcus Harmes, 'Orthodox puritans and dissenting bishops: the reformation of the English episcopate, CA. 1580–1610', *Comitatus: A Journal of Medieval and Renaissance Studies* (vol. 39, September 2008), pp. 199–218.
70 See especially William Prynne's assertion that the High Commission and Star Chamber were reminiscent of the Inquisition. Prynne argued that the Star Chamber was Jesuitical in origin. William Prynne, *The Church of Englands Old Antithesis to New Arminianisme VVhere in 7. anti-Arminian Orthodox Tenents, are Euidently Proued; their 7. opposite Arminian (once popish and Pelagian) Errors are Manifestly Disproued, to be the Ancient, Established, and Vndoubted Doctrine of the*

Church of England; by the Concurrent Testimony of the Seuerall Records and Writers of our Church, from the beginning of her Reformation, to this Present. By William Prynne Gent. Hospitij Lincolniensis (London: [Printed by Augustine Mathewes and Elizabeth Allde for Michael Sparke]1629).

71 Darrel, *An Apologie*, fl.2
72 John Darrel, *A True Narration of the Strange and Grevous Vexation by the Devil of 7.Persons in Lancashire, and of William Somers of Nottingham* (1600), pp. 10, 20.
73 Darrel, *A True Narration*, p. 23.
74 John Darrel, *A True Relation of the Grievous Handling of William Sommers of Nottingham* (London: Thomas Harper, 1641), sig.A4.
75 Darrel, *An Apologie*, fl.4.
76 Harsnet, *Discovery*, sig. Ee2.
77 Ibid., sig. Nn.1.
78 *A Briefe Narration*, sig. B3.
79 Harsnet, *Discovery*, sig. B1.
80 Ibid., sig. B.2.
81 *A Briefe Narration*, sig.B4.
82 Harsnet, *Discovery*, sig. B.4.
83 Ibid., sig. C1.
84 Ibid., sig. C2.
85 Ibid., sig. C4.
86 Ibid., sig. C4.
87 Ibid., sig. D3.
88 *The Triall of Maist. Dorrell*, p. 35.

Chapter 4

1 Nicholas Tyacke establishes a definition of Arminian as meaning a rejection of the grace of Predestination; see Tyacke, 'Puritanism, Arminianiam and Counter-Revolution' in Conrad Russell (ed.), *Origins of the English Civil War* (London: Macmillan, 1973), p. 130.
2 On Arminius, see *The Writings of James Arminius vols.1–3* (trans. James Nichols and W. R. Bagnall), (Grand Rapids, Michigan, 1959).
3 For a discussion of the early impact of these pre-Laudian bishops, see Christopher Durston, *James I* (London: Routledge, 1993) p. 61, and especially Peter Lake, 'Lancelot Andrewes, John Buckeridge, and Avant-Garde conformity at the court of James I', in Linda Levy Peck (ed.), *The Mental World of the Jacobean Court* (Cambridge: Cambridge University Press, 1991), pp. 113–33.

4   Christopher Dow, *Innovation Unjustly Charged upon the Present Church and State* (London: Iohn Clark, 1637); Peter Heylyn, *Cyprianus Anglicus: or the Life and Death of William Laud, Archbishop of Canterbury* (Dublin, 1719); Heylyn, *A Briefe and Moderate Answer to the Seditious and Scandalous Challenge of Henry Burton, late of Friday-Streete* (London: Ric. Hodgkinsonne, 1637); Heylyn, *A Briefe Relation of the Death and Sufferings of the Most Reverend and Renowned Prelate, the L.Archbishop of Canterbury with a More Perfect Copy of his Speech, and Other Passages on the Scaffold, than hath beene hitherto Imprinted* (Oxford, 1644).

5   William Prynne, *A Briefe Suruay and Censure of Mr Cozens his Couzening Deuotions Prouing both the Forme and Matter of Mr Cozens his Booke of Priuate Deuotions, or the Houres of Prayer, Lately Published, to be Meerely Popish: to differ from the Priuate Pprayers authorized by Queene Elizabeth 1560. to be Transcribed out of Popish Authors, with which they are here Paralleled: and to be Scandalous and Preiudiciall to our Church, and Aduantagious onely to the Church of Rome. By William Prynne Gent. Hospitij Lincolniensis* (London: [By Thomas Cotes], 1628), p. 3.

6   Robert Surtees, *The History and Antiquities of the County Palatinate of Durham* (London: Nichols, Son and Bentley, 1816), vol. I, p. cvii. On Smart's reactions to the music in Durham Cathedral, see Brian Crosby, 'John Cosin and music', in Margot Johnson (ed.), *John Cosin: Papers Presented to a Conference to Celebrate the 400th Anniversary of His Birth* (Durham: Turnstone Ventures, 1997), pp. 166–7.

7   'To cozen' had been in use since the 1570s to mean 'to cheat, defraud'.

8   The contemporary meaning of 'cozening' is revealed in a contemporary play on words which alluded to having 'cousen'd [deceived] Dr. Cosin'; Peter Le Huray, *Music and the Reformation in England 1549–1660* (London: Herbert Jenkins, 1967), p. 50.

9   Prynne, *A Brief Survey*, p. 99.

10 Ibid., p. 3.

11 On Cosin's alleged popish tendencies, as stridently asserted by Prynne, see John Spurr, *The Post-Reformation: Religion, Politics and Society in Britain 1603–1714* (London: Pearson, 2006), p. 66.

12 The collapse of episcopal rule in the 1640s reflected the collapse of other organs of authority bound up with episcopal rule, such as the Star Chamber and press censorship. These points are discussed in Michael Mendle, 'De facto freedom, de facto authority: press and parliament, 1640–1643', *Historical Journal* (vol. 38, no. 2, 1995), pp. 151–77.

13 Judith Maltby (ed.), 'The Short Parliament (1640) Diary of Sir Thomas Aston', (*Camden Society,* fourth series, vol. 35, 1988), p. 93.

14 The demands of the Grand Remonstrance are recorded in Wilbur Cortez Abbot (ed.), *The Writings and Speeches of Oliver Cromwell* (Cambridge: Harvard

University Press, 1939), vol. 1., p. 143. For a general background to the proceedings in Parliament, see J. P. Kenyon, *The Stuarts* (London: Fontana, 1966), p. 31.

15 Laud indicated that he was confronted with evidence from his diary at his trial; Laud, *Works* (Oxford: John Henry Parker, 1847–60), vol. IV, p. 213.

16 On Prynne's editing of the diary, see Kevin Sharpe, *The Personal Rule of Charles I* (New Haven: Yale University Press, 1992), p. 285. For the results of Prynne's editing, see *A Fresh Discovery of some Prodigious New Wandering-blazing Stars* (1645).

17 Hugh Trevor-Roper, *Archbishop Laud* (2nd edn), (London: Phoenix Press, 2000), p. 243.

18 Trevor-Roper, *Archbishop Laud*, p. 294. On earlier appointments, see Margaret Steig, *Laud's Laboratory: The Diocese of Bath and Wells in the Early Seventeenth Century* (London: Associated University Presses, 1982).

19 For a discussion of this point, see Robert Ashton, *The English Civil War: Conservatism and Revolution 1603–1649* (London: Phoenix, 1997), pp. 73–4, 112–3.

20 William Prynne, *The Church of Englands Old Antithesis to New Arminianisme VVhere in 7. anti-Arminian Orthodox Tenents, are Euidently Proued; their 7. opposite Arminian (once popish and Pelagian) Errors are Manifestly Disproued, to be the Ancient, Established, and undoubted Doctrine of the Church of England; by the Concurrent Testimony of the Seuerall Records and Writers of our Church, from the beginning of her Reformation, to this Present. By William Prynne Gent. Hospitij Lincolniensis* (London: [Printed by Augustine Mathewes and Elizabeth Allde for Michael Sparke] 1629). Most notably in Julian Davies draws heavily on what Laud's enemies had to say; *The Caroline Captivity of the Church: Charles I and the Remolding of Anglicanism, 1625–1641* (Oxford: Clarendon Press, 1992).

21 The Laudian Church has of course attracted immense scholarly interest, from Mandell Creighton in the nineteenth century to recent debates. These include Nicholas Tyacke, *Anti-Calvinists: The Rise of English Arminianism, c. 1590–1640* (Oxford: Clarendon Press, 1987); Peter White, 'The rise of Arminianism Reconsidered', *Past and Present*, (vol. 101, 1983), pp. 34–54; Sharpe, *Personal Rule*. For a cogent survey of more recent historical writing on Laud and the Church in his period, see Alexandra Walsham, 'The parochial roots of Laudianism revisited: Catholics, anti-Calvinists and "parish Anglicans" in early Stuart England', *Journal of Ecclesiastical History*, (vol. 49, no. 4, 1998), pp. 620–51.

22 Sharpe, *Personal Rule*, p. 285.

23 *CSP Dom Charles I 1636–37* (ed. John Bruce), (London, Longmans, Green, Reader and Dyer, 1867), p. 299.

24 Laud, *Works*, vol. IV, p. 290.

25 John Mason, *The Midnight-Cry. A Sermon Preached on the Parable of the Ten Virgins* (1691), pp. 20–6. On Mason, see Philip C. Almond, 'John Mason and his

religion: an enthusiastic millenarian in late 17th century England', *The Seventeenth Century* (vol. 24, no. 1, 2009), pp. 156–76.

26 See Michael Questier, 'Arminianism, Catholicism, and Puritanism in England during the 1630s', *Historical Journal* (vol. 49, no. 1, 2006), pp. 53–78. On the emerging terminology of Arminianism, see also Hillel Schwartz, 'Arminianism and the English Parliament, 1624–1629', *Journal of British Studies* (vol. 12, no. 2, 1973), pp. 41–68.

27 I. M. Green, 'The persecution of "scandalous" and "malignant" parish clergy during the English Civil War', *English Historical Review* (vol. 94, no. 372, 1979), p. 510.

28 John Cosin, *A Collection of Private Devotions* (ed. P. G. Stanwood), (London: Oxford University Press, 1967).

29 Laud was closely associated with both edifices, and the design of the latter structure is ascribed to Inigo Jones, a known associate of Laud; Paley Baildon, 'Lincoln's Inn Chapel', *Transactions of St Paul's Ecclesiology Society*, (vol. 4, 1900), pp. 252–62; K. E. Campbell, *A Brief History and Account of St Katherine Cree Church* (1999); Maija Jansson, 'The impeachment of Inigo Jones and the pulling down of St Gregory's by St Paul's', *Renaissance Studies* (vol. 17, no. 4, 2003), pp. 716–46; John Newman, 'Inigo Jones and the politics of architecture', in Kevin Sharpe and Peter Lake (eds), *Culture and Politics in Early Stuart England* (Stanford: Stanford University Press, 1993), pp. 229–55.

30 Lake, 'Serving God and the times: the Calvinist conformity of Robert Sanderson', *Journal of British Studies* (vol. 27, no. 2, 1988), p. 82. Tyacke, *Anti-Calvinists*, p. 4.

31 Patrick Collinson, *The Religion of Protestants* (Oxford: Oxford University Press, 1982). Collinson here departed from the interpretations and terminology of the *Elizabethan Puritan Movement*.

32 The presence of Calvinist beliefs on the episcopal bench is interpreted in Daniel J. Steere, '"Quo vadis?": Bishop Joseph Hall and the demise of Calvinist conformity in early seventeenth-century England' (Georgia State University PhD, 2000). On English Calvinism, see also Peter Lake, 'Calvinism and the English Church', *Past and Present* (no. 114, 1987), pp. 32–76.

33 Soteriology referring to doctrines on salvation; on the Elect see Peter White, *Predestination, Policy and Polemic: Conflict and Consensus in the English Church from the Reformation to the Civil War* (Cambridge: Cambridge University Press, 2002), p. 18.

34 White's arguments have been put forth in a series of articles in *Past and Present*, especially 'The rise of Arminianism reconsidered', pp. 34–54. A useful summary of the exchanges between White and other scholars including Tyacke is in Margo Todd, 'The Godly and the Church: new views of Protestantism in early modern Britain', *Journal of British Studies* (vol. 28, no. 4, 1989), pp. 418–20.

35 H. Hajzyk, 'The Church in Lincolnshire c.1595–c.1649' (University of Cambridge PhD, 1980), p. 102.

36 An alternative voice on these matters is provided by H. T. Blethen, who argues that the distance between Williams and Laud has been exaggerated; Blethen, 'The altar controversy and the royal supremacy, 1627–1641', *Welsh Historical Review* (vol. 9, 1978), pp. 142–54. The battles between Laud and Williams were more often fought out by Laud's subordinates; for instance, Williams's *The Holy Table* was written in 1637 as a riposte to Peter Heylyn's *A Coale from the Altar. Or An Ansvver to a Letter Not Long Since Written to the Vicar of Gr. Against the Placing of the Communion Table at the east end of the Chancell; and Now of Late Dispersed Abroad to the Disturbance of the Church. First sent by a Judicious and Learned Divine for the Satisfaction of his Private Friend; and by him Commended to the Presse, for the benefit of others* (Printed [by Augustine Mathewes] for Robert Milbourne, 1636).

37 Sharpe, *Personal Rule*, p. 285; Davies, *Caroline Captivity*, chap. 6.

38 Clergy associated with Laud, including Ambrose Fisher, Edward Boughen and Cosin, offered more novel defences of confirmation than did Laud, who confined himself to offering long-standing conforming statements on the practice; James F. Turrell, '"Until Such Time as He Be Confirmed": the Laudians and confirmation in the seventeenth-century Church of England', *The Seventeenth Century* (vol. 20, no. 2, 2005), p. 211.

39 Peter Heylyn, *A Brief and Moderate Answer to the Seditious and Scandalous Challenges of Henry Burton, late of Friday Streete* (London: for Ric. Hodgkinsonne, 1637), pp. 9–10.

40 Laud, *Works*, vol. IV, p. 3.

41 Ibid., p. 5.

42 Kate Aughterson (ed.), *The English Renaissance: An Anthology of Sources and Documents* (London: Routledge, 1998), p. 56.

43 Laud, *Works*, vol. IV, p. 6.

44 'The Autobiography of Sir John Bramston K.B.' (*Camden Society*, first series, vol. 32, 1845), p. 81.

45 Peter King, 'The episcopate during the Civil Wars, 1642–1649', *English Historical Review* (vol. 83, no. 328, 1968), p. 524; C. S. Knighton, 'The Lord of Jerusalem: John Williams as Dean of Westminster', in C. S. Knighton and Richard Mortimer (eds), *Westminster Abbey Reformed 1540–1640* (Aldershot: Ashgate, 2003), p. 258.

46 Alan Ford, *James Ussher: Theology, History, and Politics in Early-Modern Ireland and England* (Oxford: Oxford University Press, 2007), p. 229.

47 Peter Heylyn, *Cyprianus Anglicus*, p. 497.

48 Peter King, 'The episcopate during the Civil Wars, 1642–49', p. 526.

49 Anon., *The Coppy of a Letter Sent from Iohn Lord Finch, late Lord Keeper, to his Friend Dr. Cozens: with a Commemoration of the Favours Dr. Cozens Shewed him in his Vice-Chancellorship. Unto VVhivh is annexed a good Admonition to Protestants* (1641), p. 3.

50 Anon., *The Coppy of a Letter*, p. 4.
51 Attributes of Laudian worship are discussed in Richard J. W. Beran, 'John Cosin: bishop and liturgist', in Margot Johnson (ed.), *John Cosin: Papers Presented to a Conference to Celebrate the 400th Anniversary of his Birth* (Durham: Turnstone Ventures, 1997), p. 74.
52 Heylyn, *A Briefe Relation*, p. 119.
53 Ibid., p. 123.
54 Henry Walker, *The Prelates Pride: or the Manifestation that the Bishops Lordly Government from the Originall Institution, is not De Iure Divino, by Dvine Right; but Meerly Humane and Contrary Both to the Holy Word of God, the Practise of the Apostles, and of the Primitive Churches in the Purest Times* (1641), p. 1.
55 Walker, *The Prelates Pride*, p. 2.
56 For the original publication of the text, see *Rome's Masterpeece: or, the Grand Conspiracy of the Pope and his Iesuited Instruments, to extirpate the Protestant Religion* (London: for Michael Sparke, 1644).
57 Cited in Laud, *Works*, vol. IV, p. 485.
58 Laud, *Works*, vol. IV, p. 482. Clarendon also recorded contemporary perceptions and accusations that the King was 'conniving at and tolerating, Popery'; Edward Hyde, Earl of Clarendon, *The History of the Rebellion and Civil Wars in England* (ed. W. D. Macray), (Oxford: Clarendon Press, 1888), vol. II, p. 276.
59 However, authentic writings by Laud also allude to this issue; Laud recorded in his diary a strange encounter with a man in Greenwich in 1633 who offered him a position in the Curia; Laud, *Works*, vol. III, p. 239.
60 Laud, *Works*, vol. IV, p. 493.
61 Ibid., p. 495. On the Scottish liturgy, see Ian Breward, *Archbishop Laud: Reforming Liturgy and Fostering National Unity* (Heildelberg, Victoria: The Prayer Book Society in Australia, 2001).
62 Laud, *Works*, vol. IV, p. 290.
63 Anon., *The Bishop of Canterbvry His Confession. Wherein is declared his constant Resolution, his Plots, and indeavours, to introduce Popery into England, and to advance the Roman Catholick Religion* (London, [1643]), p. 4.
64 Anon., *The Bishop of Canterbvry*, p. 1.
65 Ibid., pp. 6, 3.
66 Anon., *The Last Advice of William Laud, late Arch-Bishop, to his Episcopall Brethren; and Especially to Bishop Wren, Who Still Remaines Prisoner in the Tower* (London: for J. B., 1644), p. 4.
67 Charles Carlton, 'The Dream Life of Archbishop Laud', *History Today* (vol. 36, iss.12, 1986), p. 9.
68 Quoted in Stanford Lehmberg, *English Cathedrals: A History* (London: Hambledon and London, 2005), p. 183.

69 The title page of *A Prophecie of the Life, Reigne and Death of William Laud, Archbishop of Canterbury* (Printed for R.A., 1644) showed a devil presenting Laud with a cardinal's hat on a platter.
70 Laud, *Works*, vol. IV, p. 226.
71 On its dissemination, see Jesse Lander, 'Foxe's *Book of Martyrs*: printing and popularizing the *Acts and Monuments*', in Claire McEachen and Deborah Sliger (eds), *Religion and Culture in Renaissance England* (Cambridge: Cambridge University Press, 1997), pp. 69–92.
72 On the provision of Bibles in English churches, see I. M. Green, *Print and Protestantism in Early Modern England* (Oxford: Oxford University Press, 2000), p. 68.
73 William Laud, *A Speech Delivered in the Star Chamber, on Wednesday the XIVth of June MDCXXXVII at the Censure of Iohn Bastwick, Henry Burton and William Prinn, concerning pretended innovation in the Church* (London: Richard Badger, 1637), p. 11.
74 Judith Maltby, 'Petitions for episcopacy and the Book of Common Prayer on the eve of the Civil War 1641–42', in Stephen Taylor (ed.), *From Cranmer to Davidson: A Church of England Miscellany* (Woodbridge: Boydell Press/Church of England Record Society vol. 7, 1999), pp. 116, 119.
75 BL Add.MS 34216.
76 Laud, *Works*, vol. VI, p. 71.
77 Anon., *A Discovrse Presented to those who seeke the Reformation of the Church of England: Wherein is Shewed that new Chvrch Discipline is Daungerous both to Religion, and also to the Whole State. Together with the Opinions of Certaine Reuerend and Learned Divines, Concerning the Fundamentall Poynts of the true Protestant Religion* (Oxford: W. W. and I. B., 1645).
78 Laud, *A Speech Delivered in the Star Chamber*, p. 7.
79 Heylyn, *A Briefe and Moderate Answer*, p. 163.
80 See *The Copy of the Petition presented to the Honourable Houses of Parliament, by the Lord Arch-Bishop of Canterbury* (London: Io. Smith, 1642).
81 Heylyn, *A Briefe Relation*, p. 7.
82 Ibid., p. 8.
83 Peter Heylyn indicated the problematic construction of Laud's defence for his treason trial and bemoaned the lack of resources available to the Archbishop, complaining that his papers had been removed from his quarters at the Tower of London. Heylyn, *A Briefe Relation*, p. 8.
84 Laud, *Works*, vol. IV, p. 230.
85 Laud indicated that many of the charges against him were preoccupied with external aspects of religion; Laud, *Works*, vol. IV, p. 230.
86 Laud, *Works*, vol. IV, p. 210. The practical demands of worship underpinned other defences of apparently popish worship. Bishop Pierce of Bath and Wells explained

that having the communion table at the east end of the chancel, set altar-wise, was not so much popish but simply left more room for the communicants; Lambeth Palace Library MS 943, p. 475. On the background to this quarrel, see Phyllis Hembry, *The Bishops of Bath and Wells, 1540–1640: Social and Economic Problems* (London: Athlone Press, 1967), p. 231.

87 *CSP DomCharles I* 1640–41 CCCCLXXIX.
88 Ibid.
89 Laud, *Works*, vol. IV, p. 219.
90 Ibid., p. 211.
91 Ibid., p. 211.
92 Kenneth Fincham and Nicholas Tyacke, *Altars Restored: The Changing Face of English Religious Worship, 1547-c.1700* (Oxford: Oxford University Press, 2008), p. 177.
93 Laud, *Works*, vol. IV, p. 215.
94 As such, Laud's residences became targets for mobs during the 1640s; Laud, *Works* vol. III, p. 84.
95 Laud, *Works*, vol. IV, p. 209.
96 Ibid., p. 209.
97 Ibid., p. 209.
98 Ibid., p. 209.
99 On the conversion and reconversion of the high ranking, see also Christopher Haigh, 'From monopoly to minority: Catholicism in early modern England', *Transactions of the Royal Historical Society* (fifth series, vol. 31, 1981), p. 137.
100 Laud, *Works*, vol. VI, p. 59.
101 Ibid., pp. 55–6.
102 Ibid., p. 65.
103 Ibid., p. 53.
104 Ibid., p. 53.
105 See my article 'Episcopal identity and authority in Restoration England', *Reformed Theological Review* (vol. 71, no. 1, 2012), pp. 45–69.

Chapter 5

1 See Brian P. Levack, *The Civil Laywers in England, 1603–1641: A Political Study* (Oxford: Clarendon Press, 1973), pp. 36, 96.
2 Patrick Collinson, 'Episcopacy and reform in England in the later sixteenth century', in *Godly People: Essays on English Protestantism and Puritanism* (London: The Hambledon Press, 1983), pp. 155–90.
3 Joseph Hall, *The Shaking of the Olive-tree. The Remaining Works of that Incomparable Prelate Joseph Hall, D. D. Late Lord Bishop of Norwich. With Some*

Specialities of Divine Providence in his Life. Noted by his own Hand. Together with his Hard Measure: VVritten also by himself (London: Printed by J. Cadwel for J. Crooke, 1660), pp. 342–3; Ussher's views are in *Report on the Manuscripts of the Right Honourable Viscount De L'Isle & Dudley*, (London: Historical Manuscripts Commission, 1925–66), vol. VI, p. 368. He also anonymously published *Directions Propovnded and Hvmbly Presented to the High Court of Parliament, Concerning the Booke of Common Prayer And Episcopall Government. Written by a Reverend and Learned Divine now Resident in this City* (London: for Iohn Thomas, 1641) and had another work posthumously published: *The Reduction of Episcopate Unto the Form of Synodical Government Received in the Antient Church: Proposed as an Expedient for the Compremising of the Now Differences, and the Preventing of Those Troubles that May Arise About the Matter of Church-Government* (London: T. N for G. B. and T. C, 1660).

4 The print form of Duck's early-seventeenth-century work is *The Life of Henry Chichele, Archbishop of Canterbury, who lived in the times of Henry the V. and VI. Kings of England* (London: Ri. Chiswell, 1699); however, it was circulating earlier in the seventeenth century. John Gauden, *Analysis: The Loosing of St Peters Bands; Setting Forth the True Sense and Solution of the Covenant in Point of Conscious so Far as it Relates to the Government of the Church by Episcopacy*, (London: J. Best for Andrew Crook, 1660).

5 [Thomas Bedford], *Luthers Predecessors: or an Answere to the Qvestion of the Papists: Where was your Church before Luther?* (London: Felix Kingston for George Winder, 1624); Edward Boughen, *An Account of the Church Catholick: Where it was before the Reformation: And, Whether Rome were or bee the Chvrch Catholick* (London: E. Cotes for Richard Royston, 1653); [Gregory Hascard], *A Discourse About the Charge of Novelty Upon the Reformed Church of England, Made by the Papists Asking of us the Question, Where was our Religion before Luther?* (London: T. Basset, 1685).

6 Humphrey Prideaux, *The Validity of the Orders of the Church of England Made out Against the Objections of the Papists, in Several Letters to a Gentleman of Norwich that Desired Satisfaction Therein* (London: Printed by John Richardson for Brabazon Aylmer, 1688).

7 Levack, *Civil Lawyers in England*, p. 181.

8 For some details of Duck's life and career, see Helen Pierce, 'Anti-Episcopacy and graphic satire in England, 1640–1645', *Historical Journal* (vol. 47, no. 4, 2004), p. 824.

9 See Pierce, 'Anti-Episcopacy', p. 824.

10 Jonathan Arnold, *Dean John Colet of St Paul's: Humanism and Reform in Early Tudor England* (London: I.B. Tauris, 2007), p. 48.

11 John Colet, *Joannes Coleti Super Opera Dionysii: Two Treatises on the Hierarchies of Dionysius, by John Colet, D. D.* (trans. J. H. Lupton), (London: George Bell and sons, 1869), p. 53.

12 See M. R. Sommerville, 'Richard Hooker and his contemporaries on episcopacy: an Elizabethan consensus', *Journal of Ecclesiastical History* (vol. 35, no. 2, 1984), pp. 177–87.

13 On the licensing of preachers by bishops, see Mark E. VanderSchaaf, 'Archbishop Parker's efforts towards a Bucerian discipline in the Church of England', *Sixteenth Century Journal* (vol. 8, no. 1, 1977), p. 96.

14 On the Court of Faculties, see Christopher Hill, *Society and Puritanism in Pre-Revolutionary England* (London: Mercury Books, 1966), p. 112. Hill also addresses the disciplinary powers of bishops in the High Commission; *Society and Puritanism*, p. 349.

15 Lancelot Andrewes composed liturgies for consecrating churches and church furnishings; see his *Minor Works* in the *Library of Anglo-Catholic Theology* (ed. J. P. Wilson and James Bliss) (Oxford: John Henry Parker, 1841–54), vol. xi., pp. 158–63.

16 See Patrick Collinson, 'The Reformer and the Archbishop: Martin Bucer and an English Bucerian', *Journal of Religious History* (vol. 6, no. 4, 1971), p. 313.

17 James F. Turrell, '"Until Such Time as He Be Confirmed": the Laudians and confirmation in the seventeenth-century Church of England', *The Seventeenth Century* (vol. 20, no. 2, 2005), pp. 204–5.

18 Cited in Patrick Collinson, John Craig and Brett Usher (eds), *Conferences and Combination Lectures in the Elizabethan Church: Dedham and Bury St Edmunds* (Woodbridge: Boydell Press/Church of England Record Society, 2003), p. xxvi.

19 On the period assessed by Duck, see B. Wilkinson, 'Fact and fancy in fifteenth-century English History', *Speculum* (vol. 42, no. 4, 1967), p. 673.

20 Chichele and other medieval primates including John Morton and John Peckam also received attention in Archbishop Parker's history of the archbishopric of Canterbury, *De Antiquitate Britannicae Ecclesiae &Priuilegiis Ecclesiae Cantuariensis cum Archiepiscopis eiusdem 70.* (London, 1572), and in other catalogues of bishops produced in the seventeenth century, including Anon., *Catalogue of All the Bishops which have Governed in the Church of England and Wales, Since the Conversion of the Saxons. Together with the Honourary Offices Which They or Any of Them Have Enjoyed in the Civil Government* (London, 1674), John Harington, *A Supplie or Addicion to the Catalogue of Bishops to the Yeare 1608* (ed. R. H. Miller), (Potomac, Maryland: Jose Porrua Turanzas S. A., 1979).

21 Duck, *The Life of Henry Chichele*, dedicatory epistle.

22 In his own lifetime, Chichele had been accused of anti-papalism, a charge that he denied and which emerged from a complex controversy regarding parliamentary legislation concerning Church lands; Edward Jacob, *The Fifteenth Century 1399–1485* (Oxford: Oxford University Press, 1961), p. 233.

23 Duck, *Life of Henry Chichele*, dedicatory epistle.

24 Ibid.
25 Thomas James, *An Apologie for Iohn Wicliffe, Shewing his Conformitie with the Now Church of England* (Oxford: Joseph Barnes, 1608).
26 John Spurr, *The Post-Reformation: Religion, Politics and Society in Britain 1603–1714* (London: Pearson, 2006), p. 146; Gauden's place in episcopal debates of the 1650s is discussed in William Abbott, 'James Ussher and "Ussherian" episcopacy, 1640–1656: the Primate and his reduction manuscript', *Albion* (vol. 22, no. 2, 1990), p. 256.
27 Edward Hyde, Earl of Clarendon, *Life and Continuation of his Life* (Oxford: Clarendon Press, 1761), vol. II, pp. 119–20.
28 See James C. Spalding and Maynard F. Brass, 'Reduction of episcopacy as a means to unity in England, 1640–62', *Church History* (vol. 30, no. 4, 1961), pp. 414–32. On the links between Ussher and Gauden, see Ronald Harris, *Clarendon and the English Revolution* (London: Hogarth Press, 1983), p. 260.
29 Cited in Alan Ford, *James Ussher: Theology, History and Politics in Early-Modern Ireland and England* (Oxford: Oxford University Press, 2007), p. 1.
30 John Milton, *Of Reformation Touching Church Discipline in England* (New Haven: Yale University Press, 1916).
31 John Gauden, *Hieraspistes: A Defence by Way of Apology for the Ministry and Ministers of the Church of England* (London, 1653), p. 219.
32 Gauden, *Loosing of St Peters Bands*, p. 8.
33 'I. W.', *Certaine Reasons Why the Booke of Common-Prayer Being Corrected Shovld Continue* (London: A. N. for Richard Lownds, 1641); Anon., *The Protestation Of the Two and Twenty Divines, For the Setling of the Church: And the Particulars by Them Excepted Against in the Liturgie: Not that the Book of Common Prayer of the Church of England Should be Utterly Abolished, but Purged of all Innovations and Absurdities* (London: H. Beck, 1642 or 1643).
34 On Scandinavian bishoprics, see Einar Molland, 'A short historical sketch' in Leslie Stannard Hunter (ed.), *Scandinavian Churches: A Picture of the Development and Life of the Churches of Denmark, Finland, Iceland, Norway and Sweden* (London: Faber and Faber, 1965), p. 37.
35 Felicity Heal, *Of Prelates and Princes: A Study of the Economic and Social Position of the Tudor Episcopate* (Cambridge: Cambridge University Press, 1980), p. 209.
36 Richard Hooker, *Of the Laws of Ecclesiastical Polity* (ed. P. G. Stanwood), (Cambridge, Massachusetts: Harvard University Press, 1981), vol. III.11.16.
37 John Whitgift, *Works* (ed. J. Ayre) (Cambridge: Cambridge University Press, 1853), vol. II, p. 400.
38 *Dr Reignolds His Letter to that Worthy Councellor, Sir Francis Knolles, Concerning Some Passages in D. Bancroft's Sermon at Pavles Crosse, Feb. 9. 1588 in the Parliament time* (London: W. I., 1641), p. 8. On Dr John Rainolds and

the controversy which followed the delivery of Bancroft's sermon, see Diarmaid MacCulloch, 'Richard Hooker's Reputation', *English Historical Review* (vol. 117, no. 473, 2002), pp. 774–5, 777.

39 Bancroft became Archbishop of Canterbury in 1604. The Paul's Cross sermon of 1588 was preached in retaliation to the publication of the Marprelate Tracts. The sermon was published in 1588 but the comments from Reynolds to Knollys may have come from the 1634 re-issue; Bancroft, *A Sermon Preached at Pavls Crosse* (London, 1634).

40 Cited in Edward Stillingfleet, *The Unreasonableness of Separation, or, An Impartial Account of the History, Nature, and Pleas of the Present Separation from the Communion of the Church of England: To which Several Late Letters are Annexed, of Eminent Protestant Divines Abroad* (London: by T. N. for Henry Mortlock, 1681) p. 449. Little is known of Monsieur Claude but he is not to be confused with the earlier Claude in the *Acts and Monuments*.

41 Herbert Thorndike, *An Epilogue to the Tragedy of the Church of England, Being a necessary consideration and Brief Resolution of the Chief Controversies in Religion that divide the Western Church: Occasioned by the Present Calamity of the Church of England* (London: J. M. and T. R. for J. Martin, J. Allestry and T. Dicas, 1659), p. 195. Thorndike's work is examined in E. C. Miller, 'The doctrine of the Church in the thought of Herbert Thorndike (1598–1672)', (Oxford University D. Phil, 1990).

42 Stillingfleet, *The Unreasonableness of Separation*, pp. 14, 18.

43 BL Birch MS 4236 fl. 92.

44 Gauden, *Loosing of St. Peters Bands*, p. 9.

45 Maurice Lee Jr., 'James VI and the revival of episcopacy: 1596–1600', *Church History* (vol. 43, no. 1, 1974), pp. 50–64.

46 Allen B. Birchler, 'Archbishop John Spottiswoode: Chancellor of Scotland, 1635–1638', *Church History* (vol. 39, no. 3, 1970), p. 318.

47 Lancelot Andrewes, *Selected Sermons and Lectures* (ed. Peter McCullough), (Oxford: Oxford University Press, 2005), p. 342.

Chapter 6

1 See especially Bernard J. Verkamp, *The Indifferent Mean: Adiaphorism in the English Reformation to 1554* (Ohio and Detroit, Michigan: Ohio University Press and Wayne State University Press, 1977).

2 David Loades, *Politics and the Nation 1450–1660: Obedience, Resistance and Public Order* (London: William Collins and Sons/Fontana, 1974), p. 256.

3 See especially Sydney Anglo, *Images of Tudor Kingship* (London: Seaby, 1992) and Caroline A. Edie, 'The public face of royal ritual: sermons, medals and civic

ceremony in later Stuart coronations', *Huntingdon Library Quarterly* (vol. 53, 1990), pp. 311–36; a more recent discussion of the intersection between authority and appearance is provided in Kevin Sharpe, 'Representation and negotiations: texts, images, and authority in early modern England', *Historical Journal* (vol. 42, no. 3, 1999), pp. 853–81.

4 Helen Pierce, 'Anti-Episcopacy and graphic satire in England, 1640–1645', Historical Journal (vol. 47, no. 4, 2004), pp. 809–48.

5 A useful survey of the period is Mark Knights, *Politics and Opinion in Crisis, 1678–1681* (London: Cambridge University, 1994).

6 [George Hooper], *The Church of England Free from the Imputation of Popery* (London: W. Abington, 1683). Later editions appeared in 1699 and 1716.

7 J. R. Tanner (ed.), *English Constitutional Conflicts of the Seventeenth Century 1603–1689* (Cambridge: Cambridge University Press, 1966), pp. 240–1.

8 For example, see John Williams's *A Sermon of Apparell, Preached before the Kings Majestie and the Prince his Highnesse at Theobalds, the 22. Of February, 1619* (London: John Bill, 1620), p. 4. On Reformed reactions to clothing more generally, see Catherine Richardson, *Clothing Culture, 1350–1650* (Aldershot: Ashgate, 2004), p. 130.

9 Such as Bishop John Aylmer's sermon on this topic recorded in Sir John Harington, *Nugae Antiquae* (London: Verner and Hood, 1804) vol. I, p. 362.

10 *Certaine Sermons of Homilies Appointed to be Read in Churches, In the Time of the Late Queene Elizabeth of Famous Memory* [1623], (eds Mary Ellen Rickey and Thomas B. Stroup), (Gainesville, Florida: Scholars' Facsimiles, 1968).

11 C. R. Boxer, *The Dutch Seaborne Empire 1600–1800* (Harmondsworth: Penguin, 1973), p. 43.

12 Stow's *Annals*, 13 November 1600, cited in Jennifer Harrison, 'The relationship between the Elizabethan Privy Council and the Corporation of London 1588 to 1603' (University of Queensland PhD, 1988), pp. 301–2.

13 J. S. Morrill, 'The Church in England, 1642–9', in J. S. Morrill (ed.), *Reactions to the English Civil War 1642–1649* (New York: St Martin's Press, 1982), Chapter 4.

14 See also B. Reay, 'Radicalism and religion in the English Revolution: an introduction', in J. M. McGregor and B. Reay (eds), *Radical Religion in the English Revolution* (Oxford: Oxford University Press, 1984), p. 9.

15 BL Add. MS 4236 fl. 92.

16 J. Ogilby refers to Juxon's 'age and weakness' when officiating at Charles II's coronation and notes Juxon spent much of the ceremony resting in St Edward's Chapel; *A Brief Narrative of His Majestie's Solemn Coronation with his Magnificent Proceeding, and Royal Feast in Westminster* (London, 1662), p. 173.

17 John Sudbury, *A Sermon Preached at the Consecration of the Right Reverend Fathers in God, Gilbert Lord Bishop of London, Humphry Lord Bishop of Sarum, George*

Lord Bishop of Worcester, Robert Lord Bishop of Lincolne, George Lord Bishop of St Asaph (London: R. Royston, 1660); William Sancroft, *A Sermon Preached in St Peter's Westminster, on the first Sunday in Advent, at the Consecration of the Right Reverend in God, John Lord Bishop of Durham, William Lord Bishop of S. David's, Beniamin L. Bishop of Peterborough, Hugh Lord Bishop of Landaff, Richard Lord Bishop of Carlisle, Brian Lord Bishop of Chester, and John Lord Bishop of Exceter* (London: T. Roycroft for Robert Beaumont, 1660).

18 Gilbert Sheldon, *David's Deliverance and Thanksgiving: A Sermon Preached before the King at Whitehall* (London: Timothy Garthwaite, 1660).

19 Anna Keay, *The Magnificent Monarch: Charles II and the Ceremonies of Power* (London: Continuum Books, 2008), p. 146.

20 A general overview of the appropriation of episcopal and cathedral revenues is given in Ian Gentles, 'The sales of bishops' lands in the English Revolution, 1646–60', *English Historical Review* (vol. 95, no. 376, 1980), pp. 573–96. On the damage to Canterbury Cathedral, see J. C. Robertson, 'The condition of Canterbury Cathedral at the Restoration in A.D.1660', *Archaeologia Cantiana* (vol. 10, 1876), pp. 95–6.

21 R. W. Symonds, 'The bishop's chair in St Paul's Cathedral', *Burlington Magazine* (vol. 77, no. 453, 1940), pp. 200–1; Compton was bishop when divine service was first held in the Cathedral in 1697.

22 William M. Marshall, *George Hooper 1640–1727: Bishop of Bath and Wells* (Sherborne: Dorset Publishing, 1976), pp. 71–8.

23 Timothy Rosendale, *Liturgy and Literature in the Making of Protestant England* (Cambridge: Cambridge University Press, 2007), p. 123.

24 J. W. Blench, *Preaching in England in the late 15th and 16th Centuries: A Study of English Sermons 1450-c.1600* (Oxford: Basil Blackwell, 1964), p. 303.

25 [John Fieldes], *First Admonition to Parliament* (Hemel Hempsted, 1572 [?]).

26 *First Admonition to Parliament*, n.p.

27 The volume of tracts appeared even though the Restoration again placed printing under the control of royal prerogative; Colin Clair, *A History of Printing in Britain* (London: Cassell, 1965), p. 153.

28 John Charles Ryle, *Light from Old Times; or, Protestant Facts and Men* (London: Chas. J. Thynne, 1902), p. 10.

29 Peter Lake, *The Boxmaker's Revenge: 'Orthodoxy', 'Heterodoxy' and the Politics of the Parish in Early Stuart London* (Stanford: Stanford University Press, 2001), p. 308.

30 Leopold G. Wickham Legg, *English Orders for Consecrating Churches in the Seventeenth Century* (London: Henry Bradshaw Society, 1911), p. 41.

31 On the building and consecrating of churches in Stuart London, see J. F. Merritt, 'Puritans, Laudians, and the phenomenon of church-building in Jacobean London', *Historical Journal* (vol. 41, no. 4, 1998), pp. 935–60. On the convergence between vestments and consecration ceremonies, see Kenneth Fincham and Nicholas

Tyacke, *Altars Restored: The Changing Face of English Religious Worship, 1547-c.1700* (Oxford: Oxford University Press, 2008), p. 240.

32　Sharpe, 'Representations and negotiations', p. 853.

33　[Alexander Nowell], *A Catechism or Institution of Christian Religion, to be Learned of all Youth, next after the Little Catechism Appointed in the Book of Common Prayer* (London: E. Cotes for the Company of Stationers, [1572],1663). On the expansion of the catechism over the seventeenth century, see Massey Hamilton Shepherd, The Oxford American Prayer Book Commentary (New York: Oxford University Press, 1950), p. 581.

34　*Book of Common Prayer*, 'Concerning Ceremonies, why some be abolished and some retained'.

35　Martin Luther, *Luther's Large Catechism* (trans. J. N. Lenker), (Minneapolis: Augsburg Publishing House, 1967), p. 127.

36　On the symbolic significance of clothing, see Jennifer Loach, 'The function of ceremonial in the reign of Henry VIII', *Past and Present* (vol. 142, no. 1, 1994), pp. 43–68.

37　Neither wigs nor mitres were specifically dealt with in canon law; see J. Mayo, *A History of Ecclesiastical Dress* (London: Holmes & Meier Publishers, 1984), pp. 81–2. Visual evidence for the developments of episcopal appearance is collected in John Ingamells, *The English Episcopal Portrait 1559–1835: A Catalogue* (published privately by the Paul Mellon Centre for Studies in British Art, 1981).

38　Medieval vestments are usefully explained in Virginia Davis, *William Wyckham: A Life* (London: Continuum Books, 2007), pp. 52–3.

39　Cited in Andrew Browning (ed.), *English Historical Documents: 1660–1714* (London: Routledge, 1966), p. 417.

40　Such as the carving at Brent Knoll in Somerset; Stephen Friar, *A Companion to the English Parish Church* (Stroud: Alan Sutton Publishing, 1996), p. 47.

41　D. Calderwood, *The History of the Kirk of Scotland* (eds T. Thomson and D. Laing), (Edinburgh: Woodrow Society, 1842–9), vol. 6, pp. 597–8.

42　S. R. Gardiner (ed.), 'Documents relating to the proceedings against William Prynne, in 1634 and 1637' (*Camden Society*, new series, XVIII, 1877), p. 39.

43　Anon., *Englands Reioycing at the Prelats Downfall* (1641), p. 3.

44　John Milton, *Of Reformation Touching Church Discipline in England* (New Haven: Yale University Press, 1916), p. 71.

45　On the sumptuary laws, see Wilfrid Hooper, 'The Tudor Sumptuary Laws', *English Historical Review* (vol. 30, no. 119, 1915), pp. 433–49; on their repeal, see N. E. Harte, 'State control of dress and social change', in D. C. Coleman and A. H. John (eds), *Trade, Government and Economy in Pre-Industrial England: Essays presented to F.J. Fisher* (London: Weidenfeld and Nicolson, 1976), pp. 148–51.

46　On the cloth trade, see Sybil M. Jack, *Trade and Industry in Tudor and Stuart England* (London: George, Allen and Unwin, 1977), p. 106.

47 Pierce, 'Anti-Episcopacy', pp. 819–20.
48 George Digby, *The Third Speech of the Lord George Digby, to the House of Commons, Concerning Bishops, and the Citie Petition, the 9th of Febr 1640* (for Tho. Walkley, 1640), p. 9. Lord Falkland used 'a paire of Lawne sleeves' as a metaphor to describe the unfortunate transformative effect which episcopal office had on clergymen; Oliver Lawson Dick (ed.), *Aubrey's Brief Lives* (Harmondsworth: Penguin, 1949), p. 474.
49 Michael Jaffé, 'Van Dyck Studies I: The Portrait of Archbishop Laud', *Burlington Magazine* (vol. 124, no. 955, 1982), p. 603.
50 On Cranmer's appearance, see S. Hubert Burke, *The Men and Women of the English Reformation, From the Days of Wolsey to the Death of Cranmer* (London: R. Washbourne, 1870), p. 205.
51 G. E. Corrie (ed.), *Sermons of Hugh Latimer, sometime Bishop of Worcester, Martyr, 1555* (Cambridge: Cambridge University Press, 1844), p. 208.
52 [Alexander Leighton], *A Decade of Grievances: Presented and Approved to the Right Honourable and High Court of Parliament against the Hierarchy or Government of the Lord Bishops* (1641), title page.
53 For the image, see Anon., *Canterburie[s] Pilgrimage: or the Testimony of an Accused Conscience* (London: for H. Walker, 1641).
54 Christopher Hodgkins, 'The Church legible: George Herbert and the externals of worship', *The Journal of Religion* (vol. 71, no. 2, 1991), p. 218.
55 Todd Butler, *Imagination and Politics in Seventeenth Century England* (Aldershot: Ashgate, 2008), p. 115.
56 These writers and their works are discussed in William Gibson, 'Dissenters, Anglicans and the Glorious Revolution: the collection of cases', *The Seventeenth Century* (vol. 22, no. 1, 2007), p. 4.
57 Marshall, *George Hooper*, p. 164.
58 See Peter Lake, 'Matthew Hutton – a puritan bishop?', *History* (vol. 64, no. 211, 1979), pp. 182–204.
59 The tombs of Matthew and Frewen are described in Hugh Murray, *Monuments in York Minster: An Illustrated Inventory* (Friends of York Minster, 2001), pp. 5, 57.
60 Examples abound from the monument to James Montague (d.1618) in Bath Abbey, Bishop John Thornborough's tomb (1627) in Worcester Cathedral, John Whitgift's in Croydon Minster, Edmund Guest's brass in Salisbury Cathedral and Samuel Harsnet's brass in Chigwell Church; see Peter Sherlock's monograph for a comprehensive discussion; *Monuments and Memory in Early Modern England* (Aldershot: Ashgate, 2008), pp. 120, 190, 193, 209.
61 R. A. Beddard suggests that Dolben was memorialized in a way to confront popery; Beddard, 'The character of a Restoration prelate: Dr. John Dolben', *Notes and Queries* (November, 1970), p. 421.

62 Peter Sherlock, 'Episcopal tombs in early modern England', *Journal of Ecclesiastical History* (vol. 55, no. 4, 2004), p. 673.
63 A further notable instance of an opulent episcopal tomb is George Abbot's iconographically enigmatic monument in Guildford; Joseph Burke, 'Archbishop Abbot's tomb at Guildford: a problem in early Caroline Iconography', *Journal of the Warburg and Courtauld Institutes* (vol. 12, 1949), pp. 179–89.
54 Muriel McCarthy, 'Archbishop Marsh and his library', *Dublin Historical Record* (vol. 29, no. 1, 1975), pp. 2–23.
65 Stanford Lehmberg, *English Cathedrals: A History* (London: Hambledon and London, 2005), p. 200.
66 The architectural implications of these disasters are discussed in Peter Kidson, Peter Murray and Paul Thompson, *A History of English Architecture* (London: Pelican, 1965), pp. 190–1; There had been some earlier building activity in settlements outside London's walls, which had necessitated the building of churches; Peter Guillery, 'Suburban models, or Calvinism and continuity in London's seventeenth-century church architecture', *Architectural History* (vol. 48, 2005), p. 70.
67 Pat Mussett, 'Some aspects of church furnishing in Cosin's time', in Margot Johnson (ed.), *John Cosin: Papers Presented to a Conference to Celebrate the 400th Anniversary of his Birth* (Durham: Turnstone Ventures, 1997), p. 191.
68 His Visitation of Durham Cathedral in 1662 shows his personal involvement in the decorative schemes; *The Correspondence of John Cosin, D. D. Lord Bishop of Durham* (ed. George Ornsby), (Edinburgh: Blackwood and sons, 1869), vol. I, p. 335.
69 William Holden Hutton, 'Tenison, Thomas', *Dictionary of National Biography* (1885–1900), vol. 56.
70 For the guidance of which was published Edward Lowe, *A Short Direction for the Performance of Cathedral Service* (Oxford: William Hall for Richard Davis, 1661).
71 T. G. Bonney, 'Lichfield', in T. G. Bonney (ed.), *Cathedrals and Abbeys of England and Wales* (London: Bracken Books, 1985), p. 121.
72 Hooper, *Imputation of Popery*, p. 2.
73 Ibid., p. 18.
74 Ibid., p. 7.
75 Ibid., p. 19.
76 Ibid., p. 19.
77 Anon., *A Dispute upon the Question of Kneeling in the Acte of Receiving the Sacramental bread and wine, proving it to be unlawfull* (London, 1608); Anon., *The Protestation of the Two and Twenty Divines, For the Settling of the Church: And the Particulars by them Excepted Against in the Liturgie: Not that the Book of Common*

Prayer of the Church of England Should be Utterly Abolished, but Purged of all Innovations and Absurdities (London: H. Beck, 1642 or 1643).
78   Hooper, *Imputation of Popery*, p. 19.
79   See Sybil M. Jack, 'In praise of queens: the public presentation of the virtuous consort in seventeenth-century Britain', in Susan Broomhall and Stephanie Tarbin (eds), *Women, Identities and Communities in Early Modern Culture* (Aldershot: Ashgate, 2008), pp. 211–25.
80   Sharpe, 'Representations and negotiations', p. 854.
81   Ibid., p. 854.
82   Hooper, *Imputation of Popery*, p. 25.
83   Ibid., p. 27.
84   Compton's evidence was cited in Edward Stillingfleet, *The Unreasonableness of Separation, or, An Impartial Account of the History, Nature, and Pleas of the Present Separation from the Communion of the Church of England: To which Several Late Letters are Annexed, of Eminent Protestant Divines Abroad* (London: by T. N. for Henry Mortlock, 1681), p. 449.
85   Hooper, *Imputation of Popery*, p. 7.
86   Ibid., p. 25.
87   Ibid., p. 8.
88   Ibid., p. 18.
89   Ibid., p. 6.
90   See especially Louise Campbell's chapter 'A diagnosis of religious moderation' in Luc Racaut and Alec Ryrie (eds), *Moderate Voices in the European Reformation* (Aldershot: St Andrew's Studies in Reformation History, 2005), pp. 32–50.
91   Hooper, *Imputation of Popery*, p. 6.
92   Ibid., p. 14.
93   Ibid., p. 13.
94   Ibid., p. 8.
95   Ibid., p. 2.
96   Ibid., p. 3.
97   Ibid., p. 14.
98   Anon., *The Case of the Cross in Baptism Considered. Wherein is Shewed That there is Nothing in it, as it is used in the Church of England, That Can be Any Just Reason of Separation From It* (London: Fincham Gardiner, 1684), p. 4.
99   Anon., *The Case of Kneeling at the Holy Sacrament Stated and Resolved* (London: for T. Basset and B. Took, 1685), p. 3.
100   Hooper, *Imputation of Popery*, p. 19.
101   Ibid., p. 19.
102   Ibid., p. 28.
103   Ibid., p. 29.

Conclusion

1. On these ideas, see Edward O. Smith Jr, 'The Elizabethan doctrine of the prince as reflected in the sermons of the episcopacy, 1559–1603', *Huntingdon Library Quarterly* (vol. 28, no. 1, 1964), pp. 1–17.
2. Richard Eedes, *Six Learned and Godly Sermons: Preached Some of Them Before the Kings Maiestie, Some Before Queen Elizabeth* (London: Adam Islip, for Edward Bishop, 1604), p. 63.
3. [Thomas Tenison], *An Argument for Union Taken from the True Interest of those Dissenters in England Who Profess, and call themselves Protestants* (London: Tho. Baffet, Benj. Tooke and F. Gardiner, 1683), p. 5.
4. Jeffrey R. Collins, 'The Restoration Bishops and the Royal Supremacy', *Church History* (vol. 68, no. 3, 1999) p. 551.
5. See Christopher Hill, *Society and Puritanism in Pre-Revolutionary England* (London: Mercury Books, 1966), p. 112.
6. Parker's endeavours in historical and antiquarian studies, as well as the polemical impulses that ran through them, are assessed in Timothy Graham and Andrew G. Watson (eds), *The Recovery of the Past in Early Elizabethan England: Documents by John Bale and John Joscelyn from the Circle of Matthew Parker* (Cambridge: Published for the Cambridge Bibliographical Society by Cambridge University Press, 1998); see also Benedict Scott Robinson, '"Darke speech": Matthew Parker and the Reforming of History', *Sixteenth Century Journal* (vol. 29, no. 4, 1998), pp. 1061–83.
7. *The First and Second Prayer Books of Edward VI* (London: Everyman Edition, 1910), pp. 460–2.

Bibliography

Manuscript sources

London: British Library
Additional Manuscripts 4236.
Additional Manuscripts 4274.
Additional Manuscripts 4358.
Additional Manuscripts 22, 473.
Additional Manuscripts 25, 899.
Additional Manuscripts 27, 632.
Additional Manuscript 28, 7571.
Additional Manuscripts 29, 546.
Additional Manuscripts 29, 584.
Additional Manuscripts 34, 216.
Additional Manuscripts 34, 268.
Additional Manuscripts 40, 160.
Additional Manuscripts 46, 370.
Birch Manuscripts 4236.
Cotton Manuscripts Cleo.E. iv.
Egerton Manuscripts 1048.
Royal MS 17 XXIIb.
Stowe Manuscripts 117.
London: Lambeth Palace Library
Register of John Tillotson.
Register of John Whitgift.
Register of William Sancroft.
CM XVI/14 – 'A roll containing the names and dates of consecration and translation of the Archbishops of Canterbury from Pecham to Abbot'.
CM XI/92 – Royal letter patent setting up a commission to reform the liturgy and canons and ecclesiastical courts.
LPL MS 943
MS 4251 – Commonplace Book of Archbishop Thomas Tenison.
London: Parliamentary Archives, House of Lords
BRY MSS – Braye Manuscripts, volumes one and two.

HC/LB/1/102 – William Prynne, Fourth Part of a Brief Register Kalendar.
HL/PO/JO/10/1/136A – Petition of Archbishop Laud from prison.

London: National Archives (formerly Public Record Office)
MS SP9/251 – The Address of the Lords Spiritual and Temporal and Commons, to the King's Most Excellent Majesty for maintaining the Church of England, as by Law Established; with His Majesty's Most Gracious Answer thereunto, 1689.
SP 9/247 – His Majesties Declaration for the Dissolution of His Late Privy-Council, and for constituting a New one, made in the Council Chamber at Whitehall, April the Twentieth, 1679.
SP 9/251 – Mercurious Librarius, or, a catalogue of Books Printed and Published in Michaelmass Term, 1668.
SP 84/156, ff. 113–119 – Letter to William Laud from William Boswell, concerning a plot against the King and Archbishop.

York Minster Library
York Minster Library Additional Manuscripts 18: *The Diary and Journal of his Grace Toby Matthew, Lord Archbishop of York from the 3rd Sept. MDLXXXIII to the 23rd Sunday after Trinity MDCXXII.*

Primary (pre-1700) sources in print

Anon., *An Answere to a Sermon Preached the 17 of April Anno D. 1608, by George Downame Doctour of Divinitie and Intitvled, A sermon defendinge the honorable function of Bishops; wherein All his reasons, brought to prove the honorable function of our L. Bishops, to be divine inftitution; are answered and refuted*, 1609.

—, *The Bishop of Canterbvry His Confession. Wherein is declared his constant Resolution, his Plots, and indeavours, to introduce Popery into England, and to advance the Roman Catholick Religion*, London, 1643.

—, *The Booke of Common Prayer, now used in the Church of England, Vindicated from the aspertion of all Schismaticks, Anabaptists, Brownists, and Separatists*, London: Iohn Thomas, 1641.

—, *A Briefe Narration of the Possession, Dispossession, and, Repossession of William Sommers and of Some Proceedings against Mr Iohn Dorrell Preacher, with Aunsweres to such Obiections as are made to Prove the Pretended Counterfeiting of the said Sommers. Together with certaine depositions taken at Nottingham concerning the said matter*, [Amsterdam?: S. n.], 1598.

—, *Canterburie[s] Pilgrimage: Or the Testimony of an accused Conscience*, London: For H. Walker, 1641.

—, *The Case of the Cross in Baptism Considered. Wherein is Shewed That there is nothing in it, as it is used in the Church of England, That Can be Any Just Reason of Separation From It*, London: Fincham Gardiner, 1684.

—, *The Case of Kneeling at the Holy Sacrament Stated and Resolved*, London: For T. Basset and B. Took, 1685.

—, *Catalogue of All the Bishops which have Governed in the Church of England and Wales, Since the Conversion of the Saxons. Together with the Honourary Offices Which They or Any of Them Have Enjoyed in the Civil Government*, London, 1674.

—, *The Coppy of a Letter Sent from Iohn Lord Finch, late Lord Keeper, to his Friend Dr. Cozens: With A Commemoration of the Favours Dr. Cozens Shewed him in his Vice-Chancellorship. Unto VVhich is Annexed a Good Admonition to Protestants*, 1641.

—, *The Copy of the Petition presented to the Honourable Houses of Parliament, by the Lord Arch-Bishop of Canterbury*, London: Io. Smith, 1642.

—, *The Dangers of the New Discipline, To The State and Church*, Oxford: For W. R., 1642.

—, *A Discovrse Presented to those who seeke the Reformation of the Church of England: Wherein is Shewed that new Chvrch Discipline is Daungerous both to Religion, and also to the Whole State. Together with the Opinions of Certaine Reuerendand Learned Divines, Concerning the Fundamentall Poynts of the true Protestant Religion*, Oxford: W. W. and I. B., 1645.

—, *A Dispute vpon the Qvestion of Kneeling in the Acte of Receiving the Sacramental bread and wine, proving it to be unlawfull*, London, 1608.

—, *Dr Reignolds His Letter to that Worthy Councellor, Sir Francis Knolles, Concerning Some Passages in D. Bancroft's Sermon at Pavles Crosse, Feb. 9. 1588 in the Parliament time*, London: W. I., 1641.

—, *Englands Glory in her Royal King and Honorable Assemblying the High Court Parliament, above her former usurped Lordly Bishops Synod*, 1641.

—, *Englands Reioycing at the Prelats Downfall*, 1641.

—, *An Exact Copy of a Letter sent to William Laud late Arch-bishop of Canterbury, now Prisoner in the Tower*, London: H. W. and T. B., 1641.

—, *The First and Large Petition of the Citie of London and Other Inhabitants Thereabouts*, 1641.

—, *Forty Four Queries Propounded to all the Clergy-Men of the Liturgy, by one whom they trained up in, and according to the best things set forth in the Book of Common Prayer*, London, 1662.

—, *The Last Advice of William Laud, late Arch-Bishop, to his Episcopall Brethren; and especially to Bishop Wren, who still remaines Prisoner in the Tower*, London: For J. B., 1644.

—, *The Most Strange and Admirable Discoverie of the Three Witches of Warboys, Convicted, and Executed at the Last Assizes at Huntington, for the Bewitching of the Five Daughters of Robert Throckmorton Esquire*, London: The Widow Orwin, for Thomas Man and John Winnington, 1593.

—, *The Petition and Articles Exhibited in Parliament Against Dr. Fvller, Deane of Ely, and Vicar of S. Giles Cripplegate, With The Petition Exhibited in Parliament against Timothy Hutton, Curate of the said Parish, By the Parishioners of Saint Giles*, London, 1641.

—, *Prelatique Preachers None of Christ's Teachers*, London, 1662.

—, *A Prophecie of the Life, Reigne and Death of William Laud, Archbishop of Canterbury*, Printed for R. A., 1644.

—, *The Protestation Of the Two and Twenty Divines, For the Setling of the Church: And the Particulars by Them Excepted Against in the Liturgie: Not that the Book of Common Prayer of the Church of England Should be Utterly Abolished, but Purged of all Innovations and Absurdities*, London: H. Beck, 1642 or 1643.

—, *Reformation Sure and Stedfast: Or, A Seasonable Sermon for the Present times. Shevving the Life and Death of Reformation*, London: J. D. for Henry Overton, 1641.

—, *A Relation of the Conference Between William Laud, Late Lord Archbishop of Canterbury, and Mr. Fisher the Jesuit*, London: Ralph Holt for Thomas Bassett, Thomas Dring and John Leigh, 1676.

—, *Rome's Masterpeece: Or, the Grand Conspiracy of the Pope and his Iesuited Instruments, to extirpate the Protestant Religion*, London: For Michael Sparke, 1644.

—, *Seasonable Reflections, on a late Pamphlet, Entituled, A History of Passive Obedience Since the Reformation: Wherein the true Notion of Passive Obedience is Settled and Secured from the Malicious Interpretations of ill-designing Men*, London: Robert Clavell, 1689/90.

—, *The Second Table, or, A Catalogue of all the Bishops which have Governed in the Church of England and Wales, since the conversion of the Saxons. Together with the Honourary offices which they or any of them have enjoyed in the civil Government*, London, 1674.

—, *A Summarie Ansvvere to al the Material Points in any of Master Darel his Bookes More Especiallie to that One Booke of his, Intituled, the Doctrine of the Possession and Dispossession of Demoniaks out of the Word of God. By Iohn Deacon. Iohn Walker. Preachers*, Londini: Impensis Geor. Bishop, 1601.

—, *A Suruey Of the Booke of Common Prayer, By way of 197. Quares grounded vpon 58. places, ministering iust matter of question, with a View of London Ministers exceptions. All humbly propounded*, 1606.

—, *To the Kings Most Excellent Majessty. The Due Account and Humble Petition of the Ministers of the Gospel, Lately Commissioned for the Review and Alteration of the Liturgy*, London, 1661.

—, *The Triall of Maist. Dorrell, or A Collection of Defences Against Allegations Not Yet Suffered to Receiue Convenient Answere Tending to Cleare Him From the Imputation of Teaching Sommers and Others to Counterfeit Possession of Divells. That the Mist of Pretended Counterfetting being Dispelled, the Glory of Christ his Royall Power in Casting out Divels (at the Prayer and Fasting of his People) may Evidently Appeare* Middelburg: R. Schilders, 1599.

—, *A Vindication of the Proceedings of His Majesties Ecclesiastical Commissioners, Against the Bishop of London, and the fellows of Magdalen College*, Tho.Milbourn for Richard Faneway, 1688.

—, *A Word to a Wavering Levite: Or an Answer to Dr Sherlock's Reasons Concerning the Taking of Oaths with Reflections Thereupon, by a London Apprentice of the Church of England*, London, 1690.

Abbott, Wilbur Cortez (ed.), *The Writings and Speeches of Oliver Cromwell* (2 vols), Cambridge: Harvard University Press, 1939.

Akrigg, G. P. V. (ed.), *Letters of King James VI and I*, Berkeley: University of California Press, 1984.

Allestry, Richard, *A Sermon Preached at Hampton Court On the 29th of May 1662. Being the Anniversary of His Sacred Majesty's Most Happy Return*, London: J Flesher for John Martin, James Allestry and Thomas Dicas, 1662.

Allington, John, *The Regal Proto-Martyr; or, The Memorial to the Martyrdom of Charles the First. In a Sermon Preached upon the First Fast of Publick Appointment for it*, London: J. W. for W. Gilbert, 1672.

Almack, Edward (ed.), *Eikon Basilike: The Pourtaicture of His Sacred Majestie in his Solitude and Sufferings*, London: De la More Press, 1903.

'Almoni, Peloni', *A Compendius Discourse, proving Episcopacy to be of Apostolicall, and Conseqvently of Divine Institution*, London: E. G. for Richard Whitaker, 1641.

Andrewes, Lancelot, *Minor Works* in *The Library of Anglo-Catholic Theology* (5 vols), (ed. J. P. Wilson and James Bliss), Oxford: John Henry Parker, 1841–54.

—, *Private Prayers* (ed. Hugh Martin), London: SCM Press, 1957.

—, *Selected Sermons and Lectures* (ed. Peter McCullough), Oxford: Oxford University Press, 2005.

Arminius, Jacob, *The Writings of James Arminius vols.1–3* (trans. James Nichols and W. R. Bagnall), Grand Rapids, Michigan, 1959.

Articles Agreed Upon By the Arch-Bishops and Bishops of Both Provinces, and the Whole Clergie, In the Convocation Holden at London, in the year 1562. For the Avoiding of Diversities of Opinions, and for the Establishing of Consent Touching True Religion. Reprinted by His Majesties Commandment: With His Royal Declaration Prefixed Thereunto, London: Bonham Norton and Iohn Bill, 1630.

Articles Exhibited Against William, Archbishop of Canterbury [1640], New York: Da Capo Press, 1971.

Atterbury, Francis, *An Answer to Some Considerations on the Spirit of Martin Luther and the Original of the Reformation*, Oxford, 1687.

Aubrey, John, *Brief Lives* (ed. Richard Barber), Woodbridge: Boydell, 1975.

—, *Aubrey's Brief Lives* (ed. Oliver Lawson Dick), Harmondsworth: Penguin, 1949.

Aughterson, Kate (ed.), *The English Renaissance: An Anthology of Sources and Documents*, London: Routledge, 1998.

Bale, John, *Select Works of John Bale*, (ed. H. Christmas), Cambridge: Cambridge University Press, 1849.

Bancroft, Richard, *A Sermon Preached at Pavls Crosse being the first Sunday in the Parleament, anno. 1588. by Richard Bancroft ... Wherein some things are now added, which then were omitted, either through want of time, or default in memorie*, Imprinted at London: By I. I[ackson] for Gregorie Seton 1588 [1634].

Barlow, William, *The Summe and Substance of the Conference, which, it pleased his Excellent Maiestie to haue with the Lords, Bishops, and other of his Clergie*, London: John Windet, 1604.

Barrow, Isaac, *A Sermon Preached on the fifth of November, MDCLXXIII*, London: J. D. for Brabazon Aylmer, 1679.

Baxter, Richard, *Autobiography* (eds. J. M. Lloyd and N. H. Keeble), London: Dent, 1974.

—, *Five Disputations of Church-Government and Worship*, London: R. W. for Nevil Simmons, 1659.

—, *The Saints' Everlasting Rest, or, a Treatise on the Blessed stated of the Saints, in their Enjoyment of God in Heaven: To which are Added, Dying Thoughts* (ed. Benjamin Fawcett), Edinburgh: Waugh and Innes, 1833.

—, *Select Political Writings*, New Haven: Durrie and Peck, 1831.

Bayne, Peter (ed.), *Documents Relating to the Settlement of the Church of England by the Act of Uniformity of 1662*, London: Kent, 1862.

Becon, Thomas, *Prayers and Other Pieces of Thomas Becon, S. T. P. Chaplain to Archbishop Cranmer, Prebendary of Canterbury, etc.* (ed. John Ayre), Cambridge: Cambridge University Press, 1844.

Bedford, Thomas, *Luthers Predecessors: Or an Answere to the Qvestion of the Papists: Where was your Church before Luther?*, London: Felix Kingston for George Winder, 1624.

Bell, Thomas, *The Tryall of the New Religion. Contayning a Plaine Demonstration that the late Faith and Doctrine of the Church of Rome, is indeede the New Religion*, London: William Iaggard, 1608.

Bisbie, Nathaniel, *The Bishop Visiting: Or a Sermon on I Cor. XI. Xxxiv*, London: Walter Kettilby, 1686.

—, *Prosecution no Persecution: Or, the Difference Between Suffering for Disobedience and Faction, and Suffering for Righteousness, and Christ's Sake*, London: Walter Kettilby, 1682.

Black, Joseph (ed.), *The Martin Marprelate Tracts: A Modernized and Annotated Edition*, Cambridge: Cambridge University Press, 2008.

Bold, Samuel, *A Brief Account of the First Rise of the Name Protestant; and what Protestantism is*, London, 1688.

Bond, R. B. (ed.), *Certain Sermons or Homilies (1547) and A Homily Against Disobedience*, Toronto: Toronto University Press, 1987.

Book of Common Prayer, Crown Copyright, multiple editions from 1662.

Boughen, Edward, *An Account of the Church Catholick: Where it was before the Reformation: And, Whether Rome were or bee the Chvrch Catholick*, London: E. Cotes for Richard Royston, 1653.

Bramhall, John, *The Works of the Most Reverend Father in God, John Bramhall, D. D.*, Oxford: John Henry Parker, 1842–5.
Bramston, John, 'The Autobiography of Sir John Bramston K. B.', *Camden Society*, first series, vol. 32, 1845.
Browning, Andrew (ed.), *English Historical Documents Vol. VI: 1660–1714*, London: Routledge, 1966.
Bruce, John (ed.), 'Annals of the First Years of the Reign of Queen Elizabeth by Sir John Hayward, Knt. D. C. L.', *Camden Society*, first series, vol. 7, 1840.
— (ed.), 'Correspondence of King James VI of Scotland with Sir Robert Cecil and others in England', *Camden Society*, first series, no. 78, 1861.
— (ed.), 'Letters of Queen Elizabeth and King James VI. of Scotland', *Camden Society*, first series, no. 46, 1849.
— (ed.), 'The Diary of John Manningham, of the Middle Temple, and of Bradbourne, Kent, Barrister-at-Law, 1602–3', *Camden Society*, first series, vol. 99, 1868.
Bruce, John and Thomason Perowne, Thomas (eds), *The Correspondence of Matthew Parker D. D., Archbishop of Canterbury*, Cambridge: Cambridge University Press, 1853.
Buchanan, Colin (ed.), *The Savoy Conference Revisited*, Cambridge: Grove, 2002.
Burnet, Gilbert, *An Apology for the Church of England with Relation to the Spirit of Persecution for which She Is Accused*, Amsterdam, 1688.
—, *The Bishop of Salisbury's Speech in the House of Lords, upon the Bill against Occasional Conformity*, London: R. Chiswell, 1704.
—, *The Case of Compulsion in matters of Religion stated*, London: T.S, 1688.
—, *An Exhortation to Peace and Union: A Sermon Preached at St.Lawrence-Jury at the Election of the Lord Mayor of London on the 29th of September, 1681*, London: R. Chiswell, 1681.
—, *An Exposition of the XXXIX Articles of the Church of England*, Oxford: Oxford University Press, 1845.
—, *History of his own Time* (six vols), (ed. Martin Joseph Routh), Hildesheim: Georg Olms Verlagsbuchhandlung, 1969.
—, *The History of the Reformation of the Church of England* (3 vols), Oxford: Clarendon Press, 1816.
—, *Life of the Most Reverend Father in God John Tillotson, arch-bishop of Canterbury*, London: E. Curll, 1717.
—, *Reflections on the Relation of the English Reformation, late Printed at Oxford*, Amsterdam: For J. S., 1688.
Calendar of State Papers Domestic: 1619–1623 (ed. Mary Anne Everett Green), London: Longmans, Brown, Green, Longmans and Roberts, 1858.
Calendar of State Papers Domestic: Charles I 1636–37 (ed. John Bruce), London, Longmans, Green, Reader and Dyer, 1867.
Calendar of State Papers Domestic: Charles I 1640–41 (ed. William Douglas Hamilton), London: Longmans and co., 1882.

Calendar of State Papers Domestic: James II (3 vols), (ed. E. K. Timings), London: HMSO, 1960–72.

Camden, William, *History of the Most Renowned and Victorious Princess Elizabeth, Late Queen of England* (selected chapters edited by Wallace T. MacCaffrey), Chicago: University of Chicago Press, 1970.

Cardwell, Edward (ed.), *Documentary Annals of the Reformed Church of England*, Oxford: Oxford University Press, 1844.

—, *History of the Conferences* (2 vols), Oxford: Oxford University Press, 1840.

—, *Synodalia: A Collection of Articles of Religion, Canons, and Proceedings of Convocations in the Province of Canterbury, from the year 1547 to the year 1717*, Oxford: Oxford University Press, 1842.

Carlson, Leland H. (ed.), *The Writings of Henry Barrow, 1587–1590*, London: George Allen and Unwin, 1962.

Cave, William, *A Discourse Concerning the Unity of the Catholick Church Maintained in the Church of England*, London: B. Tooke, 1684.

—, *A Sermon Preached before the King at Whitehall, January xxiii, 1675/6*, London: William Godbid for Richard Chiswell, 1676.

Charles II, King of England, *His Majesties Letters to the Bishop of London and the Lord Mayor*, London: L. Jenkins, 1681.

Chetwind [or Chetwynd], John (ed.), *A Brief View of the State of the Church of England, As it stood in Q. Elizabeths and King James his Reigne, to the yeare 1608. Being a Character and History of the Bishops of those times. And may serve as an additional Supply to Doctor Goodwins Catalogue of Bishops*, London: Jos. Kirton, 1653.

Clagett, William, *An Answer to the Dissenters Objections Against the Common Prayers, And Some Other Parts of Divine-Service Prescribed in the Liturgie of the Church of England*, London: T. Basset, B. Took and F. Gardiner, 1683.

—, *The Difference of the Case, Between the Separation of Protestants from the Church of Rome, And the Separation of Dissenters from the Church of England*, London: Thomas Basset and Fincham Gardiner, 1683.

Clarendon, Edward, Earl of, *The History of the Rebellion and Civil Wars in England* (6 vols), (ed. W. D. Macray), Clarendon Press, 1888.

—, *Life and Continuation of his Life* (3 vols), Oxford: Clarendon Press, 1761.

Clarke, Samuel, *England's Remembrancer, A True and Full Narrative of Those Two Never to be Forgotten Deliverances: One From the Spanish Invasion in 88. The Other from the Hellish Powder Plot, November 5. 1605. Whereunto is Added The Like Narrative of that Signal Judgment of God upon the Papists, by the Fall of the House in Black-Fryers London, upon their fifth of November, 1623*, London: J. Hancock, 1677.

—, *A General Martyrologie: Containing a Collection of all the Greatest Persecutions which have Befallen the Church of Christ, from the Creation to our Present Times. Whereunto are added, The Lives of Thirty-Two Divines, Famous in their Generations for Learning and Piety, and Most of them Great Sufferers in the Cause of Christ*, London: For William Birch, 1677.

—, *Lives of Sundry Eminent Persons in this Later Age in Two Parts: I. of Divines, II. of Nobility and Gentry of both Sexes/by Samuel Clark; Printed and Reviewed by Himself Just before his Death; to which is Added his Own Life and the Lives of the Countess of Suffolk, Sir Nathaniel Barnardiston, Mr. Richard Blackerby and Mr. Samuel Fairclough, Drawn up by Other Hands*, London: For Thomas Simmons, 1682.

—, *The Marrow of Ecclesiastical History: Divided into Two Parts: The First, Containing the Life of Our Blessed Lord & Saviour Jesus Christ, With The Lives of the Ancient Fathers, School-Men, First Reformers, and Modern Divines: The Second, Containing the Lives of Christian Emperors, Kings and Sovereign Princes: Whereunto are Added the Lives of Inferiour Christians, Who Have Lived in These Latter Centuries: And Lastly, are Subjoyned the Lives of Many of Those, Who by their Vertue and Valor Obtained the Sir-Name of Great, Divers of Which, Give Much Light to Sundry Places of Scripture, Especially to the Prophecies Concerning the Four Monarchies: Together with Lively Effigies of the Most Eminent of them Cut in Copper*, London: For W. B., [William Birch], 1675.

Colet, John, *Joannes Coleti Super Opera Dionysii: Two Treatises on the Hierarchies of Dionysius, by John Colet, D. D.* (trans. J. H. Lupton), London: George Bell and sons, 1869.

Compton, Henry, *The Lord Bishop of London's Fourth Letter to the Clergy of his Dioceses*, London, 1683.

—, *The Bishop of London's Eighth Letter to his Clergy, upon a Conference how they Ought to Behave Themselves under the Toleration*, London: Benj. Motte, 1692.

—, *The Bishop of London's Ninth Conference with his Clergy upon the Fifth and Tenth Injunctions Given by the King*, London: Benj. Motte, 1699.

Cooper, J. P., (ed.), 'Wentworth Papers 1597–1628', *Camden Society*, fourth series, vol. 12, 1973.

Copie of the Proceedings Of some Worthy and Learned Divines, Appointed by the Lords to Meet at the Bishop of Lincolnes in Westminster. Touching Innovations in the Doctrine and Discipline of the Church of England. Together With Considerations upon the Common-Prayer Book, London, 1641 and 1660.

Corrie, G. E. (ed.), *Sermons of Hugh Latimer, Sometime Bishop of Worcester, Martyr, 1555*, Cambridge: Cambridge University Press, 1844.

Cosin, John, *A Collection of Private Devotions* (ed. P. G. Stanwood), London: Oxford University Press, 1967.

—, *The Correspondence of John Cosin, D. D. Lord Bishop of Durham* (2 vols), (ed. George Ornsby), Edinburgh: Blackwood and sons, 1869.

—, *Two Letters of the Right Reverend Father in God Doctor John Cosin, late Lord Bishop of Durham, With Annotations on the Same. Also The Opinion of the Reverend Peter Heylin, D. D. Concerning the Metrical Version of DAVID's Psalms. With Remarks and Observations upon them. By R. Watson, D. D.*, London: P. Leach for Nich. Woolfe, 1686.

—, in *Two Treatises on the Church; the first by Thomas Jackson, D. D. the Second by Robert Sanderson, D. D., to which is Added a Letter of Bishop Cosin on the Validity of the Orders of the Foreign Reformed Churches*, London: Elliot Stock, 1901.

—, *Works* (5 vols), Oxford: John Henry Parker, 1843–55.

Covell, William, *A Modest and Reasonable Examination of Some Things in Use in the Church of England*, London: Clement Knight, 1603.

Coverdale, Miles, *Remains* (ed. George Pearson), Cambridge: Cambridge University Press, 1846.

Cox, J. E. (ed.), *Miscellaneous Writings and Letters of Thomas Cranmer, Archbishop of Canterbury, Martyr, 1556*, Cambridge: Cambridge University Press, 1844.

Cranmer, Thomas, *Works* (ed. G. E. Duffield), Appleford: Sutton Courtney Press, 1964.

Cross, Claire (ed.), 'The Letters of Sir Francis Hastings, 1574–1609', *Somerset Record Society*, vol. 69, 1969.

—, (ed.) *The Royal Supremacy in the Elizabethan Church*, London: George Allen and Unwin, 1969.

Daniell, David (ed.), *Tyndale's Old Testament*, New Haven: Yale University Press, 1992.

Darrel, John, *A Brief Apologie Prouing the Possession of William Sommers. Written by Iohn Dorrell, a Faithful Minister of the Gospell: But Published without his Knowledge, with a Dedicatorie Epistle Disclosing Some Disordered Procedings against the Saide Iohn Dorrell*, Middelburg: R. Schilders, 1599.

—, *A Detection of that Sinnful Shameful, Lying, and Ridiculous Discours of Samuel Harshnet*, 1600.

—, *A True Narration of the Strange and Grevous Vexation by the Devil of 7. Persons in Lancashire, and of William Somers of Nottingham*, 1600.

—, *A True Relation of the Grievous Handling of William Sommers of Nottingham*, London: Thomas Harper, 1641.

Deacon, John, *A Briefe Narration of the Possession, Dispossession, and, Repossession of William Sommers and of Some Proceedings against Mr Iohn Dorrell Preacher, with Aunsweres to Such Obiections as are Made to Prove the Pretended Counterfeiting of the Said Sommers. Together with Certaine Depositions taken at Nottingham concerning the said matter* [Amsterdam?: S. n.], Anno M. D. XCVIII [1598].

de Beer, E. S. (ed.), *Diary of John Evelyn*, Oxford: Oxford University Press, 1955.

de Beze, Theodore, *Icones* (ed. John Horden), Menston: The Scolar Press, 1971.

Digby, George, *The Third Speech of the Lord George Digby, to the House of Commons, Concerning Bishops, and the Citie Petition, the 9th of Febr 1640*, for Tho. Walkley, 1640.

Donne, John, *Pseudo-Martyr* (ed. Anthony Raspa), Montreal and Kingston: McGill-Queen's University Press, 1993.

—, *Psevdo-Martyr. Wherein Ovt of Certaine Propositions and Gradations, This Conclusion is euicted. That Those Which are of the Romane Religion in this Kingdome, may and ought to thake the Oath Allegeance*, London: W. Stansby for Walter Burre, 1610.

Dow, Christopher, *Innovation Unjustly Charged upon the Present Chvrch and State*, London: Iohn Clark, 1637.

Downame, George, *Two Sermons, the one Commending the Ministrie in General and the Other Defending the Office of Bishops in Particular, both Preached and Since Enlarged by George Downame Doctor of Diuinitie*, London: Felix Kyngston, 1608.

Duck, Arthur, *The Life of Henry Chichele, Archbishop of Canterbury, who Lived in the Times of Henry the V and VI. Kings of England*, London: Ri. Chiswell, 1699.

Dugdale, William, *The History of St Paul's Cathedral in London, From its Foundation Untill These Times*, London: Longman, Hurst, Rees, Orme and Brown, 1818.

—, *Monasticon Anglicanum*, London: Sam Keble, 1693.

Eedes, Richard, *Six Learned and Godly Sermons: Preached Some of Them before the Kings Maiestie, Some before Queen Elizabeth*, London: Adam Islip for Edward Bishop, 1604.

Eikon Basilike: The Pourtraicture of His Sacred Majestie in his Solitude and Sufferings, London: For R. Royston, 1648.

Fenner, Dudley, *A Briefe and Plaine Declaration, Concerning the Desires of all Those Faithfull Ministers, That Haue and do Seeke for the Discipline and Reformation of the Church of Englande: Which May Serve for a Iust Apologie, Against the False Accusations and Slanders of their Aduersaries*, London: Robert Walde-graue, 1584.

Ferne, Henry, *Certain Considerations of Present Concernment: Touching this Reformed Church of England. With a Particular Examination of An: Champny (Doctor of the Sorbon) his Exceptions Against the Lawful Calling and Ordination of the Protestant Bishops and Pastors of this Church*, London: Printed by J. G. for R. Royston, at the Angel in Ivie-lane, 1653.

—, *Of the Division between the English and Romish Church upon the Reformation*, London: J. G. for Richard Royston, 1652.

Field, Richard, *Of the Church: Fiue Bookes*, London: Imprinted by Humfrey Lownes, for Simon Waterson, 1606.

Fieldes, John, *First Admonition to Parliament*, Hemel Hempsted, 1572 [?].

Fisher, Ambrose, *A Defence of the Litvrgie of The Church of England, or The Booke of Common Prayer, In a Dialogue betweene Novatus and Irenaevs*, London: W. S. for Robert Milbourne, 1630.

Foster, C. W. (ed.), *The State of the Church in the Reigns of Elizabeth and James I, as Illustrated by Documents Relating to the Diocese of Lincoln*, Lincoln: Lincoln Record Society, 1926.

Foxe, John, *Book of Martyrs: Being a History of the Persecution of the Protestants*, London: Ward, Lock, Bowden and Co., 1888.

—, *Martyrologia, or, Records of Religious Persecution: Being a New and Comprehensive Book of Martyrs, of Ancient and Modern Times, Compiled Partly from the Acts and Monuments of John Foxe, and Partly from other Genuine and Authentic Documents, Printed and in Manuscript* (3 vols), London: J. Mason, 1848–51.

Fulke, William, *Stapleton's Fortress Overthrown; A Rejoinder to Martiall's Reply; A Discovery of the Dangerous Rock of the Popish Church Commended by Sanders* (ed. Richard Gibbings), Cambridge: Cambridge University Press, 1848.

Fuller, Thomas, *A Sermon of Reformation. Preached at the Church of the Savoy, Last Fast Day, July 27, 1643*, London, 1643.

—, *Worthies of England*, London: Allen and Unwin, 1952.

Gardiner, S. R. (ed.), *Constitutional Documents of the Puritan Revolution*, Oxford: Oxford University Press, 1899.

—, (ed.),'Debates in the House of Commons in 1625', *Camden Society*, new series, no. 6, 1873.

—, (ed.), 'Documents relating to the proceedings of against William Prynne, in 1634 and 1637', *Camden Society*, new series, no. 18, 1877.

— (ed.), 'The Hamilton Papers, 1638–1650', *Camden Society*, new series, no. 27, 1880.

—, (ed.), 'Notes on the Debates in the House of Lords, officially taken by Henry Elsing, Clerk of the Parliaments, A. D. 1621', *Camden Society*, first series, vol. 103, 1870.

—, 'Parliamentary Debates in 1610', *Camden Society*, first series, vol. 81, 1860.

—, 'Reports of Cases in the Courts of Star Chamber and High Commission', *Camden Society*, new series, no. 39, 1886.

Gauden, John, *Analysis: The Loosing of St Peters Bands; Setting Forth the True Sense and Solution of the Covenant in Point of Conscious so Far as it Relates to the Government of the Church by Episcopacy*, London: J. Best for Andrew Crook, 1660.

—, *Considerations Touching the Liturgy of the Church of England. In Reference to his Majesties late Gracious Declaration and in order to an Happy Union in Church and State*, J. G. for John Playford, 1661.

—, *Hieraspistes: A Defence by Way of Apology for the Ministry and Ministers of the Church of England*, London, 1653.

—, *A Pillar of Gratitude Humbly Dedicated to the Glory of God*, London: F. M. for Andrew Crook, 1661.

—, *Tears, Sighs and Complaints, and Prayers of the Church of England: Setting Forth Her Former Constitution, Compared with Her Present Condition*, London: J. G. for R. Royston, 1659.

Gibson, E. C. S. (ed.), *The First and Second Prayer Books of Edward VI*, London: J. M. Dent, 1910.

Gillespie, George, *A Late Dialogue Betwixt a Civilian and a Divine, Concerning the Present Condition of the Church of England*, London: Robert Bellock, 1644.

Glanvill, Joseph, *Some Discourse, Sermons and Remains, 1681* (ed. Rene Wellek), New York: Garland Publishing, 1979.

Godwin, Francis, *A Catalogue of the Bishops of England, since the First Planting of Christian Religion in this Island*, London: Thomas Adams, 2nd edn, 1615.

Goodman, Godfrey, *The Court of King James the First; to which are Added Letters Illustrative of the Personal History of the Most Distinguished characters in the Court of that Monarch and His Predecessors* (2 vols), London: Richard Bentley, 1839.

Graham, Timothy, and Andrew G. Watson (eds.), *The Recovery of the Past in Early Elizabethan England: Documents by John Bale and John Joscelyn from the Circle of Matthew Parker*, Cambridge: Published for the Cambridge Bibliographical Society by Cambridge University Press, 1998.

Hales, John, *A Tract Concerning Schism and Schismaticks: Wherein is briefly Discovered the Original Causes of all Schism*, London, 1700.

Hall, Joseph, *The Shaking of the Olive-tree. The Remaining Works of that Incomparable Prelate Joseph Hall, D. D. Late Lord Bishop of Norwich. With Some Specialities of Divine Providence in his Life. Noted by his own Hand. Together with his Hard Measure: VVritten also by himself*, London: Printed by J. Cadwel for J. Crooke, 1660.

—, *Works* (6 vols), (ed. Philip Wynter), Oxford: Oxford University Press, 1843.

Haller, William and Davies, Godfrey (ed.), *The Leveller Tracts, 1647–53*, Gloucester, MA, P. Smith, 1944.

Harington, Sir John, *Nugae Antiquae* (2 vols), London: Verner and Hood, 1804.

—, *A Supplie or Addicion to the Catalogue of Bishops to the Yeare 1608* (ed. R. H. Miller), Potomac, Maryland: Jose Porrua Turanzas S.A., 1979.

—, *A Tract on the Succession to the Crown (A. D. 1602)*, London: J. B. Nichols, 1880.

The Harleian Miscellany; or, a Collection of Scarce, Curious and Entertaining Pamphlets and Tracts (10 vols), London: For Robert Dutton, 1808.

Harper-Bill, C., *The Register of John Morton, Archbishop of Canterbury 1486–1500*, Canterbury and York Society, 1987–91.

Harsnet, Samuel, *A Discouery of the Fraudulent Practises of Iohn Darrel Bacheler of Artes in his Proceedings Concerning the Pretended Possession and Dispossession of William Somers at Nottingham: Of Thomas Darling, the Boy of Burton at Caldwall: And of Katherine Wright at Mansfield, & Whittington: And of his Dealings with one Mary Couper at Nottingham, Detecting in Some Sort the Deceitfull Trade in These Latter Dayes of Casting out Deuils*, London: Imprinted by [John Windet for] Iohn Wolfe, 1599.

Hascard, Gregory, *A Discourse About the Charge of Novelty Upon the Reformed Church of England, Made by the Papists Asking of us the Question, Where was our Religion before Luther?*, London: T. Basset, 1685.

Heylyn, Peter, *Cyprianus Anglicus: Or the Life and Death of William Laud, Archbishop of Canterbury*, Dublin, 1719.

—, *A Briefe and Moderate Answer to the Seditious and Scandalous Challenge of Henry Burton, late of Friday-Streete*, London; Ric. Hodgkinsonne, 1637.

—, *A Briefe Relation of the Death and Sufferings of the Most Reverend and Renowned Prelate, the L. Archbishop of Canterbury with a More Perfect Copy of his Speech, and Other Passages on the Scaffold, than hath beene hitherto Imprinted*, Oxford, 1644.

—, *A Coale from the Altar. Or An Ansvver to a Letter Not Long Since Written to the Vicar of Gr. Against the Placing of the Communion Table at the east end of the Chancell; and Now of Late Dispersed Abroad to the Disturbance of the Church. First sent by a Judicious and Learned Divine for the Satisfaction of his Private Friend; and by him Commended to the Presse, for the benefit of others*, Printed [by Augustine Mathewes] for Robert Milbourne, 1636.

—, *The Way and Manner of the Reformation of the Church of England Declared and Justified against the Clamors and Objections of the Opposite Parties*, London, 1657.

Hickes, George, *Some Discourses upon Dr. Burnet and Dr. Tillotson, Occasioned by the Late Funeral Sermon of the Former upon the Later*, London, 1695.

His Maiesties Commission Giuing Power to Enquire of the Decayes of the Cathedral Church of St Paul in London, London: Robert Barker, 1631 and New York: Da Capo Press, 1971.

His Maiesties Commission, and Further Declaration: Concerning the Reparation of Saint Pauls Church, London: Robert Barker, 1633 and New York: Da Capo Press, 1971.

Hobbs, Mary (ed.), *The Sermons of Henry King (1592–1669), Bishop of Chichester*, Aldershot: Scolar Press, 1992.

Hooke, Elias, *The Spirit of Martyrs Revived*, London, 1682.

—, *Truth Seeks no Corners. Being a Vindication of the People Called Quakers*, London, 1679.

Hooker, Richard, *Of the Laws of Ecclesiastical Polity* (3 vols), (ed. P. G. Stanwood), Cambridge, MA: Harvard University Press, 1981.

Hooper, George, *The Church of England Free from the Imputation of Popery*, London: W. Abington, 1683.

Hooper, John, *Early Writings* (ed. Samuel Carr), Cambridge: Cambridge University Press, 1843.

Howe, John, *An Answer to Dr. Stillingfleet's Mischief of Separation, Being a Letter Written out of the Country to a Person of Quality in the City*, London: S. W for S. Tydmarsh, 1680.

Humfrey, John, *An Answer to Dr. Stillingfleet's Book of the Unreasonabless of Separation so far as it Concerns the Peaceable Designe, with some Animadversions upon the Debate between Him and Mr. Baxter, concerning the National Church, and the Head of it*, London: Thomas Packhurft, 1682.

Hutton, Thomas, *A Defence of the Ministers Reasons, for Refusal of Subscription to the Booke of Common Prayer, and of Conformitie*, Oxford: Joseph Barnes, 1605.

—, *The Second Parte of the Defense of the Ministers Reasons for Refusal of Subscription to the Book of Common Praier, and of Conformitie, &c.*, London: John Windet, 1606.

Isham, Sir Gyles (ed.), *Correspondence of Bishop Duppa and Sir Justinain Isham*, Northampton Record Society, xvii, 1950–1.

'I. W.', *Certaine Reasons Why the Booke of Common-Prayer Being Corrected Shovld Continue*, London: A. N. for Richard Lownds, 1641.

Jacob, Henry, *Reasons Taken out of God's Word and the best Humane Testimonies Proving a Necessitie of Reforming our Churches in England*, 1604.

James I, *The Workes of the Most High and Mighty Prince, James, by the Grace of God Kinge of Greate Brittaine, France & Ireland Defender of ye Faith etc*, London: By James [Montague] Bishop of Winton & Deane of His Majesties Chappell Royall, 1616.

James II, *His Majesties Most Gracious Speech to both Houses of Parliament on Saturday the 18th of March*, 1688.

James, Thomas, *An Apologie for Iohn Wicliffe, Shewing his Conformitie with the Now Church of England*, Oxford: Joseph Barnes, 1608.

Jessopp, A., (ed.), 'Visitations of the Diocese of Norwich A. D. 1492–1532', *Camden Society*, new series, 1888.

Jones, William, *The True Inquisition*, London, 1633.
Jonson, Ben, *The Devil is an Ass* (ed. Peter Happé), Manchester: Manchester University Press, 1996.
Joscelyn, John, *Life of the 70. Archbishop of Canterbury*, Zurich [?], 1574.
Ken, Thomas, *Ichabod: Or, Five Groans of the Church*, Cambridge: For J. Greaves, 1663.
Kenyon, J. P. (ed.), *The Stuart Constitution: Documents and Commentary, 1603–1688*, Cambridge: Cambridge University Press, 1966.
Ketley, Joseph (ed.), *The Two Liturgies, AD. 1549 and AD. 1552: With Other Documents Set Forth by Authority in the Reign of King Edward VI*, Cambridge: Cambridge University Press, 1844.
King Charles, His Speech Made upon the Scaffold at Whitehall-Gate Immediately before his Execution On Tuesday the 30 of Jan. 1648 With a Relation of the Manner of his Going to Execution, London: Peter Cole, 1649.
Latimer, Hugh, *Sermons*, London: Everyman, 1906.
Laud, William, *A Relation of the Conference Between William Laud, Late Lord Archbishop of Canterbury, and Mr. Fisher the Jesuit*, London: Ralph Holt for Thomas Bassett, Thomas Dring and John Leigh, 1676.
—, *A Speech Delivered in the Star Chamber, on Wednesday the XIVth of June MDCXXXVII at the Censure of Iohn Bastwick, Henry Burton and William Prinn, concerning pretended innovation in the Church*, London: Richard Badger, 1637.
—, *Works* (7 vols), Oxford: John Henry Parker, 1847–60.
Laune, Thomas de, *A Plea for the Non-Conformists, Giving the True State of the Dissenters Case*, London: For the Author, 1684.
Law, Thomas Graves (ed.), 'Archpriest Controversy: Documents Relating to the Dissensions of the Roman Catholic Clergy, 1597–1602', *Camden Society*, new series, no. 40, 50, 57, 1886–1920.
Leighton, Alexander, *A Decade of Grievances: Presented and Approved to the Right Honourable and High Court of Parliament against the Hierarchy or Government of the Lord Bishops*, 1641.
—, *An Appeal to the Parliament; or Sion's Plea against the Prelacie*, 1628.
le Neve, John, *Fasti Ecclesiae Anglicanae; or, an Essay Towards Deducing a Regular Succession of all the Principal Dignitaries in Each Cathedral, Collegiate Church or Chapel*, In the Savoy: Printed by J. Nutt, 1716.
Lloyd, William, *Considerations Touching the True Way to Suppress Popery in this Kingdom*, London, 1677.
Lodington, Thomas, *The Honour of the Clergy Vindicated from the Contempt of the Laity in a Sermon*, London: Joseph Clarke, 1673.
Long, Thomas, *The Case of Persecution, Charg'd on the Church of England, Consider'd and Discharg'd, In order to her Justification and a Desired Vnion of Protestant Dissenters* [1685], London: Freeman Collins for Richard Baldwin, 1689.
Lowe, Edward, *A Short Direction for the Performance of Cathedral Service*, Oxford: William Hall for Richard Davis, 1661.

Luther, Martin, *Luther's Large Catechism* (trans. J. N. Lenker), Minneapolis: Augsburg Publishing House, 1967.

MacDonald, Michael (ed.), *Witchcraft and Hysteria in Elizabethan London*, London: Tavistock/Routledge, 1991.

Maclean, John (ed.), 'Letters of Sir Robert Cecil to Sir George Carew', *Camden Society*, first series, no. 88, 1864.

Maimbury, Lewis, *A Peaceable Method for the Re-uniting of Protestants and Catholicks*, G. W., 1686.

Maltby, Judith (ed.), 'The Short Parliament (1640) Diary of Sir Thomas Aston', *Camden Society*, fourth series, vol. 35, 1988.

—, 'Petitions for episcopacy and the Book of Common Prayer on the eve of the Civil War 1641–42', in Stephen Taylor (ed.), *From Cranmer to Davidson: A Church of England Miscellany*, Woodbridge: Boydell Press/Church of England Record Society vol. 7, 1999.

Manby, Peter, *A Reformed Catechism, in Two Dialogues concerning the English Reformation. Collected For the Most Part, Word for Word, out of Dr. Burnet, John Foxe, and other Protestant Historians*, London: Nathaniel Thompson, 1687.

March, John, *A Sermon Preached Before the Mayor of Newcastle 30th January*, 1677.

Marescot, Michel, *A True Discourse, Upon the Matter of Martha Brossier of Romorantin, Pretended to be Possessed by a Devill* (trans. Abraham Hartwell), London, 1599.

Marshall, Nathaniel, *The Penitential Discipline of the Primitive Church, for the First Four Hundred Years after Christ* [1714], Oxford: John Henry Parker, 1844.

'Martin Marprelate', *The Epistle [September–November 1588]* (ed. Edward Arber], London: English Scholars Library of Old and Modern Works, 1880.

Mason, John, *The Midnight-Cry. A Sermon Preached on the Parable of the Ten Virgins*, 1691.

Matthews, A. G. (ed.), *Walker Revised: Being a Revision of John Walker's Sufferings of the Clergy during the Grand Rebellion, 1642–60*, Oxford: Clarendon Press, 1948.

McClure, Norman (ed.), *Letters of John Chamberlain* (2 vols), Philadelphia: American Philosophical Society, 1939.

McCullough, Peter (ed.), *Lancelot Andrewes: Selected Sermons and Lectures*, Oxford: Oxford University Press, 2005.

Milton, John, in *Complete Poems and Selected Prose* (ed. M. Y. Hughes), New York: Odyssey Press, 1957.

—, *Of Reformation Touching Church Discipline in England*, New Haven: Yale University Press, 1916.

Milward, Peter (ed.), *Religious Controversies of the Jacobean Age: A Survey of the Printed Sources*, London: The Scolar Press, 1978.

Montagu, Richard, *A Gagg for the new Gospell? No: A Nevv Gagg for an Old Goose VVho Would Needes Vndertake to Stop all Protestants Mouths for Euer, with 276. Places out of their owne English Bibles. Or an Ansvvere to a Late Abridger of Controuersies, and Belyar of the Protestants Doctrine. By Richard Mountagu. Published by authoritie*, London: William Barret, 1624.

Moore Smith, G. C. (ed.), 'Extracts from the Days of the Reformation, chiefly from the manuscripts of John Foxe the Martyrologist, with two contemporary biographies of Archbishop Cranmer', *Camden Society*, first series, vol. 77, 1860.

—, 'Extracts from the papers of Thomas Woodcock (ob.1695)', *Camden Society*, third series, vol. 13, 1907.

Morice, Ralph, 'Cranmer and Canterbury School'[1579], in J. G Nichols (ed.), 'Narratives of the Days of the Reformation', *Camden Society*, first series, no. 77, 1859.

Morley, George, *The Bishop of Worcester's Letter To a Friend for Vindication of Himself from Mr. Baxter's Calumny*, London: R. Norton for Timothy Garthwait, 1662.

—, *A Modest Advertisement Concerning the Present Controversie about Church-Government; Wherein the maine Grounds of that Booke, intituled, The Unlawfulnesse and Danger of Limited Prelacie. Are Calmly Examined*, London: Robert Bostock, 1641.

Muller, J. A. (ed.), *The Letters of Stephen Gardiner*, Cambridge: Cambridge University Press, 1933.

Neal, Daniel, *History of the Puritans; or, the Rise, Principles, and Sufferings of the Protestant Dissenters to the Aera of the Glorious Revolution* (ed. Edward Parsons), London: Longman, Hurst, Rees, Orme, and Brown, 1811.

'N. F', *Vnparallel'd Reasons for Abollishing Episcopacy*, London: For S. S., 1642.

Nichols, J. G. (ed.), 'Diary of Henry Machyn A. D. 1550 to A. D. 1563', *Camden Society*, first series, no. 42, 1848.

—, *Literary Remains of Edward VI*, Roxburgh Club, 1857.

—, 'Reminiscences of John Loude or Louthe, Archdeacon of Nottingham' [1579], in 'Narratives of the Days of the Reformation', *Camden Society* first series, no. 77, 1859.

Nichols, Josias, *Abrahams Faith: That is, The Old Religion. Wherein is Tavght, that the Religion Now Publikely Taught and Defended by Order in the Church of England, is the Onely True Catholike, Auncient, and Vnchangeable Faith of Gods Elect*, London: Thomas Wight, 1602.

—, *The Plea of the Innocent Wherein is Auerred; that the Ministers & People Falsley Termed Puritanes, are Iniuriouslie Slaundered for Enemies of Troublers of the State. Published for the Common Good of the Church and Common Wealth of this Realme of England as a Countermure against all Sycophantising Papsts, Statising Priestes, Neutralising Atheistes, and Satanising Scorners of all Godlinesse, Trueth and Honestie. Written: By Iosias Nichols, a faithfull minister of the Ghospell of Christ: And an humble seruant, of the English Church*, [R. Schilders](?), 1602.

Nicholson, William (ed.), *Remains of Edmund Grindal*, Cambridge: Cambridge University Press, 1843.

Nowell, Alexander, *A Catechism or Institution of Christian Religion, to be Learned of all Youth, next after the Little Catechism Appointed in the Book of Common Prayer*, London: E. Cotes for the Company of Stationers, [1572], 1663.

Nuttall, G. F., and Chadwick, Owen (eds.), *From Uniformity to Unity 1662–1962*, London: SPCK, 1962.

Ogilby, J., *A Brief Narrative of His Majestie's Solemn Coronation with his Magnificent Proceeding, and Royal Feast in Westminster*, London, 1662.

Ormerod, Oliver, *The Picture of a Puritaine*, London, 1605.

Paget, John, *A Defence of Chvrch-Government, Exercised in Presbyteriall, Classicall & Synodical Assemblies; According to the Practise of the Reformed Churches*, London: H. A for Thomas Underhill, 1641.

Palmer, Samuel, *A Vindication of the Learning, Loyalty, Morals and Most Christian Behaviour of the Dissenters Toward the Church of England, In Answer to Mr Wesley's Defence of his Letter Concerning the Dissenters Education in their Private Academies. And to Mr Sacheverel's Injurious Reflections upon them*, London: J. Lawrence, 1705.

Parker, Matthew, *De Antiquitate Britannicae Ecclesiae & Priuilegiis Ecclesiae Cantuariensis cum Archiepiscopis eiusdem 70.*, London, 1572.

Parker, T. H. L. (ed.), *English Reformers*, London: SCM Press, 1966.

Paule, Sir George, *The Life of the Most Reverend and Religious Prelate, John Whitgift, Lord Archbishop of Canterbury*, London: Printed by Thomas Snodham, 1612.

Pelling, Edward, *A Sermon Preached on 30th January 1678/79*, 1679.

Perkins, William, *The Works of William Perkins* (ed. Ian Breward), Appleford: Sutton Courtenay Press, 1970.

—, *Workes*, Printed at London by John Legatt, printer to the Vniuersitie of Cambridge [and Cantrell Legge], 1616–18.

Pilkington, James, *Works* (ed. James Scholefield), Cambridge: Cambridge University Press, 1842.

Potter, George R., and Simpson, Evelyn M. (ed.), *The Sermons of John Donne* (6 vols), Berkeley: University of California Press, 1953.

Prideaux, Humphrey, *The Validity of the Orders of the Church of England Made out Against the Objections of the Papists, in Several Letters to a Gentleman of Norwich that Desired Satisfaction Therein*, London: Printed by John Richardson for Brabazon Aylmer, 1688.

Proceedings and Trial in the Case of the Most Reverend Father in God William, Lord Archbishop of Canterbury, London: For Thomas Basset, 1689.

Prynne, William, *A Briefe Suruay and Censure of Mr Cozens his Couzening Deuotions Prouing both the Forme and Matter of Mr Cozens his Booke of Priuate Deuotions, or the Houres of Prayer, Lately Published, to be Meerely Popish: To differ from the Priuate Prayers authorized by Queene Elizabeth 1560. to be Transcribed out of Popish Authors, with which they are here Paralelled: And to be Scandalous and Preiudiciall to our Church, and Aduantagious onely to the Church of Rome. By William Prynne Gent. Hospitij Lincolniensis*, London: [By Thomas Cotes], 1628.

—, *The Church of Englands Old Antithesis to New Arminianisme VVhere in 7. anti-Arminian Orthodox Tenents, are Euidently Proued; their 7. opposite Arminian (once popish and Pelagian) Errors are Manifestly Disproued, to be the Ancient, Established, and Vndoubted Doctrine of the Church of England; by the Concurrent Testimony of the Seuerall Records and Writers of our Church, from the beginning of her Reformation,* to this Present. By William Prynne Gent. Hospitij Lincolniensis, London: [Printed by Augustine Mathewes and Elizabeth Allde for Michael Sparke], 1629.

—, *A Fresh Discovery of Some Prodigious New Wandering-blazing Stars*, 1645.

—, *A New Discovery of the Prelates Tyranny in their late prosecutions of Mr William Pryn, and eminent Lawyer; Dr. John Bastwick, a learned physition; and Mr Henry Burton, a reverent Divine*, London: For M. S. [Michael Spark], 1641.

—, *The Substance of a Speech made in the House of Commons by Wil. Prynn of Lincolns Inn Esquire 4th Dec. 1648*, London: Michael Spark, 1649.

—, *A Looking-glasse for all Lordly Prelates Wherein they may cleerely behold the True Divine Originall and Laudable Pedigree, whence they are Descended; Together with their Holy Lives and Actions Laid Open in a Double Parallel, the First, betweene the Divell; the Second, betweene the Iewish High-Priests, and Lordly Prelates; and by their double dissimilitude from Christ, and his Apostles*, [London?], 1636.

Pulton, A., *A True and Full Account of a Conference Between Dr Tenison and A. Pulton, One of the Masters in the Savoy*, London: Nathaniel Thompson, 1687.

Rawlet, John, *A Dialogue Betwixt Two Protestants*, London: Samuel Tidmarsh, 1685.

Reasons of the Present Judgement of the University of Oxford concerning the Solemne League and Covenant, The Negative Oath, The Ordinances concerning Discipline and Worship: Approved by the Generall Consent in a Full Convocation, 1, Jan. 1647, and Presented to Consideration, London, 1647.

Remarkable Passages: First A prayer for the Parliament. As also the Arch-Bishop of Canterburies Letter to the Archbishop of Yorke, and the Lord Keeper, to put in Practice the Kings desires. With a Petition to His Majestie, by divers Noblemen and Gentlemen estated in Ireland, and now residing in London. Also A New Declaration from Both Houses of Parliament, London[?]: W. O., 1642.

Rickey, Mary Ellen and Stroup, Thomas B. (eds), *Certaine Sermons of Homilies Appointed to be Read in Churches, In the Time of the Late Queene Elizabeth of Famous Memory* [1623], Gainesville, Florida: Scholars' Facsimiles, 1968.

Robinson, H. (ed.), *Zurich Letters*, Cambridge: Cambridge University Press, 1842.

Rogers, Thomas, *Catholic Doctrine of the Church of England: An Exposition of the Thirty-Nine Articles of the Church of England* [1621] (ed. J. J. S. Perowne), Cambridge: Cambridge University Press, 1854.

Rushworth, John, *Historical Collections* (8 vols), London: J. A. for Robert Boulter, 1682.

Saltmarsh, John, *Examinations, or, A Discovery of some Dangerous Positions Delivered in a Sermon of Reformation Preached in the Church of the Savoy Last Fast Day, July 26, by Tho. Fuller B. D. and since printed*, London: For Lawrence Blacklock, 1643.

Sancroft, William, *The Archbishop of Canterbury's Instructions to the Clergy of the Church of England*, London: For H. Jones, 1689.

—, *A Sermon Preached in St Peter's Westminster, on the first Sunday in Advent, at the Consecration of the Right Reverend in God, John Lord Bishop of Durham, William Lord Bishop of S. David's, Beniamin L. Bishop of Peterborough, Hugh Lord Bishop of*

Landaff, Richard Lord Bishop of Carlisle, Brian Lord Bishop of Chester, and John Lord Bishop of Exceter, London: T. Roycroft for Robert Beaumont, 1660.

—, *A Sermon Preach'd to the House of Peers, Novemb. 13th 1678. Being the Feast Day Appointed by the King to Implore the Mercies of Almighty God in the Protection of his Majesties Sacred Person, and His Kingdom*, In the Savoy: Printed by Tho. Newcomb for Robert Beaumont, 1678.

—, *A Vindication of the Arch-Bishop and severall other Bishops from the Imputations and Calumnies Cast upon them by the Author of the Modest Enquiry*, London, 1690.

Sanderson, Robert, *Episcopacy Not Prejudicial to Royal Power*, London: Robert Pawlet [1661], 1678.

—, *Two Sermons: The Former, Concerning the Right use of Christian Liberty, Preached at S.Pauls Crosse, London, the Later, Concerning the perswasion of conscience, Preached At a Metropolitical Visitation at Grantham, Lincoln*, London: M. F. for R. Daulman, and L. Fawne, 1630.

Sandys, Edwin, *Sermons* (ed. John Ayre), Cambridge: Cambridge University Press, 1841.

Say and Seale, William Lord Viscount, *Tvvo Speeches in Parliament of the Right Honourable William, Lord Vicount Say and Seale Mr. of his Majesties Court of Wards and Liveries, and one of his Majesties Most Honourable Privie Councell, the First upon the Bill against Bishops Power in Civill Affaires and Courts of Judicature. The Other a Declaration of Himself Touching the Liturgie, and Separation*, London: Thomas Underhill, 1641.

Saywell, William, *The Reformation of the Church of England Justified, According to the Canons of the Council of Nice*, Cambridge: John Hayes, printer to the University, 1688.

Scott, A. F. (ed.), *The Stuart Age*, New York: Apollo Editions, 1974.

Scott, Walter (ed.), *Somers Tracts* (13 vols), London: T. Cadell, 1809–1815.

Shaw, John, *Origo Protestantium: Or, An Answer to a Popish Manuscript (of N.N's.) That Would Fain Make the Protestant Catholick Religion Bear date at the Very Time when the Roman Popish Commenced in the World. Wherein Protestacy is Demonstrated to be Elder than Popery*, London: For H. Brome, 1677.

Sheldon, Gilbert, *David's Deliverance and Thanksgiving: A Sermon Preached before the King at Whitehall*, London: Timothy Garthwaite, 1660.

Smith, John, *Select Discourses, 1660* (ed. Rene Wellek), London: J. Flesher for W. Morden, 1660; re-issued New York: Garland Publishing, 1978.

Sommerville, J. P. (ed.), *King James VI and I: Political Writings*, Cambridge: Cambridge University Press, 1994.

Sparke, Thomas, *A Brotherly Perswasion to Vnitie and Vniformitie in Iudgment and Practice Tovching the Received and Present Ecclesiasticall Government, and the Authorised Rites and Ceremonies of the Church of England*, London: Nicholas Okes for Roger Iackton, 1607.

—, *A Sermon Preached at Whaldon in Buckinghamshyre the 22 November 1593 at the buriall of the Right Honourable, Arthur Lorde Grey of Wilton, Knight of the most Honourable order of the Garter*, Oxford: Ioseph Barnes, 1593.

Sprat, Thomas, *A Sermon preached before the Honourable House of Commons at St Margaret's Westminster, January 30th 1677/78*, London: T. N. for Henry Brome, 1678.

Steel, Mr, 'How the uncharitable and dangerous contentions that are among Professors of the true Religion, may be allayed?', in *Casuistical Morning Exercises*, London: James Aftwood for John Dunton, 1690.

Stillingfleet, Edward, *An Answer to some Papers Lately Printed, Concerning the Authority of the Catholick Church in Matters of Faith, and the Reformation of the Church of England*, London: Ric. Chiswel, 1686.

—, *The Mischief of Separation. A Sermon Preached at the Guild-Hall Chappel, May 11. MDCLXXX. Being the First Sunday in Easter-Term, Before the Lord Mayor, &c.*, London: Henry Mortlock, 1680.

—, *A Rational Account of the Grounds of Protestant Religion: Being a Vindication of the Lord Archbishop of Canterbury's Relation of a Conference, etc. From the Pretended Answer by J. C.*, London: Rob. White for Henry Mortlock, 1665.

—, *The Reformation Justify'd: In a Sermon Preached at Guild-Hall Chappel Septemb. 21. 1673. Before the Lord Major and Aldermen, &c.*, London: Robert White for Henry Mortlock, 1674.

—, *The Unreasonableness of Separation, or, An Impartial Account of the History, Nature, and Pleas of the Present Separation from the Communion of the Church of England: To which Several Late Letters are Annexed, of Eminent Protestant Divines Abroad*, London: By T. N. for Henry Mortlock, 1681.

—, *A Vindication of their Majesties Authority to Fill the Sees of the Deprived Bishops: In a Letter out of the Country. Occasioned by Dr. B–'s Refusal of the Bishoprick of Bath and Wells*, London: For Ric. Chiswell, 1691.

Strype, John, *Annals of the Reformation and other Various Occurrences in the Church of England during Queen Elizabeth's Happy Reign*, Oxford: Clarendon Press, 1824.

—, *Historical Collections of the Life and Acts of the Right Reverend Father in God John Aylmer*, New York: Burt Franklins Reprints, 1974.

—, *The Life and Acts of John Whitgift, D. D.* (3 vols), Oxford: Clarendon Press, 1829.

—, *The History of the Life and Acts of the Most Reverend Father in God, Edmund Grindal*, New York: Burt Franklin Reprints, 1974.

—, *Memorials of the Most Reverend Father in God Thomas Cranmer, Sometime Lord Archbishop of Canterbury* (ed. P. E. Barnes), London: George Routledge and Co., 1853.

Sudbury, John, *A Sermon Preached at the Consecration of the Right Reverend Fathers in God, Gilbert Lord Bishop of London, Humphry Lord Bishop of Sarum, George Lord Bishop of Worcester, Robert Lord Bishop of Lincolne, George Lord Bishop of St Asaph*, London: R. Royston, 1660.

Tanner, J. R. (ed.), *Constitutional Documents of the Reign of James I*, Cambridge: Cambridge University Press, 1952.

—, *English Constitutional Conflicts of the Seventeenth Century 1603–1689*, Cambridge: Cambridge University Press, 1966.

Taylor, John, *Some Small And Simple Reasons, Delivered in a Hollow-tree, in Waltham Forrest, in a Lecture, on the 33. Of March last. By Aminadab Blower A Devout Bellows-mender of Pimlico*, 1643.

Taylor, Stephen (ed.), *From Cranmer to Davidson: A Church of England Miscellany*, Woodbridge: Boydell Press/Church of England Record Society vol. 7, 1999.

Tenison, Thomas, *An Argument for Union Taken from the True Interest of those Dissenters in England Who Profess, and Call Themselves Protestants*, London: Tho. Basset, Benj. Tooke and F. Gardiner, 1683.

—, *Articles of Visitation and Inquiry Concerning Matters Ecclesiastical; Exhibited to the Ministers, Church-wardens, and Side-men, Of every Parish within the Diocese of Canterbury, At the Primary Visitation of the Most Reverend Father in God, Thomas, By Divine Providence Lord Archbishop of Canterbury, His Grace, Primate of all England, and Metropolitan*, 1695.

—, *His Grace the Lord Archbishop of Canterbury's Letter to the Reverend Dr. Batteley, Archdeacon of that Diocese, Concerning the late Act against Popery, to be Communicated to the Clergy of his Archdeaconry*, London: Charles Bill, 1700.

—, *Mr Pulton Consider'd in his Sincerity, Reasonings, Authorities. Or a Just Answer to what He Hath Hitherto Published in His True Account: His True and Full Account*, London: Richard Chiswell, 1687.

Thomson, Elizabeth McClure (ed.), *The Chamberlain Letters: A Selection of the Letters of John Chamberlain Concerning life in England from 1597 to 1626*, London: John Murray, 1966.

Thorndike, Herbert, *An Epilogue to the Tragedy of the Church of England, Being a Necessary Consideration and Brief Resolution of the Chief Controversies in Religion that Divide the Western Church: Occasioned by the Present Calamity of the Church of England*, London: J. M. and T. R. for J. Martin, J. Allesty and T. Dicas, 1659.

—, *The Theological Works of Herbert Thorndike, Sometime Prebendary of the Collegiate Church of St Peter, Westminster* (5 vols), Oxford: John Henry Parker, 1854.

Tillotson, John, 'A Discourse Against Transubstantiation' in 'Wickliffe' (alias S. G. Winchester), *The People's Right Defended; Being An Examination of the Romish Principle of withholding the Scriptures from the Laity*, Philadelphia: W. F. Geddes, 1831.

—, 'The Protestant Religion Vindicated from the charge of Singularity and Novelty' [1680], in *Three Restoration Divines: Barrow, South, Tillotson: Selected Sermons*, Bibliotheque de la Faculte de Philosophe et lettres de'l'Universite de Liege, 1967, 1976.

'T. W.', *Some Queries to the Protestants Concerning the English Reformation*, London: Nathaniel Thompson, 1687.

Ussher, James, *Directions Propovnded and Hvmbly Presented to the High Court of Parliament, Concerning the Booke of Common Prayer And Episcopall Government. Written by a Reverend and Learned Divine now Resident in this City*, London: For Iohn Thomas, 1641.

—, *The Bishop of Armaghes Direction, Concerning the Lyturgy, and Episcopall Government*, London: For A. D. and C. D, 1642.

—, *The Reduction of Episcopate Unto the Form of Synodical Government Received in the Antient Church: Proposed as an Expedient for the Compremising of the Now Differences, and the Preventing of Those Troubles that May Arise About the Matter of Church-Government*, London: T. N for G. B. and T. C, 1660.

Vane, Henry, *Sir Henry Vane: His Speech in the House of Commons, at a Committee for the Bill Against Episcopall-Government*, London: For Francis Constable, 1641.

Walker, Henry, *The Prelates Pride: Or the Manifestation that the Bshops Lordly Government from the Originall Institution, is not De Iure Divino, by Dvine Right; but Meerly Humane and Contrary Both to the Holy Word of God, the Practise of the Apostles, and of the Primitive Churches in the Purest Times*, 1641.

Walton, Izaak, *The Lives of John Donne, Sir Henry Wotton, Richard Hooker, George Herbert and Robert Sanderson* [1640, 1651, 1665, 1670, 1678], (ed. George Saintsbury), London: Oxford University Press, 1927.

Walwyn, William, *The Writings of William Walwyn* (eds Jack R. McMichael and Barbara Taft), London: University of Georgia Press, 1989.

Ward, Seth, *The Case of Joram. A Sermon Preached before the House of Peers in the Abby-Church at Westminster, January 30 1673/4*, London: Andrew Clark for James Collins, 1674.

Warner, George F. (ed.), 'Correspondence of Sir Edward Nicholas' (3 vols), *Camden Society*, new series, no. 45, 1849.

Webster, Tom and Shipps, Kenneth (eds), *The Diary of Samuel Rogers, 1634–1638*, Woodbridge: Boydell Press/Church of England Record Society, vol. 11, 2004.

Westfaling, Herbert, *A Treatise of Reformation in Religion, Diuided into Seuen Sermons Preached in Oxford*, London: George Bishop, 1582.

Whitgift, John, *Works* (3 vols), (ed. John Ayre), Cambridge: Cambridge University Press, 1851–3.

Williams, John, *The Holy Table, & and Thing more Anciently, Properly, and Literally used under the New Testament, then that of an Altar: Written Long ago by a Minister in Lincolnshire, in Answer to D. Coal; a Judicious Divine of Q. Maries Days* [London]: Printed [by Nicholas Okes] for the Diocese of Lincoln, 1637.

—, *A Sermon of Apparell, Preached before the Kings Majestie and the Prince his Highnesse at Theobalds, the 22. Of February, 1619*, London: John Bill, 1620.

Wilson, Thomas, *A Sermon on the Martyrdom of King Charles I. Preached January 30 1681. With a Relation of Some Rebellious Practices and Principles of Fanaticks*, London: Walter Davies, 1682.

Woodcock, Thomas, 'How doth Practical Godliness better rectifie the Judgment than doubtful Disputations?(Sermon on Rom. xiv. i)' in *Morning Exercises. The Forth Volume. By Several Ministers in and about London, Preached in October, 1689*, London: James Astwood for John Dunton, 1690.

'W.P', *The Great Case of Liberty of Conscience Once More Briefly Debated and Defended, by the Authority of Reason, Scripture, and Antiquity*, 1670.

Wyatt, William, *A Sermon Preached to those who had been Scholars of St Paul's School. in Guild-Hall Chapel, London, 1678/9*, London: For Benj. Tooke, 1679.

York, Anne, Duchess of, *The Church of England Truly Represented, According to Dr. Heylins History of the Reformation, In Justication Of her Royal Highness the Late Dutchess of Yorks Paper*, London: Printed for the Author, 1686.

Young, Edward, *A Sermon Preached at Lambeth January the 25th. At the Consecration of the Right Reverend Father in God, Thomas, Lord Bishop of Bath and Wells*, London: William Grantham, 1685.

Secondary sources in print

Abbott, William M., 'James Ussher and "Ussherian" episcopacy, 1640–1656: The Primate and his Reduction Manuscript', *Albion*, vol. 22, no. 2, 1990, pp. 237–59.

Akrigg, G. P. V., *Jacobean Pageant, or the Court of James I*, London: Hamish Hamilton, 1962.

Almond, Philip C., *Demonic Possession and Exorcism in Early Modern England: Contemporary Texts and their Cultural Contexts*, Cambridge: Cambridge University Press, 2004.

—, 'John Mason and his religion: An enthusiastic millenarian in late 17th century England', *The Seventeenth Century*, vol. 24, no. 1, 2009, pp. 156–76.

—, *The Witches of Warboys: An Extraordinary Story of Sorcery, Sadism and Satanic Possession*, London: I. B. Tauris, 2007.

Anglo, Sydney, *Images of Tudor Kingship*, London: Seaby, 1992.

Aquilina, Ivan D., *Bp John Cosin: Liturgist*, unpublished paper, 2006.

Archer, Stanley, 'Hooker on Apostolic Succession: The two voices', *Sixteenth Century Journal*, vol. 24, no. 1, 1993, pp. 67–74.

Arnold, Jonathan, *Dean John Colet of St Paul's: Humanism and Reform in Early Tudor England*, London: I. B. Taurus, 2007.

Arthur, Anthony, *The Tailor-King: The Rise and Fall of the Anabaptist Kingdom of Münster*, New York: St Martin's Press, 1999.

Ashton, Robert, *The English Civil War: Conservatism and Revolution 1603–1649*, London: Phoenix, 1997.

Aston, Margaret, *England's Iconoclasts*, Oxford: Oxford University Press, 1998.

—, 'Iconoclasm in England: Official and clandestine', in Peter Marshall (ed.), *The Impact of the English Reformation 1500–1640*, London: Arnold, 1977, pp. 167–92.

—, *The King's Bedpost: Reformation and Iconography in a Tudor Group Portrait*, Cambridge: Cambridge University Press, 1993.

Atkins, Jonathan M., 'Calvinist bishops, church unity and the rise of Arminianism', *Albion*, vol. 18, no. 3, 1986, pp. 411–21.

Ayris, Paul, 'Continuity and change in diocese and province: The role of a Tudor bishop', *Historical Journal*, vol. 39, no. 2, 1996, pp. 291–313.

—, 'The rule of Thomas Cranmer in diocese and province', *Reformation and Renaissance Review*, vol. 7, no. 1, 2005, pp. 69–110.

Ayris, Paul and Selwyn, David (eds), *Thomas Cranmer: Churchman and Scholar*, Woodbridge: Boydell Press, 1993.

Babbage, Stuart Barton, *Puritanism and Richard Bancroft*, London: SPCK, 1962.

Baildon, Paley, 'Lincoln's Inn Chapel', *Transactions of St Paul's Ecclesiology Society*, vol. 4, 1900, pp. 252–62.

Barnes, Thomas G., 'Due process and slow process in the late Elizabethan-early Stuart Star Chamber', *The American Journal of Legal History*, vol. 6, no. 3, 1962, pp. 221–49.

Beales, D., Best, G. (eds), *History, Society and the Churches: Essays in Honour of Owen Chadwick*, Cambridge: Cambridge University Press, 1985.

Beddard, R. A., 'The character of a Restoration prelate: Dr. John Dolben', *Notes and Queries*, November, 1970, p. 421–32.

—, 'Wren's Mausoleum for Charles I and the cult of the Royal Martyr', *Architectural History*, vol. 27, 1984, pp. 36–47.

Beer, Barrett L., 'Episcopacy and reform in Mid-Tudor England', *Albion*, vol. 23, no. 2, 1991, pp. 231–52.

Bell, G. K. A., *Christian Unity: The Anglican Position*, London: Hodder and Stoughton, 1948.

Bellany, Alastair, 'A poem on the Archbishop's Hearse: Puritanism, libel and sedition after the Hampton Court Conference', *Journal of British Studies*, vol. 34, no. 1, 1995, pp. 137–64.

Beran, Richard J. W., 'John Cosin: Bishop and liturgist', in Margot Johnson (ed.), *John Cosin: Papers Presented to a Conference to Celebrate the 400th Anniversary of his Birth*, Durham: Turnstone Ventures, 1997, pp. 73–90.

Bernard, G. W., 'The Making of Religious Policy, 1533–1546: Henry VIII and the Search for the Middle Way', *Historical Journal*, vol. 41, no. 2, 1998, pp. 321–49.

Birch, Thomas (ed.), *The Court and Times of James the First* (2 vols), New York: AMS Press, 1973.

—, *The Life of the Most Reverend Dr. John Tillotson, Lord Archbishop of Canterbury, Compiled Chiefly from his Original Papers and Letters*, London: J. Fox and R. Tomson, 1752.

Birchler, Allen B., 'Archbishop John Spottiswoode: Chancellor of Scotland, 1635–1638', *Church History*, vol. 39, no. 3, 1970, pp. 317–26.

Black, Joseph, 'The rhetoric of reaction: The Martin Marprelate tracts (1588–89), anti-Martinism, and the uses of print in early modern England', *Sixteenth Century Journal*, vol. 28, 1997, pp. 707–28.

Black, J. William, 'From Martin Bucer to Richard Baxter: "discipline" and Reformation in sixteenth-and-seventeenth-century England', *Church History*, vol. 70, no. 4, 2001, pp. 644–73.

Black, Pamela M., 'Matthew Parker's search for Cranmer's "Great notable written books"', *The Library*, vol. 29, 1974, pp. 312–22.

Blench, J. W., *Preaching in England in the late 15th and 16th Centuries: A Study of English Sermons 1450-c.1600*, Oxford: Basil Blackwell, 1964.

Blethen, H. T., 'The altar controversy and the royal supremacy, 1627–1641', *Welsh Historical Review*, vol. 9, 1978, pp. 142–54.

Boas, Frederick S., *University Drama in the Tudor Age*, Oxford: Clarendon Press, 1914.

Bondos-Greene, Stephen A., 'The end of an era: Cambridge Puritanism and the Christ's College election of 1609', *Historical Journal*, vol. 25, no. 1, 1982, pp. 197–208.

Bonney, T. G., 'Lichfield', in T. G. Bonney (ed.), *Cathedrals and Abbeys of England and Wales*, London: Bracken Books, 1985, pp. 114–23.

— (ed.), *Cathedrals and Abbeys of England and Wales*, London: Bracken Books, 1985.

Bosher, Robert, *The Making of the Restoration Settlement: The Influence of the Laudians, 1649–1662*, Oxford: Oxford University Press, 1951.

Bowker, Margaret, 'The Supremacy and the episcopate: The struggle for control, 1534–1540', *Historical Journal*, vol. 18, no. 2, 1975, pp. 227–43.

Boxer, C. R., *The Dutch Seaborne Empire 1600–1800*, Harmondsworth: Penguin, 1973.

Braddick, Michael, *God's Fury, England's Fire: A New History of the English Civil Wars*, London: Penguin, 2009.

Bradshaw, C., 'David or Josiah? Old Testament kings as exemplars in Edwardian religious polemic', in B. Gordon (ed.), *Protestant History and Identity in Sixteenth Century Europe* (2 vols), Aldershot: St Andrew's Studies in Reformation History, 1996, pp. 79–90.

Braunmuller, A. R., 'Robert Carr, Earl of Somerset, as collector and patron', in Linda Levy Peck (ed.), *The Mental World of the Jacobean Court*, Cambridge: Cambridge University Press, 1991, pp. 230–50.

Breward, Ian, *Archbishop Laud: Reforming Liturgy and Fostering National Unity*, Heildelberg, Victoria: The Prayer Book Society in Australia, 2001.

Brigden, Susan, *New Worlds, Lost Worlds: The Rule of the Tudors 1485–1603*, London: Viking, 2000.

Briggs, Robin, *Witches and Neighbours: The Social and Cultural Context of European Witchcraft*, 2nd edn, Oxford: Blackwell, 2002.

Broedel, Hans Peter, 'To preserve the manly form from so vile a crime: Ecclesiastical anti-sodomitic rhetoric and the gendering of Witchcraft in the *Malleus Maleficarum*', *Essays in Medieval Studies*, vol. 19, 2002, pp. 136–49.

Broomhall, Susan, and Tarbin, Stephanie (eds), *Women, Identities and Communities in Early Modern Culture*, Aldershot: Ashgate, 2008.

Brownlow, Frank Walsh, *Shakespeare, Harsnett, and the Devils of Denham*, London and Toronto: Toronto University Press, 1993.

Burke, Joseph, 'Archbishop Abbot's tomb at Guildford: A problem in early Caroline Iconography', *Journal of the Warburg and Courtauld Institutes*, vol. 12, 1949, pp. 179–89.

Burke, S. Hubert, *The Men and Women of the English Reformation, From the Days of Wolsey to the Death of Cranmer*, London: R. Washbourne, 1870.

Butler, Todd, *Imagination and Politics in Seventeenth Century England*, Aldershot: Ashgate, 2008.

Calderwood, D., *The History of the Kirk of Scotland* (7 vols), (eds T. Thomson and D. Laing), Edinburgh: Woodrow Society, 1842–9.

Campbell, K. E., *A Brief History and Account of St Katherine Cree Church*, London: Printed for St Katherine Cree Church, 1999.

Campbell, Louise, 'A diagnosis of religious moderation' in Luc Racaut and Alec Ryrie (eds), *Moderate Voices in the European Reformation*, Aldershot: St Andrew's Studies in Reformation History, 2005, pp. 32–50.

Capp, Bernard, '*A Door of Hope* re-opened: The Fifth Monarchy, King Charles and King Jesus', *Journal of Religious History*, vol. 32, no. 1, 2008, pp. 16–30.

Carlson, Leland H., 'The Court of High Commission: A newly discovered Elizabethan Letters Patent, 20 June 1589', *Huntingdon Library Quarterly*, vol. 45, no. 4, 1982, pp. 295–315.

Carlton, Charles, 'The dreamlife of Archbishop Laud', *History Today*, vol. 36, iss. 12, 1986, pp. 9–14.

Carpenter, Edward, *Cantuar: The Archbishops in their Office*, London: Cassell, 1971.

—, *The Protestant Bishop: Being the Life of Henry Compton, 1632–1713 Bishop of London*, London: Longmans, Green and Co., 1956.

Champion, J. A. I., *The Pillars of Priestcraft Shaken: The Church of England and its Enemies, 1660–1730*, Cambridge: Cambridge University Press, 1992.

Chibi, Andrew A., 'The social and regional origins of the Henrician episcopacy', *Sixteenth Century Journal*, vol. 29, no. 4, 1998, pp. 955–73.

Christophers, Richard A., *George Abbot Archbishop of Canterbury 1562–1633: A Bibliography*, Charlottesville: The University Press of Virginia, 1966.

Clair, Colin, *A History of Printing in Britain*, London: Cassell, 1965.

Clark, George, *The Oxford History of England: The Later Stuarts 1660–1714*, Oxford: Clarendon Press, 1955.

—, *A History of the Royal College of Physicians of London*, Oxford: Clarendon Press for The Royal College of Physicians, 1964.

Clark, Peter, 'Josias Nichols and religious radicalism, 1555–1639', *Journal of Ecclesiastical History*, vol. 28, no. 2, 1977, pp. 133–50.

Clarke, F. A., *Thomas Ken*, London: Methuen, 1896.

Clarke, Thomas, *A Life of Gilbert Burnet, Bishop of Salisbury*, Cambridge: Cambridge University Press, 1907.

Clifton, R., 'Fear of Popery' in Conrad Russell (ed.), *Origins of the English Civil War*, London: Macmillan, 1973, pp. 144–67.

—, 'The popular fear of Catholics during the English Revolution', *Past and Present*, no. 52, 1971, p. 23–55.

Coffey, John, 'The martyrdom of Sir Henry Vane the Younger: From apocalyptic witness to heroic Whig', in Thomas S. Freeman, and Thomas F. Mayer (eds), *Martyrs and Martyrdom in England in England, c.1400–1700*, Woodbridge: The Boydell Press, 2007, pp. 221–39.

Coleman, D. C. and John, A. H. (eds), *Trade, Government and Economy in Pre-Industrial England: Essays presented to F. J. Fisher*, London: Weidenfeld and Nicolson, 1976.

Collett, Barry, 'Civil War, communal guilt and reconciliation in England: The *Book of Common Prayer* of 1662', *Parergon*, vol. 21, no. 2, 2004, pp. 107–26.

Collins, Jeffrey R., 'The Restoration bishops and the Royal Supremacy', *Church History*, vol. 68, no. 3, 1999, pp. 549–80.

Collinson, Patrick, *Archbishop Grindal 1519–1583: The Struggle for a Reformed Church*, Berkeley: University of California Press, 1979.

—, 'A comment: Concerning the name Puritan', *Journal of Ecclesiastical History*, vol. 31, no. 4, 1980, pp. 483–8.

—, 'The downfall of Archbishop Grindal and its place in Elizabethan political and ecclesiastical history', in *Godly People: Essays on English Protestantism and Puritanism*, London: The Hambledon Press, 1983a, pp. 371–97.

—, *Elizabethan Essays*, London: The Hambledon Press, 1994.

—, *The Elizabethan Puritan Movement*, London: Cape, 1967.

—, 'Episcopacy and reform in England in the later sixteenth century', in *Godly People: Essays on English Protestantism and Puritanism*, London: The Hambledon Press, 1983b, pp. 155–190.

—, 'From iconoclasm to iconophobia: The cultural impact of the Second English Reformation', in Peter Marshall (ed.), *The Impact of the English Reformation 1500–1640*, London: Arnold, 1997, pp. 278–308 [1985 Stenton Lecture].

—, *Godly People: Essays on English Protestantism and Puritanism*, London: The Hambledon Press, 1983.

—, 'The Jacobean religious settlement: The Hampton Court Conference', in Howard Tomlinson (ed.), *Before the English Civil War Essays in Early Stuart Politics and Government*, London: Macmillan, 1983, pp. 27–51.

—, 'John Field and Elizabethan Puritanism', in *Godly People: Essays on English Protestantism and Puritanism*, London: Hambledon Press, 1983, pp. 335–70.

—, 'The "nott conformytye" of the young John Whitgift', *Journal of Ecclesiastical History*, vol. 15, no. 2, 1964, pp. 192–9.

—, 'The Protestant Cathedral', in Patrick Collinson, Nigel Ramsey and Margaret Sparks (eds), *A History of Canterbury Cathedral*, Oxford: Oxford University Press, 1995, pp. 154–203.

—, 'The Reformer and the Archbishop: Martin Bucer and an English Bucerian', *Journal of Religious History*, vol. 6, no. 4, 1971, pp. 305–30.

—, *The Religion of Protestants*, Oxford: Oxford University Press, 1982.

Collinson, Patrick, Craig, John and Usher, Brett (eds), *Conferences and Combination Lectures in the Elizabethan Church: Dedham and Bury St Edmunds*, Woodbridge: Boydell Press/Church of England Record Society, 2003.

Collinson, Patrick, Ramsey, Nigel and Sparks, Margaret (eds), *A History of Canterbury Cathedral*, Oxford: Clarendon Press, 1995.
Cragg, Gerald R., *Puritanism in the Period of the Great Persecution, 1660–1688*, New York: Russell and Russell, 1971.
Cressy, David, *Bonfires and Bells: National Memory and the Protestant Character in Elizabethan and Jacobean England*, London: Weidenfeld and Nicolson, 1989.
—, *Travesties and Transgressions*, Oxford: Oxford University Press, 2000.
Croft, Pauline, 'The religion of Robert Cecil', *Historical Journal*, vol. 34, no. 4, 1991, pp. 773–96.
—, 'The reputation of Robert Cecil: Libels, political opinion and popular awareness in the early seventeenth century', *Transactions of the Royal Historical Society*, sixth series, vol. 1, 1991, pp. 43–69.
—, 'Wardship in the parliament of 1604', *Parliamentary History*, vol. II, 1983, pp. 39–48.
Crosby, Brian, 'John Cosin and music', in Margot Johnson (ed.), *John Cosin: Papers Presented to a Conference to Celebrate the 400th Anniversary of his Birth*, Durham: Turnstone Ventures, 1997, pp. 164–84.
Cross, Claire, 'Churchmen and the Royal Supremacy', in Felicity Heal and Rosemary O'Day (eds), *Church and Society in England: Henry VIII to James I*, London: Macmillan, 1977, pp. 15–34.
—, *The Puritan Earl: The Life of Henry Hastings, Third Earl of Huntingdon, 1536–1595*, London: Macmillan, 1966.
Cummings, Brian (ed.), *The Book of Common Prayer: The Texts of 1549, 1559, and 1662*, Oxford: Oxford University Press, 2011.
Curtis, H. M., 'Hampton Court Conference and its aftermath', *History*, vol. 46, no. 156, 1961, pp. 1–16.
Cust, Richard, 'News and Politics in early 17th century England', *Past and Present*, vol. 112, 1986, pp. 60–90.
Cust, Richard and Hughes, Ann (eds), *Conflict in Early Stuart England: Studies in Religion and Politics 1603–1642*, London: Longman, 1989.
D'Alton, Craig, 'Cuthbert Tunstal and heresy in Essex and London', *Albion*, vol. 35, no. 2, 2003, pp. 210–28.
—, 'Heresy Hunting and Clerical Reform: William Warham, John Colet and the Lollards of Kent, 1511–12', in Ian Hunter, John Laursen, and Cary J. Nederman (eds), *Heresy in Transition: Transforming Ideas of Heresy in Medieval and Early Modern Europe*, Aldershot: Ashgate, 2005, pp. 104–14.
Danner, Dan G., 'The contributions of the Geneva Bible of 1560 to the English Protestant Tradition', *Sixteenth Century Journal*, vol. xii, no. 3, 1981, pp. 5–18.
Davies, C. M. F., and Facey, J., 'A Reformation dilemma: John Foxe and the problem of discipline', *Journal of Ecclesiastical History*, vol. 39, no. 1, 1988, pp. 37–65.
Davies, E. T., *Episcopacy and the Royal Supremacy in the Church of England in the Sixteenth Century*, Oxford: Basil Blackwell, 1950.

Davies, Julian, *The Caroline Captivity of the Church: Charles I and the Remoulding of Anglicanism, 1625–1641*, Oxford: Clarendon Press, 1992.
Davis, Virginia, *William Wyckham: A Life*, London: Continuum Books, 2007.
De Krey, Gary S., 'Rethinking the Restoration: Cases for conscience, 1667–72', *Historical Journal*, vol. 38, no. 1, 1995, pp. 53–83.
De Ricci, Seymour, *English Collectors of Books and Manuscripts (1530–1930) and their Marks of Ownership*, Cambridge: Cambridge University Press, 1930.
Dever, Mark E., 'Moderation and deprivation: A reappraisal of Richard Sibbes', *Journal of Ecclesiastical History*, vol. 43, no. 3, 1992, pp. 396–413.
Dickens, A. G., 'Robert Holgate: Archbishop of York and President of the King's Council in the North', in *Reformation Studies*, London: The Hambledon Press, 1982, pp. 323–52.
—, Tonkin, John and with the assistance of Powell, Kenneth, *The Reformation in Historical Thought*, Oxford: Blackwell, 1985.
Doerksen, Daniel W., *Conforming to the Word: Herbert, Donne and the English Church before Laud*, London: Associated University Presses, 1997.
Doran, Susan and Durston, Christopher, *Princes, Pastors and People: The Church and Religion in England 1529–1689*, London: Routledge, 1991.
Drabble, John, 'Gilbert Burnet and the history of the English Reformation: The historian and his milieu', *Journal of Religious History*, vol. 12, no. 3, 1983, pp. 351–63.
Duffy, Eamon, 'Cardinal Pole preaching: St Andrew's Day 1557', in Eamon Duffy and David Loades (eds), *The Church of Mary Tudor*, Aldershot: Ashgate, 2006, pp. 176–200.
—, *The Stripping of the Altars*, New Haven: Yale University Press, 1992.
Duffy, Eamon and Loades, David (eds), *The Church of Mary Tudor*, Aldershot: Ashgate, 2006.
Duke, A. G., and C. A. Tamse (eds), *Clio's Mirror: Historiography in Britain and the Netherlands*, Zutphen: De Walburg Press, c.1985.
Durston, Christopher, *James I*, London: Routledge, 1993.
Durston, Christopher and Eales, Jacqueline (eds), *The Culture of English Puritanism, 1560–1700*, London: Macmillan, 1996.
Dzelzainis, Martin, '"Undoubted realities": Clarendon on sacrilege', *Historical Journal*, vol. 33, no. 3, 1990, pp. 515–40.
Edie, Caroline A., 'The public face of royal ritual: Sermons, medals and civic ceremony in later Stuart coronations', *Huntingdon Library Quarterly*, vol. 53, 1990, pp. 311–36.
Elton, Geoffrey, *Reform and Reformation: England 1509–1558*, London: Arnold, 1977.
Eppley, Daniel, *Defending Royal Supremacy and Discerning God's Will in Tudor England*, Aldershot: Ashgate, 2007.
Eustace, Katherine, 'The Post-Reformation Monuments', in Patrick Collinson, Nigel Ramsey and Margaret Sparks (eds), *A History of Canterbury Cathedral*, Oxford: Oxford University Press, 1995, pp. 511–52.

Fielding, John, 'Arminianism in the Localities: Peterborough Diocese, 1603–1642', in Kenneth Fincham (ed.), *The Early Stuart Church, 1603–1642*, London: Macmillan, 1993, pp. 93–113.

Fincham, Kenneth, 'Clerical conformity from Whitgift to Laud', in Peter Lake and Michael Questier (eds), *Conformity and Orthodoxy in the English Church, c.1560–1660*, Woodbridge: The Boydell Press, 2000, pp. 125–58.

—, 'Episcopal government, 1603–1640', in Kenneth Fincham (ed.), *The Early Stuart Church, 1603–1642*, London: Macmillan, 1993, pp. 71–91.

—, *Prelate as Pastor: The Episcopate of James I*, Oxford: Clarendon Press, 1990.

—, 'Prelacy and politics: Archbishop Abbot's defence of Protestant orthodoxy', *Historical Research*, vol. 61, 1988, pp. 36–64.

—, 'Ramifications of the Hampton Court Conference in the dioceses 1603–1609', *Journal of Ecclesiastical History*, vol. 36, no. 2, 1985, pp. 208–27.

—, *Visitation Articles and Injunctions of the Early Stuart Church* (2 vols), Woodbridge: Boydell Press/Church of England Record Society, 1998.

— (ed.), *The Early Stuart Church, 1603–1642*, London: Macmillan, 1993.

Fincham, Kenneth, and Lake, Peter, 'The ecclesiastical policy of King James I', *Journal of British Studies*, vol. 24, no. 2, 1985, pp. 169–207.

—, 'The ecclesiastical policies of James I and Charles I', in Kenneth Fincham (ed.), *The Early Stuart Church, 1603–1642*, London: Macmillan, 1993, pp. 23–49.

Fincham, Kenneth and Tyacke, Nicholas, *Altars Restored: The Changing Face of English Religious Worship, 1547-c.1700*, Oxford: Oxford University Press, 2008.

Fisher, R. M., 'The origins of divinity lectureships at the Inns of Court, 1569–1585', *Journal of Ecclesiastical History*, vol. 29, no. 2, 1978, pp. 145–62.

—, 'The Reformation of clergy at the Inns of Court 1530–1580', *Sixteenth Century Journal*, vol. 12, no. 1, 1981, pp. 69–91.

Fletcher, Anthony, *The Outbreak of the English Civil War*, London: Edward Arnold, 1981.

—, 'National and local awareness in the county communities', in Howard Tomlinson (ed.), *Before the English Civil War: Essays in Early Stuart Politics and Government*, London: Macmillan, 1983, pp. 151–74.

Ford, Alan, *James Ussher: Theology, History and Politics in Early-Modern Ireland and England*, Oxford: Oxford University Press, 2007.

Forrestal, Alison, 'A Catholic model of martyrdom in the post-Reformation era: The Bishop in seventeenth-century France', *The Seventeenth Century*, vol. 20, no. 2, 2005, pp. 254–80.

Foster, Andrew, 'Archbishop Richard Neile Revisited', in Peter Lake and Michael Questier (eds), *Conformity and Orthodoxy in the English Church, c.1560–1660*, Woodbridge: The Boydell Press, 2000, pp. 159–78.

—, 'The clerical estate revitalized' in Kenneth Fincham (ed.), *The Early Stuart Church, 1603–1642*, London: Macmillan, 1993, pp. 93–113.

—, 'The function of a bishop: The career of Richard Neile, 1562-1640', in Rosemary O'Day and Felicity Heal (eds), *Continuity and Change: Personnel and Administration of the Church of England 1500-1642*, Leicester: Leicester University Press, 1976, pp. 33-54.

Fox, Levi (ed.), *English Historical Scholarship in the Sixteenth and Seventeenth Centuries*, London: Oxford University Press, 1956.

Freeman, Thomas S. and Mayer, Thomas F. (eds), *Martyrs and Martyrdom in England in England, c. 1400-1700*, Woodbridge: The Boydell Press, 2007.

Friar, Stephen, *A Companion to the English Parish Church*, Stroud: Alan Sutton Publishing, 1996.

Gentles, Ian, 'The sales of bishops' lands in the English Revolution, 1646-1660', *English Historical Review*, vol. 95, no. 376, 1980, pp. 573-96.

George, C. H., 'Puritanism as history and historiography', *Past and Present*, vol. 41, no. 1, 1968, pp. 77-104.

Gibson, William, 'Dissenters, Anglicans and the Glorious Revolution: The collection of cases', *The Seventeenth Century*, vol. 22, no. 1, 2007, pp. 1-23.

Given-Wilson, Chris, *Chronicles: The Writing of History in Medieval England*, London: Hambledon and London, 2004.

Goldie, Mark, 'The theory of religious intolerance in Restoration England', in Ole Peter Grell, Jonathan Israel and Nicholas Tyacke (eds), *From Persecution to Toleration: The Glorious Revolution and Religion in England*, Oxford: Clarendon Press, 1991, pp. 331-68.

Gordon, B., 'Calvin and the Swiss Reformed Churches', in A. Pettegree, A. Duke and G. Lewis (eds), *Calvinism in Europe, 1540-1620*, Cambridge: Cambridge University Press, 1994, pp. 64-81.

— (ed.), *Protestant History and Identity in Sixteenth Century Europe* (2 vols), Aldershot: St Andrew's Studies in Reformation History, 1996.

Graves, Michael A. R., 'Elizabethan men of business reconsidered', *Parergon*, vol. 14, no. 1, 1996, pp. 111-27.

—, *The House of Lords in the Parliaments of Edward VI and Mary I*, Cambridge: Cambridge University Press, 1981.

—, 'Thomas Norton the Parliament Man: En Elizabethan M. P., 1559-1581', *Historical Journal*, vol. 23, no. 1, 1980, pp. 17-35.

Greaves, Richard L., 'Shattered Expectations? George Fox, the Quakers, and the Restoration State, 1660-1685', *Albion*, vol. 24, 1992, pp. 237-59.

Gregory, Jeremy, 'Canterbury and the Ancien Regime: The Dean and Chapter 1660-1828', in Patrick Collinson, Nigel Ramsey and Margaret Sparks (eds), *A History of Canterbury Cathedral*, Oxford: Oxford University Press, 1995, pp. 204-55.

—, *Restoration, Reformation and Reform, 1660-1828: Archbishops of Canterbury and their Diocese*, Oxford: Clarendon Press, 2000.

—, 'The Eighteenth-Century Reformation: The Pastoral Task of Anglican Clergy after 1689', in J. Walsh, C. Haydon and S. Taylor (eds), *The Church of England c.1689 – c.1833: From Toleration to Tractarianism*, Cambridge: Cambridge University Press, 1993, pp. 67–89.

Green, I. M., 'The persecution of "scandalous" and "malignant" parish clergy during the English Civil War', *English Historical Review*, vol. 104, no. 372, 1979, pp. 507–31.

—, *Print and Protestantism in Early Modern England*, Oxford: Oxford University Press, 2000.

—, *The Re-establishment of the Church of England, 1660–1663*, Oxford: Oxford University Press, 1978.

Greig, Martin, 'Heresy hunt: Gilbert Burnet and the Convocation Controversy of 1701', *Historical Journal*, vol. 37, no. 3, 1994, pp. 569–97.

—, 'The Reasonableness of Christianity? Gilbert Burnet and the Trinitarian Controversy of the 1690s', *Journal of Ecclesiastical History*, vol. 44, no. 4, 1993, pp. 631–51.

Grell, Ole Peter, Israel, Jonathan I, and Tyacke, Nicholas (eds), *From Persecution to Toleration: The Glorious Revolution and Religion in England*, Oxford: Clarendon Press, 1991.

Guillery, Peter, 'Suburban models, or Calvinism and continuity in London's seventeenth-century church architecture', *Architectural History*, vol. 48, 2005, pp. 69–106.

Gunn, S. J., and Lindley, P. G. (eds), *Cardinal Wolsey: Church, State and Art*, Cambridge: Cambridge University Press, 1991.

Guy, John, 'The Elizabethan establishment and the ecclesiastical polity', in John Guy (ed.), *The Reign of Elizabeth I: Court and Culture in the Last Decade*, Cambridge: Cambridge University Press, 1995, pp. 126–49.

— (ed.), *The Reign of Elizabeth I: Court and Culture in the Last Decade*, Cambridge: Cambridge University Press, 1995.

Haigh, Christopher, 'From monopoly to minority: Catholicism in early modern England', *Transactions of the Royal Historical Society*, fifth series, vol. 31, 1981, pp. 129–47.

—, 'Puritan evangelism in the reign of Elizabeth I', *English Historical Review*, vol. xcii, 1977, pp. 30–58.

—, 'Success and failure in the English Reformation', *Past and Present*, vol. 173, 2001, pp. 28–49.

—, 'The taming of Reformation: Preachers, pastors and parishioners in Elizabethan and early Stuart England', *History*, vol. 85, no. 280, 2000, pp. 572–88.

—, 'The troubles of Thomas Pestell: Parish squabbles and ecclesiastical politics in Caroline England', *Journal of British Studies*, vol. 41, no. 4, 2002, pp. 403–28.

Hamilton, Donna B., and Strier, Richard (eds), *Religion, Literature and Politics in Post-Reformation England, 1540–1688*, Cambridge: Cambridge University Press, 1996.

Harmes, Marcus, 'Episcopal identity and authority in Restoration England', *Reformed Theological Review*, vol. 71, no. 1, 2012, pp. 45–69.

—, 'Orthodox puritans and dissenting bishops: The reformation of the English episcopate, CA. 1580–1610', *Comitatus: A Journal of Medieval and Renaissance Studies*, vol. 39, 2008, pp. 119–218.

—, 'The universality of discipline and the restoration of the English episcopacy 1660–1688, *Renaissance and Reformation/Renaissance and Réforme*, vol. 33, no. 1, 2010, pp. 55–79.

—, and Colclough, Gillian, 'Henry Prince of Wales, Proverbs and the English Episcopate', *Explorations in Renaissance Culture*, vol. 37, no. 2, 2011, pp. 97–115.

Harris, Tim, *Politics under the Later Stuarts: Party Conflict in a Divided Society 1660–1715*, London: Longman, 1993.

Harris, Ronald, *Clarendon and the English Revolution*, London: Hogarth Press, 1983.

Harte, N. E., 'State control of dress and social change', in D. C. Coleman and A. H. John (eds), *Trade, Government and Economy in Pre-Industrial England: Essays Presented to F. J. Fisher*, London: Weidenfeld and Nicolson, 1976, pp. 132–65.

Haugaard, William P., *Elizabeth and the English Reformation: The Struggle for a Stable Settlement of Religion*, Cambridge: Cambridge University Press, 1968.

Haynes, Alan, *Robert Cecil 1st Earl of Salisbury: Servant of Two Sovereigns*, London: Peter Owen, 1989.

Heal, Felicity, 'The Archbishops of Canterbury and the practice of hospitality', *Journal of Ecclesiastical History*, vol. 33, no. 4, 1982, pp. 544–63.

—, 'The bishops and the Act of Exchange of 1559', *Historical Journal*, vol. 17, no. 2, 1974, pp. 227–46.

—, *Of Prelates and Princes: A Study of the Economic and Social Position of the Tudor Episcopate*, Cambridge: Cambridge University Press, 1980.

—, 'The Tudors and the Church lands: Economic problems of the Bishopric of Ely during the sixteenth century', *Economic History Review*, 2nd series, vol. 26, 1973, pp. 198–217.

Heal, Felicity and O'Day, Rosemary (eds), *Church and Society in England: Henry VIII to James I*, London: Macmillan, 1977.

Heinze, Rudolph W., '"I pray to God to grant that I may endure to the end": A New Look at the Martyrdom of Thomas Cranmer', in Paul Ayris and David Selwyn (eds), *Thomas Cranmer: Churchman and Scholar*, Woodbridge: Boydell Press, 1993, pp. 261–80.

Hembry, Phillis, *The Bishops of Bath and Wells, 1540–1640: Social and Economic Problems*, London: Athlone Press, 1967.

Henderson, Lizanne, 'The survival of witchcraft prosecutions and witch belief in South-West Scotland', *Scottish Historical Review*, vol. 85, no. 1, 2006, pp. 52–74.

Hill, Christopher, *Antichrist in Seventeenth-Century England*, London: Verso, 1990.

—, *Economic Problems of the Church: From Archbishop Whitgift to the Long Parliament*, Oxford: Clarendon Press, 1956.

—, *God's Englishman: Oliver Cromwell and the English Revolution*, London: Weidenfeld and Nicolson, 1970.

—, *Society and Puritanism in Pre-Revolutionary England*, London: Mercury Books, 1966.

Hirst, Derek, *Authority and Conflict: England, 1603–1658*, London: E. Arnold, 1986.

Hoak, Dale (ed.), *Tudor Political Culture*, Cambridge: Cambridge University Press, 2002.

Hodgkins, Christopher, 'The Church legible: George Herbert and the externals of worship', *The Journal of Religion*, vol. 71, no. 2, 1991, pp. 217–41.

Holland, Susan M., 'Archbishop Abbot and the problem of "Puritanism"', *Historical Journal*, vol. 37, no. 1, 1994, pp. 23–43.

—, 'George Abbot: "The wanted Archbishop"', *Church History*, vol. 56, no. 2, 1987, pp. 172–87.

Hooper, Wilfrid, 'The Tudor Sumptuary Laws', *English Historical Review*, vol. 30, no. 119, 1915, pp. 433–49.

Horn, Joyce M. (ed.), *Fasti Ecclesiae Anglicana 1541–1857 Vol. III: Canterbury, Rochester and Winchester Dioceses*, London: The Athlone Press, 1974.

Horwitz, Henry, 'Protestant reconciliation in the Exclusion Crisis', *Journal of Ecclesiastical History*, vol. 15, no. 2, 1964, pp. 201–17.

Hoskins, W. G., *The Age of Plunder: The England of Henry VIII 1500–1547*, London: Longman, 1976.

Houlbrooke, Ralph, 'The Protestant Episcopate, 1547–1603: The pastoral contribution', in Felicity Heal and Rosemary O'Day (eds), *Church and Society in England: Henry VIII to James I*, London: Macmillan, 1977, pp. 78–98.

Houston, S. J., *James I*, London: Longman, 1973.

Howarth, David (ed.), *Art and Patronage in the Caroline Courts*, Cambridge: Cambridge University Press, 1993.

Hunt, Alice, *The Drama of Coronation: Medieval Ceremony in Early Modern England*, Cambridge: Cambridge University Press, 2008.

Hunter, Ian, Laursen, John and Nederman, Cary J., (eds), *Heresy in Transition: Transforming Ideas of Heresy in Medieval and Early Modern Europe*, Aldershot: Ashgate, 2005.

Hunter, Leslie Stannard (ed.), *Scandinavian Churches: A Picture of the Development and Life of the Churches of Denmark, Finland, Iceland, Norway and Sweden*, London: Faber and Faber, 1965.

Hurtig, Judith W., 'Seventeenth-century shroud tombs: Classical revival and Anglican context', *Art Bulletin*, vol. lxiv, no. 2, pp. 217–28.

Hutton, Ronald, *Charles the Second: King of England, Scotland and Ireland*, Oxford: Clarendon Press, 1989.

—, *The Restoration: A Political and Religious History of England and Wales 1658–1667*, Oxford: Oxford University Press, 1985.

Hutton, William Holden, 'Tenison, Thomas', *Dictionary of National Biography* (1885–1900), vol. 56, pp. 57–60.

Ingamells, John, *The English Episcopal Portrait 1559–1835: A Catalogue*, published privately by the Paul Mellon Centre for Studies in British Art, 1981.

Israel, Jonathan I., 'William III and Toleration', in Ole Peter Grell, Jonathan Israel, and Nicholas Tyacke (eds), *From Persecution to Toleration: The Glorious Revolution and Religion in England*, Oxford: Clarendon Press, 1991, pp. 129–70.

Ives, E. W. (ed.), *The English Revolution 1600–1660*, London: Edward Arnold, 1968.
Jack, Sybil M., 'The conflict of Common Law and Canon Law in early sixteenth-century England: Richard Hunne revisited', *Parergon*, New Series, no. 3, 1985, pp. 131–45.
—, 'English bishops as tax collectors in the sixteenth century', *Parergon*, vol. 14, no. 1, 1996, pp. 129–63.
—, 'In praise of queens: The public presentation of the virtuous consort in seventeenth-century Britain', in Susan Broomhall and Stephanie Tarbin (eds), *Women, Identities and Communities in Early Modern Culture*, Aldershot: Ashgate, 2008, pp. 211–25.
—, "A pattern for a King's inauguration': The coronation of James I in England', *Parergon*, vol. 21, no. 2, 2004, pp. 67–91.
—, *Trade and Industry in Tudor and Stuart England*, London: George, Allen and Unwin, 1977.
Jacob, Edward, *Archbishop Henry Chichele*, London: Nelson, 1966.
—, *The Fifteenth Century 1399–1485*, Oxford: Oxford University Press, 1961.
Jaffé, Michael, 'Van Dyck studies I: The portrait of Archbishop Laud', *Burlington Magazine*, vol. 124, no. 955, 1982, pp. 600–7.
Jansson, Maija, 'The impeachment of Inigo Jones and the pulling down of St Gregory's by St Paul's', *Renaissance Studies*, vol. 17, no. 4, 2003, pp. 716–46.
Jensen, Peter, 'The catechisms of Elizabethan England', *Reformed Theological Review*, vol. 39, no. 1, 1980, pp. 1–9.
Johnson, Margot (ed.), *John Cosin: Papers Presented to a Conference to Celebrate the 400th Anniversary of his Birth*, Durham: Turnstone Ventures, 1997.
Johnstone, Warren, 'The Anglican Apocalypse in Restoration England', *Journal of Ecclesiastical History*, vol. 53, no. 3, 2004, pp. 467–501.
Kalu, O. U., 'Bishops and puritans in early Jacobean England: A perspective on methodology', *Church History*, vol. 45, 1976, pp. 469–89.
—, 'Continuity in change: Bishops of London and religious dissent in early Stuart England', *Journal of British Studies*, vol. 18, no. 1, 1978, pp. 28–45.
Kaplan, Benjamin J., 'Possessed by the Devil?: A very public dispute in Utrecht', *Renaissance Quarterly*, vol. 49, no. 4, 1996, pp. 738–59.
Keay, Anna, *The Magnificent Monarch: Charles II and the Ceremonies of Power*, London: Continuum Books, 2008.
Kelley, Donald R., and Sacks, David Harris (eds), *The Historical Imagination in Early Modern Britain: History, Rhetoric, and Fiction, 1500–1800*, Cambridge: Cambridge University Press.
Kennedy, D. E., 'The Jacobean episcopate', *Historical Journal*, vol. 5, no. 2, 1962, pp. 175–81.
Kenyon, J. P., *The Stuarts*, London: Fontana, 1966.
Kent, F. W., and Zika Charles (eds), *Rituals, Images and Words: Varieties of Cultural Expression in Late Medieval and Early Modern Europe*, Turnhout: Brepols, 2005.
Kidson, Peter, Murray, Peter, and Thompson, Paul, *A History of English Architecture*, London: Pelican, 1965.

King, John N., 'The royal image', in Dale Hoak (ed.), *Tudor Political Culture*, Cambridge: Cambridge University Press, 2002, pp. 104-32.

King, Peter, 'Bishop Wren and the suppression of the Norwich Lecturers', *Historical Journal*, vol. 11, no. 2, 1968, pp. 237-54.

—, 'The episcopate during the Civil Wars, 1642-49', *English Historical Review*, vol. 83, no. 328, 1968, pp. 523-37.

Kingdon, Robert, 'A new view of Calvin in the light if the registers of the Geneva Consistory', in Wilhelm H. Neuser and Brian G. Armstrong (eds), *Calvinus Sincerioris Religionis Vindex: Calvin as Protector of the Purer Religion*, Sixteenth Century Essays and Studies, 1997, vol. XXXVI, pp. 21-34.

Kirby, Torrance (ed.), *A Companion to Richard Hooker*, Leiden: Brill, 2008.

Kisby, Fiona, '"When the King Goeth a Procession": Chapel ceremonies and services, the ritual year, and religious reforms at the early Tudor court, 1485-1547', *Journal of British Studies*, vol. 40, no. 1, 2001, pp. 44-75.

Knappen, M. M., 'The early Puritanism of Lancelot Andrewes', *Church History*, vol. 2, no. 2, 1933, pp. 95-104.

Knighton, C. S., 'The Lord of Jerusalem: John Williams as Dean of Westminster', in C. S. Knighton, and Richard Mortimer (eds), *Westminster Abbey Reformed 1540-1640*, Aldershot: Ashgate, 2003, pp. 233-58.

—, 'Westminster Abbey restored', in Eamon Duffy and David Loades (eds), *The Church of Mary Tudor*, Aldershot: Ashgate, 2006, pp. 77-123.

Knighton C. S., and Mortimer, Richard (eds), *Westminster Abbey Reformed 1540-1640*, Aldershot: Ashgate, 2003.

Knights, Mark, *Politics and Opinion in Crisis, 1678-1681*, London: Cambridge University Press, 1994.

Knott, J. R., *Discourses of Martyrdom in English Literature, 1563-1694*, Cambridge: Cambridge University Press, 1993.

Lacy, Andrew, '"Charles the First and Christ the Second": The creation of a political martyr', in Thomas S. Freeman and Thomas F. Mayer (eds), *Martyrs and Martyrdom in England in England, c. 1400-1700*, Woodbridge: The Boydell Press, 2007, pp. 203-20.

Lake, Peter, *Anglicans and Puritans? Presbyterianism and English Conformist Thought from Whitgift to Hooker*, London: Allen and Unwin, 1988.

—, *The Boxmaker's Revenge: 'Orthodoxy', 'Heterodoxy' and the Politics of the Parish in Early Stuart London*, Stanford: Stanford University Press, 2001.

—, 'Calvinism and the English Church', *Past and Present*, vol. 114, 1987, pp. 32-76.

—, 'The dilemma of the establishment Puritan: The case of Francis Johnson and Cuthbert Bainbrigg', *Journal of Ecclesiastical History*, vol. 29, no. 1, 1978, pp. 22-35.

—, 'Lancelot Andrewes, John Buckeridge, and avant-garde conformity at the Court of James I', in Linda Levy Peck (ed.), *The Mental World of the Jacobean Court*, Cambridge University Press, 1991, pp. 113-33.

—, 'Matthew Hutton – a puritan bishop?', *History*, vol. 64, no. 211, 1979, pp. 182-204.

—, *Moderate Puritans and the Elizabethan Church*, Cambridge: Cambridge University Press, 1982.

—, 'Moving the goal posts? Modified subscription and the construction of conformity in the early Stuart Church', in Peter Lake and Michael Questier (eds), *Conformity and Orthodoxy in the English Church, c. 1560-1660*, Woodbridge: The Boydell Press, 2000, pp. 179-210.

—, 'The Laudian style: Order, uniformity and the pursuit of the Beauty of Holiness in the 1630s', in Kenneth Fincham (ed.), *The Early Stuart Church, 1603-1642*, London: Macmillan, 1993, pp. 161-85.

—, 'Serving God and the times: The Calvinist conformity of Robert Sanderson', *Journal of British Studies*, vol. 27, no. 2, 1988, pp. 81-116.

—, 'The significance of the Elizabethan identification of the Pope as Antichrist', *Journal of Ecclesiastical History*, vol. 55, no. 2, 2004, pp. 161-78.

Lake, Peter, with Questier, Michael, *The Antichrist's Lewd Hat: Protestants, Papists and Players in Post-Reformation England*, New Haven: Yale University Press, 2002.

Lake, Peter, and Questier, Michael (eds), *Conformity and Orthodoxy in the English Church, c. 1560-1660*, Woodbridge: The Boydell Press, 2000.

Lamont, William M., 'The rise and fall of Bishop Bilson', *Journal of British Studies*, vol. 5, no. 2, 1966, pp. 22-32.

Lander, Jesse, 'Foxe's *Book of Martyrs*: Printing and popularizing the *Acts and Monuments*', in Claire McEachen and Deborah (eds), *Religion and Culture in Renaissance England*, Cambridge: Cambridge University Press, 1997, pp. 69-92.

Larner, Christina, 'Crimen Exceptum?: The crime of Witchcraft in Europe', in Brian P. Levack (ed.), *Witch-hunting in Early Modern Europe: General Studies*, New York and London: Garland Publishing Inc., 1992, pp. 79-105.

Lee Jr., Maurice, *Great Britain's Solomon: James VI and I in His Three Kingdoms*, Urbana: University of Illinois Press, 1990.

—, *Government by Pen: Scotland under James VI and I*, Urbana: University of Illinois Press, 1980.

—, 'James VI and the revival of episcopacy: 1596-1600', *Church History*, vol. 43, no. 1, 1974, pp. 50-64.

Legg, Leopold G. Wickham, *English Coronation Records*, Westminster: Archibald Constable, 1901.

—, *English Orders for Consecrating Churches in the Seventeenth Century*, London: Henry Bradshaw Society, 1911.

Lehmberg, Stanford, 'Archbishop Grindal and the Prophesyings', *Historical Magazine of the Protestant Episcopal Church*, vol. 34, 1965, pp. 87-145.

—, *Cathedrals Under Siege: Cathedrals in English Society 1600-1700*, Exeter: University of Exeter Press, 1996.

—, *English Cathedrals: A History*, London: Hambledon and London, 2005.

—, *The Reformation Parliament 1529-1536*, Cambridge: Cambridge University Press, 1970.

Le Huray, Peter, *Music and the Reformation in England 1549–1660*, London: Herbert Jenkins,1967.
Levack, Brian P., *The Civil Lawyers in England, 1603–1641: A Political Study*, Oxford: Clarendon Press, 1973.
—, 'Possession, Witchcraft and the law in Jacobean England', *Washington and Lee Legal Review*, vol. 52, 1995, pp. 1613–40.
—, (ed.), *Witch-Hunting in Early Modern Europe: General Studies*, New York and London: Garland Publishing Inc., 1992.
Levison, Wilhelm, *England and the Continent in the Eighth Century*, Oxford: Clarendon Press, 1946.
Levy, F. J., *Tudor Historical Thought*, San Marino, CA: The Huntington Library, 1967.
Litzenberger, Caroline, 'Richard Cheyney, Bishop of Gloucester: An infidel in religion?', *Sixteenth Century Journal*, vol. 25, no. 3, 1994, pp. 567–84.
Loach, Jennifer, 'The function of ceremonial in the reign of Henry VIII', *Past and Present*, vol. 142, no. 1, 1994, pp. 43–68.
Loades, David (ed.), *John Foxe and the English Reformation*, Aldershot: Scholar Press, 1997.
—, *Politics, Censorship and the English Reformation*, London: Pinter Publishers, 1991.
—, *Politics and the Nation 1450–1660: Obedience, Resistance and Public Order*, London: William Collins and Sons/Fontana, 1974.
Loomie, Albert J., 'New light on the Spanish Ambassador's purchases from Charles I's collection 1649–53', *Journal of the Warburg and Courtauld Institutes*, vol. 52, 1989, pp. 257–67.
Macaulay, Thomas Babington, *History of England from the Accession of James the Second* (6 vols), London, Everyman Edition, 1913–15.
—, *Historical Essays*, London: J. M. Dent, 1907.
MacCulloch, Diarmaid, *The Boy King: Edward VI and the Protestant Reformation*, New York: Palgrave, 1999.
—, 'Cranmer's ambiguous legacy', *History Today*, vol. 46, issue 6, 1996, pp. 23–31.
—, 'Richard Hooker's reputation', *English Historical Review*, vol. 117, no. 473, 2002, pp. 773–812.
—, *Suffolk and the Tudors: Politics and Religion in an English County, 1500–1600*, Oxford: Clarendon Press, 1986.
—, *Thomas Cranmer: A Life*, New Haven: Yale University Press, 1996.
MacDonald, Alan R., 'James VI and I, the Church of Scotland, and British ecclesiastical convergence', *Historical Journal*, vol. 48, no. 4, 2005, pp. 885–903.
Macfarlane, Alan, *Witchcraft in Tudor and Stuart England*, 2nd edn, London: Routledge, 1999.
Macinnes, C. A., *Charles I and the Making of the Covenanting Movement*, Edinburgh: Donald, 1991.
Maclure, Millar, *The Paul's Cross Sermons 1534–1642*, Toronto: University of Toronto Press, 1958.

Maltby, Judith, '"By this Book": Parishioners, the Prayer Book and the established Church', in Kenneth Fincham (ed.), *The Early Stuart Church, 1603–1642*, London: Macmillan, 1993, pp. 115–38.

—, *Prayer Book and People in Elizabethan and Early Stuart England*, Cambridge: Cambridge University Press, 1998.

Manning, R. B., 'The crisis of episcopal authority during the reign of Elizabeth I', *Journal of British Studies*, vol. 11, no. 1, 1971, pp. 1–25.

Mansfield, B. E., 'Erasmus, Luther and the problem of Church history', *Australian Journal of Politics and History*, vol. 8, 1962, pp. 41–56.

Marchant, R. A., *The Puritans and the Church Courts in the Diocese of York, 1560–1642*, London: Longmans, 1960.

Marshall, J., 'The ecclesiology of the Latitude Men 1660–1689: Stillingfleet, Tillotson and "Hobbism"', *Journal of Ecclesiastical History*, vol. 36, 1985, pp. 407–27.

Marshall, Peter (ed.), *The Impact of the English Reformation 1500–1640*, London: Arnold, 1997.

Marshall, W. G., (ed.), *The Restoration Mind*, Newark: University of Delaware Press, 1997.

Marshall, William M., *George Hooper 1640–1727: Bishop of Bath and Wells*, Sherborne: Dorset Publishing, 1976.

Mason, Thomas A., *Serving God and Mammon: William Juxon, 1582–1663, Bishop of London, Lord High Treasurer of England, and Archbishop of Canterbury*, Newark: University of Delaware Press, 1985.

Mayo, J., *A History of Ecclesiastical Dress*, London: Holmes & Meier Publishers, 1984.

McCarthy, Muriel, 'Archbishop Marsh and his library', *Dublin Historical Record*, vol. 29, no. 1, 1975, pp. 2–23.

McCullough, Peter, E., 'Making dead men speak: Laudianism, print, and the works of Lancelot Andrewes, 1625–1642', *Historical Journal*, vol. 41, no. 2, 1998, pp. 410–24.

—, *Sermons at Court: Politics and Religion in Elizabethan and Jacobean Preaching*, Cambridge: Cambridge University Press, 1998.

McEachen, Claire and Sliger, Deborah (eds), *Religion and Culture in Renaissance England*, Cambridge: Cambridge University Press, 1997.

McGrade, A. S., 'Episcopacy', in Torrance Kirby (ed.), *A Companion to Richard Hooker*, Leiden: Brill, 2008, pp. 481–502.

—, 'Richard Hooker on episcopacy and bishops, good and bad', *International Journal for the Study of the Christian Church*, vol. 2, no. 2, 2002, pp. 28–43.

McGregor, J. M., 'The Baptists: Fount of all heresy', in J. M. McGregor and B. Reay (eds), *Radical Religion in the English Revolution*, Oxford: Oxford University Press, 1984, pp. 23–63.

—, 'Paul Best and the limits of toleration in Civil War England', *Parergon*, vol. 21, no. 2, 2004, pp. 93–106.

McGregor, J. M. and Reay, B., (eds), *Radical Religion in the English Revolution*, Oxford: Oxford University Press, 1984.

McKeon, Michael, *Politics and Poetry in Restoration England: The Case of Dryden's Annus Mirabilis*, Cambridge, MA: Harvard University Press, 1975.

McMahon, S., 'John Ray (1627–1705) and the Act of Uniformity', *Notes and Records of the Royal Society*, vol. 54, no. 2, 2000, pp. 153–78.

Mendle, Michael, 'De facto freedom, de facto authority: Press and parliament, 1640–1643', *Historical Journal*, vol. 38, no. 2, 1995, pp. 151–77.

Mercer, Eric, *English Art: 1553–1625*, Oxford: Clarendon Press, 1962.

Merritt, J. F., 'The Cradle of Laudianism? Westminster Abbey, 1558–1630', *Journal of Ecclesiastical History*, vol. 52, no. 4, 2001, pp. 623–46.

—, 'Puritans, Laudians, and the phenomenon of church-building in Jacobean London', *Historical Journal*, vol. 41, no. 4, 1998, pp. 935–60.

Meza, Pedro Thomas, 'Gilbert Burnet's concept of religious toleration', *Historical Magazine of the Protestant Episcopal Church*, vol. 50, no. 3, 1981, pp. 227–42.

Millar, Oliver, 'Van Dyck and Thomas Killigrew', *Burlington Magazine*, vol. cv., no. 726, 1963, p. 409.

Miller, John, *Charles II*, London: Weidenfeld and Nicolson, 1991.

—, *The Restoration and the England of Charles II*, London: Longman, 1997.

—, *The Stuarts*, London: Hambledon Continuum, 2004.

Molland, Einar, 'A short historical sketch' in Leslie Stannard Hunter (ed.), *Scandinavian Churches: A Picture of the Development and Life of the Churches of Denmark, Finland, Iceland, Norway and Sweden*, London: Faber and Faber, 1965, pp. 34–43.

Monod, Paul Kleber, *The Power of Kings: Monarchy and Religion in Europe, 1589–1715*, New Haven: Yale University Press, 1999.

Morrill, J. S., 'The Attack on the Church of England in the Long Parliament, 1640–2', in D. Beales and G. Best (eds), *History, Society and the Churches: Essays in Honour of Owen Chadwick*, Cambridge: Cambridge University Press, 1985, pp. 105–24.

—, 'The Church in England, 1642–9', in J. S. Morrill (ed.), *Reactions to the English Civil War 1642–1649*, New York: St Martin's Press, 1982.

— (ed.), *Reactions to the English Civil War 1642–1649*, New York: St Martin's Press, 1982.

—, 'The religious context of the English Civil War', *Transactions of the Royal Historical Society*, vol. 34, 1984, pp. 155–78.

—, 'Sir William Brereton and England's Wars of Religion', *Journal of British Studies*, vol. 24, 1985, pp. 311–32.

— (ed.), *The Oxford Illustrated History of Tudor and Stuart Britain*, Oxford: Oxford University Press, 2000.

Murray, Hugh, *Monuments in York Minster: An Illustrated Inventory*, Ogleforth, York: Friends of York Minster, 2001.

Mussett, Pat, 'Some aspects of church furnishing in Cosin's time' in Margot Johnson (ed.), *John Cosin: Papers Presented to a Conference to Celebrate the 400th Anniversary of his Birth*, Durham: Turnstone Ventures, 1997, pp. 185–93.

Neuser, Wilhelm H., and Armstrong, Brian G., (eds), *Calvinus Sincerioris Religionis Vindex: Calvin as Protector of the Purer Religion*, Sixteenth Century Essays and Studies, 1997, vol. XXXVI.

New, John F. H., *Anglican and Puritan: The Basis of Their Opposition, 1558–1640*, London: Adam and Charles Black, 1964.

Newman, John, 'Inigo Jones and the politics of architecture', in Kevin Sharpe and Peter Lake (eds), *Culture and Politics in Early Stuart England*, Stanford: Stanford University Press, 1993, pp. 229–55.

—, 'Laudian Literature and the Interpretation of Caroline Churches in London', in David Howarth (ed.), *Art and Patronage in the Caroline Courts*, Cambridge: Cambridge University Press, 1993, pp. 168–86.

Nichols, Mark, 'Investigating gunpowder plot', *Recusant History*, vol. xix, no. 2, 1988, pp. 124–45.

Nussbaum, Damian, 'Appropriating Martyrdom: Fears of Renewed Persecution and the 1632 Edition of Acts and Monuments', in D. M. Loades (ed.), *John Foxe and the English Reformation*, Aldershot: The Scolar Press, 1997, pp. 178–91.

Nuttall, W. L. F. 'King Charles I's pictures and the Commonwealth sale', *Apollo*, vol. lxxii, 1965, pp. 302–9.

O'Day, Rosemary, *The Debate on the English Reformation*, London: Methuen, 1986.

O'Day, Rosemary and Heal, Felicity (eds), *Continuity and Change: Personnel and Administration of the Church of England 1500–1642*, Leicester: Leicester University Press, 1976.

Okines, A. W. R. E., 'Why was there so little government reaction to the Gunpowder Plot?', *Journal of Ecclesiastical History*, vol. 55, no. 2, 2004, pp. 275–92.

Oldridge, Darren, 'Protestant conceptions of the Devil in early Stuart England', *History*, vol. 85, no. 278, 2000, pp. 232–46.

Owen, H. G., 'The Episcopal Visitation: Its limits and limitations in Elizabethan London', *Journal of Ecclesiastical History*, vol. 11, no. 2, 1960, pp. 179–85.

Parry, Glyn J. R., 'The creation and recreation of Puritanism', *Parergon*, vol. 14, no. 1, 1996, pp. 31–55.

Patterson, W. B., *King James VI and I and the Reunion of Christendom*, Cambridge: Cambridge University Press, 1997.

Pearson, A. F. S., *Thomas Cartwright and Elizabethan Puritanism*, Cambridge: Cambridge University Press, 1925.

Peck, Linda Levy, (ed.), *The Mental World of the Jacobean Court*, Cambridge: Cambridge University Press, 1991.

Perrot, M. E. C., 'Richard Hooker and the Elizabethan Church', *Journal of Ecclesiastical History*, vol. 49, 1998, pp. 29–60.

Perry, Curtis, 'The citizen politics of nostalgia: Elizabeth in early Jacobean London', *Journal of Medieval and Renaissance Studies*, vol. 23, no. 1, 1993, pp. 89–111.

Pettegree, Andrew, *Marian Protestantism: Six Studies*, Aldershot: Scolar Press, 1996.

— (ed.), *The Reformation World*, London: Routledge, 2000.

Pettegree, A., Duke A., and Lewis, G. (eds), *Calvinism in Europe, 1540-1620*, Cambridge: Cambridge University Press, 1994.
Phillips, Walter, 'Henry Bullinger and the Elizabethan Vestiarian Controversy: An analysis of influence', *Journal of Religious History*, vol. 11, no. 3, 1981, pp. 363-84.
Pierce, Helen, 'Anti-Episcopacy and graphic satire in England, 1640-1645', *Historical Journal*, vol. 47, no. 4, 2004, pp. 809-48.
Prest, Wilfred, *Albion Ascendant: English History 1660-1815*, Oxford: Oxford University Press, 1998.
—, 'Law, learning and religion: Gifts to Gray's Inn library in the 1630s', *Parergon*, vol. 14, no. 1, 1996, pp. 205-22.
Prior, Mary, '"Reviled and crucified marriages": The position of Tudor bishops' wives', in Mary Prior (ed.), *Women in English Society, 1500-1800*, London: Methuen, 1985, pp. 118-48.
—, (ed.), *Women in English Society, 1500-1800*, London: Methuen, 1985.
Questier, Michael, 'Arminianism, Catholicism, and Puritanism in England during the 1630s', *Historical Journal*, vol. 49, no. 1, 2006, pp. 53-78.
—, 'Loyalty, religion and state power in early modern England: English Romanism and the Jacobean Oath of Allegiance', *Historical Journal*, vol. 40, no. 2, 1997, pp. 311-18.
—, 'The politics of religious conformity and the accession of James I', *Historical Research*, vol. 71, no. 174, 1998, pp. 14-30.
Quintrell, B. W., 'The Royal Hunt and the Puritans, 1604-1605', *Journal of Ecclesiastical History*, vol. 31, no. 1, 1980, pp. 41-58.
Racaut, Luc, and Ryrie, Alec (eds), *Moderate Voices in the European Reformation*, Aldershot: St Andrew's Studies in Reformation History, 2005.
Reay, B., 'Radicalism and religion in the English Revolution: An introduction', in J. M. McGregor and B. Reay (eds), *Radical Religion in the English Revolution*, Oxford: Oxford University Press, 1984, pp. 1-21.
Redworth, Glyn, *In Defence of the Church Catholic: The Life of Stephen Gardiner*, Oxford: Oxford University Press, 1990.
Reedy, Gerard, 'Interpreting Tillotson', *Harvard Theological Review*, vol. 86, no. 1, 1993, pp. 81-103.
Report on the Manuscripts of the Right Honourable Viscount De L'Isle & Dudley (6 vols), London: Historical Manuscripts Commission, 1925-66.
Rex, R. A. W., *Henry VIII and the English Reformation*, London: Macmillan, 1993.
Rice, Hugh A. L., *Thomas Ken: Bishop and Non-Juror*, London: SPCK, 1958.
Richards, Judith, 'The English accession of James VI', *English Historical Review*, no. 427, 2002, pp. 515-35.
—, 'English allegiance in a British context: Political problems and legal resolutions', *Parergon*, vol. 18, no. 2, 2001, pp. 103-21.
—, '"His Nowe Majestie" and the English Monarchy: the Kingship of Charles I before 1640', *Past and Present*, vol. 11, no. 3, 1986, pp. 70-96.
—, *Mary Tudor*, Oxford: Routledge, 2008.

Richardson, Catherine, *Clothing Culture, 1350–1650*, Aldershot: Ashgate Publishing, 2004.
Richardson, H. G. 'The coronation in medieval England', *Traditio*, vol. 16, 1960, pp. 111–75.
Rickert, Corinne H., *The Case of John Darrell: Minister and Exorcist*, University of Florida Monographs, no. 9, Winter, 1962.
Ricketts, Annabel, with Claire Gapper and Caroline Knight, 'Designing for Protestant worship: The private chapels of the Cecil family', in Spicer, Andrew and Hamilton, Sarah (eds), *Defining the Holy: Sacred Space in Medieval and Early Modern Europe*, Aldershot: Ashgate, 2005, pp. 115–36.
Ridley, Jasper, *Thomas Cranmer*, Oxford: Clarendon Press, 1962.
Ritchie, Carson I. A., 'Sir Richard Grenville and the Puritans', *English Historical Review*, vol. 77, no. 304, 1972, pp. 518–23.
Robertson, J. C., 'The condition of Canterbury Cathedral at the Restoration in A. D. 1660', *Archaeologia Cantiana*, vol. 10, 1876, pp. 95–6.
Robinson, Benedict Scott, '"Darke speech": Matthew Parker and the reforming of history', *Sixteenth Century Journal*, vol. 29, no. 4, 1998, pp. 1061–83.
Rosendale, Timothy, *Liturgy and Literature in the Making of Protestant England*, Cambridge: Cambridge University Press, 2007.
Russell, Conrad, *The Fall of the British Monarchies, 1637–1642*, Oxford: Oxford University Press, 1991.
—, 'The Reformation and creation of the Church of England', in J. S. Morrill (ed.), *The Oxford Illustrated History of Tudor and Stuart Britain*, Oxford: Oxford University Press, 2000, pp. 258–92.
— (ed.), *The Origins of the English Civil War*, London: Macmillan, 1973.
Ryle, John Charles, *Light from Old Times; or, Protestant Facts and Men*, London: Chas. J. Thynne, 1902.
Salt, J. P., 'The origin of Sir Edward Derring's attack on the ecclesiastical hierarchy', *Historical Journal*, vol. 30, no. 1, 1987, pp. 21–52.
Saslow, Edward L., 'Dryden's Authorship of the Defence of the Royal Papers', *Studies in English Literature, 1500–1900*, vol. 17, no. 3, Restoration and Eighteenth Century, 1977, pp. 387–95.
Saumarez-Smith, C., 'Wren and Sheldon', *Oxford Art Journal*, vol. 6, no. 1, 1983, pp. 45–50.
Scarisbrick, J. J., *Henry VIII*, Berkeley and Los Angeles: University of California Press, 1968.
Schwartz, Hillel, 'Arminianism and the English Parliament, 1624–1629', *Journal of British Studies*, vol. 12, no. 2, 1973, pp. 41–68.
Seaver, Paul S., *The Puritan Lectureships 1560–1662*, Stanford: Stanford University Press, 1970.
Selwyn, David, 'Cranmer's library: Its potential for Reformation studies', in Paul Ayris and David Selwyn (eds), *Thomas Cranmer: Churchman and Scholar*, Woodbridge: Boydell Press, 1993, pp. 39–72.

Sharpe, Kevin, '"So hard a text"? Images of Charles I, 1612–1700', *Historical Journal*, vol. 43, no. 2, 2000, pp. 383–405.
—, *The Personal Rule of Charles I*, New Haven: Yale University Press, 1992.
—, 'Representation and negotiations: Texts, images, and authority in early modern England', *Historical Journal*, vol. 42, no. 3, 1999, pp. 853–81.
—, and Lake, Peter (eds), *Culture and Politics in Early Stuart England*, Stanford: Stanford University Press, 1993.
Sharpe, James, *Witchcraft in Early Modern England*, Harlow: Pearson, 2001.
Sheils, William, *The Puritans in the Diocese of Peterborough 1558–1610,* Northampton: Northampton Record Society, 1979.
—, 'Some problems of government in a new diocese: The bishop and the Puritans in the diocese of Peterborough, 1560–1630', in Rosemary O'Day and Felicity Heal (eds), *Continuity and Change: Personnel and Administration of the Church of England 1500–1642*, Leicester: Leicester University Press, 1976, pp. 167–87.
Shepherd, Massey Hamilton, *The Oxford American Prayer Book Commentary*, New York: Oxford University Press, 1950.
Sherlock, Peter, 'Episcopal tombs in early modern England', *Journal of Ecclesiastical History*, vol. 55, no. 4, 2004, pp. 654–80.
—, 'Henry VII's "miraculum orbis": Royal commemoration at Westminster Abbey 1500–1700', in F. W. Kent, and Charles Zika (eds), *Rituals, Images and Words: Varieties of Cultural Expression in Late Medieval and Early Modern Europe*, Turnhout: Brepols, 2005, pp. 177–99.
—, 'The monuments of Elizabeth Tudor and Mary Stuart: King James and the manipulation of memory', *Journal of British Studies*, vol. 46, 2007, pp. 263–89.
—, *Monuments and Memory in Early Modern England*, Aldershot: Ashgate, 2008.
—, 'Monuments, reputation and clerical marriage in Reformation England: Bishop Barlow's Daughters', *Gender and History*, vol. 16, no. 1, 2004, pp. 57–82.
Simon, Walter G., *The Restoration Episcopate*, New York: Bookmen Associates, 1965.
Skidmore, Chris, *Edward VI The Lost King of England: The Struggle for the Soul of England After the Death of Henry VIII*, London: Phoenix, 2008.
Sluhovsky, Moshe, 'The Devil in the convent', *The American Historical Review*, vol. 107, no. 5, 2002, pp. 1379–411.
—, 'A divine apparition or demonic possession? Female agency and church authority in demonic possession in sixteenth-century France', *Sixteenth Century Journal*, vol. 27, no. 4, 1996, pp. 1039–55.
Smith Jr, Edward O., 'The Elizabethan doctrine of the prince as reflected in the sermons of the episcopacy, 1559–1603', *Huntingdon Library Quarterly*, vol. 28, no. 1, 1964, pp. 1–17.
Smith, Lacey Baldwin, *Tudor Prelates and Politics, 1536–1558*, Princeton: Princeton University Press, 1953.
—, *Treason in Tudor England: Politics and Paranoia*, Princeton: Princeton University Press, 1986.

Somerville, J. P., 'The Royal Supremacy and episcopacy "Jure Divino", 1603–1640', *Journal of Ecclesiastical History*, vol. 34, no. 4, 1983, pp. 548–58.

Sommerville, M. R., 'Richard Hooker and his contemporaries on episcopacy: An Elizabethan consensus', *Journal of Ecclesiastical History*, vol. 35, no. 2, 1984, pp. 177–87.

Spalding, James C., and Brass, Maynard F., 'Reduction of episcopacy as a means to unity in England, 1640–1662', *Church History*, vol. 30, no. 4, 1961, pp. 414–32.

Spellman, W. M., *The Latitudinarians and the Church of England, 1660–1700*, London: University of Georgia Press, 1993.

Spicer, Andrew, '"God will have a house": Defining sacred space and rites of consecration and early seventeenth-century England', in Andrew Spicer and Sarah Hamilton (eds), *Defining the Holy: Sacred Space in Medieval and Early Modern Europe*, Aldershot: Ashgate, 2005, pp. 207–30.

Spicer, Andrew and Hamilton, Sarah (eds), *Defining the Holy: Sacred Space in Medieval and Early Modern Europe*, Aldershot: Ashgate, 2005.

Spinks, Bryan D., 'Treasures old and new: A look at some of Thomas Cranmer's methods of liturgical compilation', in Paul Ayris and David Selwyn (eds), *Thomas Cranmer: Churchman and Scholar*, Woodridge: Boydell Press, 1993, pp. 175–88.

Spraggon, Julie, *Puritan Iconoclasm during the English Civil War*, Woodbridge: Boydell Press, 2003.

Spufford, Margaret, 'Can we count the "Godly" and the "Conformable" in the seventeenth century?', *Journal of Ecclesiastical History*, vol. 36, no. 3, 1985, pp. 428–38.

Spurr, John, 'From Puritanism to Dissent, 1660–1700', in Christopher Durston and Jacqueline Eales (eds), *The Culture of English Puritanism, 1560–1700*, London: Macmillan, 1996, pp. 234–65.

—, 'Latitudinarianism' and the Restoration Church', *The Historical Journal*, vol. 31, no. 1, 1988, pp. 61–82.

—, *The Post-Reformation: Religion, Politics and Society in Britain 1603–1714*, London: Pearson, 2006.

—, *The Restoration Church of England 1646–1689*, New Haven: Yale University Press, 1991.

—, 'Schism and the Restoration Church', *Journal of Ecclesiastical History*, vol. 41, no. 3, 1990, pp. 408–24.

Steere, Dan, "For the peace of both, for the humour of neither': Bishop Joseph Hall defends the Via Media in an age of extremes, 1601–1656', *Sixteenth Century Journal*, vol. 27, no. 3, 1996, pp. 749–65.

Steig, Margaret, *Laud's Laboratory: The Diocese of Bath and Wells in the Early Seventeenth Century*, London: Associated University Presses, 1982.

Stewart, Byron S., 'The cult of the Royal Martyr', *Church History*, vol. 38, no. 2, 1969, pp. 175–87.

Stewart, J. D., 'A militant Stoic monument: The Wren-Cibber-Gibbons Charles I Mausoleum project: Its authors, sources, meaning and influence', in W. G. Marshall (ed.), *The Restoration Mind*, Newark: University of Delaware Press, 1997, pp. 21–66.

Stoyel, A. D., 'The lost buildings of Otford Palace', *Archaeologia Cantiana*, vol. 100, 1984, pp. 259–80.

Strong, Roy, 'Edward VI and the Pope: A Tudor anti-papal allegory and its settings', *Journal of the Warburg and Courtauld Institutes*, vol. 23 no. 3/4, 1960, pp. 311–13.

—, *Gloriana: The Portraits of Elizabeth I*, London: Thames and Hudson, 1987.

—, *Henry Prince of Wales and England's Lost Renaissance*, London: Thames and Hudson, 1986.

—, *Holbein and Henry VIII*, London: Routledge, 1967.

—, *Portraits of Queen Elizabeth I*, Oxford: Clarendon Press, 1963.

—, *Tudor and Jacobean Portraits* (2 vols), London: Her Majesty's Stationary Office, 1969.

—, *The Tudor and Stuart Monarch: Pageantry, Painting, Iconography* (3 vols), Woodbridge: Boydell Press, 1995.

Styles, Philip, 'Politics and historical research in the early seventeenth century', in Levi Fox (ed.), *English Historical Scholarship in the Sixteenth and Seventeenth Centuries*, London: Oxford University Press, 1956, pp. 49–72.

Surtees, Robert, *The History and Antiquities of the County Palatinate of Durham* (4 vols), London: Nichols, Son and Bentley, 1816–40.

Sutch, Victor, *Gilbert Sheldon: Architect of Anglican Survival 1640–1676*, The Hague: M. Nijholl, 1973.

Sykes, Norman, *From Sheldon to Secker: Aspects of English Church History 1660–1768*, Cambridge: Cambridge University Press, 1959.

—, *Old Priest and New Presbyter: Episcopacy and Presbyterianism Since the Reformation with Especial Relation to the Churches of England and Scotland*, Cambridge: Cambridge University Press, 1957.

Symonds, R. W., 'The bishop's chair in St Paul's Cathedral', *Burlington Magazine*, vol. 77, no. 453, 1940, pp. 200–01.

Tatton-Brown, Tim, *Lambeth Palace: A History of the Archbishops of Canterbury and their Houses*, London: SPCK, 2000.

Thomas, Keith, *Religion and the Decline of Magic*, New York: Scribner, 1971.

Thurley, Simon, *The Royal Palaces of Tudor England: Architecture and Court Life 1460–1547*, New Haven: Yale University Press, 1993.

—, *Whitehall Palace: An Architectural History of the Royal Apartments, 1240–1698*, New Haven: Yale University Press, 1999.

Tighe, W. J., 'William Laud and the reunion of the Churches: Some evidence from 1637 and 1638', *Historical Journal*, vol. 30, no. 3, 1987, pp. 717–27.

Todd, Margo, 'The Godly and the Church: new views of Protestantism in early modern Britain', *Journal of British Studies*, vol. 28, no. 4, 1989, pp. 418–27.

Tomlinson, Howard (ed.), *Before the English Civil War: Essays in Early Stuart Politics and Government*, London: Macmillan, 1983.

Trevor-Roper, Hugh, R., *Archbishop Laud*, 2nd edn, London: Phoenix Press, 2000.

—, *Historical Essays*, London: Macmillan, 1957.

Tudor-Craig, P., 'Henry VIII and King David', in D. Williams (ed.), *Early Tudor England*, Woodbridge: Boydell Press, 1989, pp. 183–206.

Turrell, James F., '"Until Such Time as He Be Confirmed": The Laudians and confirmation in the seventeenth-century Church of England', *The Seventeenth Century*, vol. 20, no. 2, 2005, pp. 204–21.

Tyacke, Nicholas, *Anti-Calvinists: The Rise of English Arminianism, c. 1590–1640*, Oxford: Clarendon Press, 1987.

—, 'Archbishop Laud', in Kenneth Fincham (ed.), *The Early Stuart Church, 1603–1642*, London: Macmillan, 1993, pp. 51–70.

—, 'Puritanism, Arminianism and Counter-Revolution', in Conrad Russell (ed.), *The Origins of the English Civil War*, London: Macmillan, 1973, pp. 119–43.

—, 'The "Rise of Puritanism" and the legalizing of dissent, 1571–1719', in Ole Peter Grell, Jonathan I Israel and Nicholas Tyacke (eds), *From Persecution to Toleration: The Glorious Revolution and Religion in England*, Oxford: Clarendon Press, 1991, pp. 17–49.

—, (ed.), *England's Long Reformation 1500–1800*, London: University College London Press, 1998.

Usher, Brett, 'In time of persecution: New light on the secret Protestant congregation in Marian London', in David Loades (ed.), *John Foxe and the English Reformation*, Aldershot: The Scolar Press, 1997, pp. 233–51.

—, *William Cecil and Episcopacy 1559–1577*, Aldershot: Ashgate, 2003.

VanderSchaaf, Mark E., 'Archbishop Parker's efforts towards a Bucerian discipline in the Church of England', *Sixteenth Century Journal*, vol. 8, no. 1, 1977, pp. 85–103.

Venn, J. and Venn, J. A. (eds). 'Darrell, John' in *Alumni Cantabrigienses* (10 vols), (1922–1958), (online ed.). Cambridge University Press, http://venn.lib.cam.ac.uk/cgi-bin/search.pl?sur=&suro=c&fir=&firo=c&cit=&cito=c&c=all&tex=DRL575J&sye=&eye=&col=all&maxcount=50 accessed 6 March, 2012.

Verkamp, Bernard J., *The Indifferent Mean: Adiaphorism in the English Reformation to 1554*, Ohio and Detroit, Michigan: Ohio University Press and Wayne State University Press, 1977.

Wabuda Susan, 'Bishops and the Provision of Homilies, 1520 to 1547', *Sixteenth Century Journal*, vol. 25, no. 3, 1994, pp. 551–66.

Walker, Anita M. and Dickerman, Edmund H., 'A woman under the influence: A case of alleged possession in sixteenth-century France', *Sixteenth Century Journal*, vol. 22, no. 3, 1991, pp. 535–54.

Walker, D. P., *Unclean Spirits: Possession and Exorcism in France and England in the Late-Sixteenth and Early-Seventeenth Centuries*, London: The Scolar Press, 1981.

Walker, R. B., 'Lincoln Cathedral in the reign of Queen Elizabeth I', *Journal of Ecclesiastical History*, vol. 11, no. 2, 1960, pp. 186–201.

          G., *The Long European Reformation: Religion, Political Conflict, and the   onformity, 1350–1750*, London: Palgrave, 2004.

          ndra, *Charitable Hatred: Tolerance and Intolerance in England 1500–1700*, Manchester University Press, 2006.

—, '"Fanatick Hacket": Prophecy, sorcery, insanity, and the Elizabethan Puritan Movement', *Historical Journal*, vol. 41, no. 1, 1998, pp. 27–66.

—, 'The parochial roots of Laudianism revisited: Catholics, anti-Calvinists and "parish Anglicans" in early Stuart England', *Journal of Ecclesiastical History*, vol. 49, no. 4, 1998, pp. 620–51.

Wenig, Scott, 'The Reformation in the diocese of Ely during the episcopate of Richard Cox, 1559–77', *Sixteenth Century Journal*, vol. 33, no. 1, 2002, pp. 151–89.

Whinney, Margaret and Miller, Oliver, *English Art 1625–1714*, Oxford: Clarendon Press, 1957.

White, Peter, 'The rise of Arminianism reconsidered', *Past and Present*, vol. 101, 1983, pp. 34–54.

—, *Predestination, Policy and Polemic: Conflict and Consensus in the English Church from the Reformation to the Civil War*, Cambridge: Cambridge University Press, 2002.

Whiteman, E. A. O., 'The re-establishment of the Church of England, 1660–1663', *Transactions of the Royal Historical Society*, vol. 5, 1955, pp. 111–31.

Wiener, Carol Z., 'The beleaguered isle: A study of Elizabethan and Jacobean anti-Catholicism', *Past and Present*, vol. 51, 1971, pp. 27–62.

Wilkinson, B., 'Fact and fancy in fifteenth-century English History', *Speculum*, vol. 42, no. 4, 1967, pp. 673–92.

Williams, D. (ed.), *Early Tudor England*, Woodbridge: Boydell Press, 1989.

Woodward, Jennifer, 'Images of a dead queen: Historical record of mourning ceremony for Queen Elizabeth I of England', *History Today*, vol. 47, no. 11, 1997, pp. 18–23.

Woolf, Daniel, *The Idea of History in Early Stuart England*, Toronto: University of Toronto Press, 1990.

—, *Reading History in Early Stuart England*, Cambridge: Cambridge University Press, 2000.

Woolrych, Austin, 'Puritanism, politics and society', in E. W. Ives (ed.), *The English Revolution 1600–1660*, London: Edward Arnold, 1968, pp. 87–100.

Wright, C. E., 'The dispersal of the monastic libraries and the beginnings of Anglo-Saxon studies: Matthew Parker and his circle: A preliminary study', *Transactions of the Cambridge Bibliographical Society*, vol. I, 1951, pp. 208–37.

Wright, Jonathan, 'The world's worst worm: Conscience and conformity during the English Reformation', *Sixteenth Century Journal*, vol. 30, no. 1, 1999, 113–33.

Youings, Joyce, *The Dissolution of the Monasteries*, London: Allen and Unwin, 1971.

Yule, George, *Puritans in Politics: The Religious Legislation of the Long Parliament 1640–1647*, Appleford: Sutton Courtenay Press, 1981.

Unpublished dissertations

Abbott, W. M., 'The Issue of Episcopacy in the Long Parliament, 1640–1648: The Reasons for Abolition', University of Oxford D. Phil, 1981.

Anderson, M. D., 'Bishop Gilbert Burnet (1643–1715): A critical account of his conception of the Christian ministry', University of Edinburgh PhD, 1965.

Craig, William, 'The King's own conference: A reassessment of Hampton Court 1604', University of Trinity College Th. D., 2006.

Davies, K., 'The true church: The formation of the ecclesiology of the Marian exiles and its influence on the Church of England', University of Cambridge PhD, 1985.

Dowley, T. E., 'The history of the English Baptists during the great persecution, 1660–1688', University of Manchester PhD, 1976.

Elliot, Maurice John, 'Episcopacy in the thinking of Thomas Cranmer (1489–1556)', Queen's University of Belfast PhD, 2001.

Gallant, Lorraine, 'Apocalyptic and non-apocalyptic anti-episcopalianism in early modern England, 1558–1646', Dalhousie University MA, 1999.

Gavin, S. J., Joseph, 'An Elizabethan Bishop of Durham: Tobias Matthew, 1595–1606', McGill University PhD, 1972.

Gibson, K., 'Eschatology, apocalypse and millenarianism in seventeenth century Protestant thought', University of Nottingham at Trent PhD, 1999.

Greig, M., 'The thought and polemic of Gilbert Burnet, c. 1673–1705', University of Cambridge PhD, 1991.

Griffin, Martin, 'Latitudinarianism in the seventeenth-century Church of England', Yale University PhD, 1963.

Hajzyk, H, 'The Church in Lincolnshire c.1595–c.1649', University of Cambridge PhD, 1980.

Harrison, Jennifer, 'The relationship between the Elizabethan Privy Council and the Corporation of London 1588 to 1603', University of Queensland PhD, 1988.

Helman, Susannah, '"A prince of much and various knowledge and curious observation": Charles II's cultural interests through his collecting', University of Queensland PhD, 2003.

Hetet, J. S. T., 'A literary underground in Restoration England: Printers and Dissenters in the context of constraints 1660–1689', University of Cambridge PhD, 1987.

Johnston, Warren J., 'Apocalypticism in Restoration England', University of Cambridge PhD, 2000.

Kelly, Michael J., 'Canterbury Jurisdiction and Influence during the Episcopate of William Warham 1503–1532', University of Cambridge PhD, 1963.

Langton, Stephanie, 'Bishops as governors: Diocesan administration and social organization among the late Elizabethan and Jacobean episcopacy', University of Alberta MA, 2002.

MacFarlane, Jean Elizabeth, 'Antichrist in English Literature, 1380–1680', University of Florida PhD, 1980.

McKenna, H. F., 'Rude and Ignorant Commons?: Rebellion in Tudor England, 1536–1570', University of Queensland PhD, 1989.

Miller, E. C.,'The doctrine of the Church in the thought of Herbert Thorndike (1598–1672)', Oxford University D.Phil, 1990.

Pocas, Paul Peter, 'Gilbert Burnet: A case study in the genesis and development of revolutionary consciousness and activism in late Stuart England', Loyola University of Chicago PhD, 1988.
Scott-Warren, J., 'Sir John Harington as a giver of books', University of Cambridge PhD, 1997.
Shaw, Barry, 'The Elizabethan men of business and the implementation of domestic policy 1569–1584', University of Queensland PhD, 1987.
Steere, Daniel J., '"Quo vadis?": Bishop Joseph Hall and the demise of Calvinist conformity in early seventeenth-century England', Georgia State University PhD, 2000.
Vage, J. A., 'The diocese of Exeter 1519–1641: A study of church government in the age of the reformation', University of Cambridge PhD, 1991.
Wenig, Scott, 'The ecclesiastical vision and pastoral achievements of the progressive bishops under Elizabeth I, 1559–1579', University of Colorado at Boulder PhD, 1994.
Wilson, R. Paul, 'John Hooper and the English reform under Edward VI, 1547–1553', Queen's University at Kingston PhD, 1994.

Index

39 Articles of Religion   17

Abbot, George, Archbishop of
    Canterbury   3, 27, 74–5
  reputation as a puritan   39–40
  suspended   17
Act of Uniformity (1662)   37
Admonition Controversy   15, 18, 23,
    98, 121
Anabaptism   38
Andrewes, Lancelot, Bishop of
    Winchester   60, 64, 90, 99
Anne, Princess (later Queen of
    Great Britain)   1
Arminianism   59–60, 64–8, 70, 119
Arminius, Jacob   60
Aston, Sir Thomas   63
Augustine of Canterbury, Saint   7, 14–15
Ayris, Paul   11

Bancroft, Richard, Bishop of London,
    Archbishop of Canterbury   1–4,
    9, 13, 17, 38, 40, 58, 60, 62, 90,
    94, 100
  and Canons of 1604   50
  investigates Anne Gunter case   46
  investigates exorcisms   45, 52, 57
  investigates John Darrel   46, 48–9,
    51, 53–5
  investigates Mary Glover case   46, 48
  investigates William Hacket   47
  and 'Martin Marprelate' tracts   47
  ordained   47
  preaches at Paul's Cross   88–9
Barlow, William, Bishop of Bath and
    Wells   14
Bastwick, John   67
Baxter, Richard   37, 40, 85
Bedford, Thomas   81–2
Beer, Barrett   5
Bellany, Alastair   23, 33
Bewitchment *see* Possession, Demonic

'Bilson Boy'   45, 48
Bilson, Thomas, Bishop of Winchester
    17, 40
Birch, Thomas   96
bishop, bishops *see names of individual*
    bishops and bishoprics elsewhere
    in index
Bondos-Greene, Stephen   24
Bonner, Edmund, Bishop of London   13
Book of Common Prayer   8–9, 74, 88, 96,
    99, 110, 121
Boswell, Sir William   69
Boughen, Edward   82
Bradshaw, William   38
Bradstreet, Simon   32
Brigden, Susan   42
Bristol, Diocese of   8, 27
Brossier, Marthe   48, 50
Brown, Dr   74
Brown, Mr   75
Brownrigg, Ralph, Bishop of Exeter   68
Bucer, Martin   83
Buckeridge, John   64
Burton, Henry   6, 64–8, 73, 76
Busby, Richard   97

Calamy, Edward   90
Calvin, Jean   69, 88–9
Calvinism, Calvinists   41, 60, 65–7, 73,
    75, 88, 104
Canterbury Cathedral   28, 71, 79, 97,
    106–8, 119
Canterbury, Diocese of   9, 14,
    26–8, 32
Carpenter, Edward   27, 47
Cartwright, Thomas   15, 23, 98
Cave, Henry   82
Cecil, Sir Robert, Lord Salisbury
    38–9, 43
Cecil, Sir William, Lord Burghley   24
Charles I, King   3, 17–18, 42, 60–1, 65–6,
    69, 74, 81, 90

Charles II, King   90, 97, 109, 120
Chetwynd, John   29–30
Chester, Diocese of   8
Chibi, Andrew A.   3
Chichele, Henry, Archbishop of
    Canterbury   79, 81–5, 91
Chimere   3, 93–105, 111, 113, 115, 119,
    121 *see also* vestments
Civil Wars   60, 64–5, 86, 96, 97, 105,
    107–8, 115
Clark, Peter   38, 41
Clarke, Samuel   12, 38–9, 53
Claude, Monsieur   89
Colet, John   83
Collinson, Patrick   5, 23, 33, 35, 40, 65
Combination Lectures   84
Commons, House of   1, 65
    Long Parliament   18, 63, 67, 72, 121
    and 'men of business'   23
    Short Parliament   63, 67
Compton, Henry, Dean of London, Bishop
    of London   1, 3, 87, 89, 97, 104,
    111, 113
Corbet, Clement   18
Cosin, John, Vice Chancellor of
    Cambridge University, Dean of
    Peterborough, Dean of Durham,
    Bishop of Durham   39, 60, 68,
    74, 97, 107, 120
    Book of Devotions   62, 64–5, 69
    and 'cozening'   63
Cotton, Thomas   32
Covell, William   38
Coverdale, Miles, Bishop of Exeter
    14, 28
Cox, Richard, Bishop of Ely   47
Cranmer, Thomas, Archbishop of
    Canterbury   2, 4, 6, 12–14, 28,
    31–2, 113, 117, 119
    and *Book of Common Prayer*   8–9, 103
    Crowns Edward VI   7, 9, 15, 18
    Established Faculty Office   10
    mentioned in Laud's trial   61, 75–6,
        78, 120
    portrait of   101
    Register   10–11
Croft, Pauline   38, 43
Cromwell, Thomas   11–12
Croydon Palace   75–6

Darling, Thomas   52
Darrel, John   45, 57
    A Brief Apologie   53
    exorcises Will Somers   48–50
    imprisoned   46
    opponent of episcopacy   51–2,
        54–6
Davenant, John, Bishop of Salisbury   19
Davies, E. T.   23
Davies, Julian   66
Declaration of Breda (1660)   97
Denison, Stephen   41, 99
Demoniacs   46, 48–9, 51–2, 57
Denmark, Church of   4, 88
Directory for Public Worship   96
Dolben, John, Archbishop of York,   104–5
Dove, Thomas, Bishop of
    Peterborough   24
Duck, Arthur   2, 79–86, 90–1, 120
Dugdale, William   26
Durham Cathedral   62–3, 74, 97, 106–7
Durham, Diocese of   11, 14, 36, 61
Dyck, Anthony van   101–2

Edward VI, King of England   2, 5–6, 8, 29,
    31, 74, 77, 118
    coronation of   7, 9–10, 12, 15, 18
    as godly prince   16
Eedes, Richard, Dean of Worcester
    17, 118
Elizabeth I, Queen of England   6, 8,
    13–15, 17–19, 24, 27, 36, 50,
    62–3, 71, 74, 77, 83, 88
    as godly ruler   16, 30
    and Prophesyings   35
Episcopacy *see* Episcopate
Episcopate
    abolished by Long Parliament   18, 63,
        67, 72, 79, 118, 121
    in House of Lords   7, 9, 19, 93, 119
    imparity of ministers   15, 51, 56
    jure divino   5, 89
    marriages of bishops   9, 26
    order for consecrating bishops   8–9
    preaching duties   11, 19, 42
    revenues of   5, 8–9, 11–12, 15–17, 59,
        118–19
    responsibilities of   9, 15, 84, 99
    and Royal Supremacy   16–17, 80

visitations 9–11, 15, 17–18, 36, 93, 98, 101–2
and witchcraft 3–4, 46–7, 50–2, 56–7
Exclusion Crisis 95
Exeter Cathedral 100, 106
exorcisms 4, 6, 45–58

Faculty Office 10, 83, 119
Falkland, Lord 67–8
Farrar, Robert, Bishop of St David's 15, 117
Fenner, Dudley 39
Field, John 34–5
Field, Richard 19
Finch, Lord 68
Fincham, Kenneth 3, 11, 25, 34, 75
Fliche, Gerlach 101
Fowler, Edward 104
Foxe, John 5, 13
and *Book of Martyrs* (*Acts and Monuments*) 15, 71–2
Frewen, Accepted, Archbishop of York 104
Fulke, William 39
Fuller, Thomas 28–9

Gardiner, Stephen, Bishop of Winchester 12
Gatehouse Prison (London) 46
Gauden, John, Bishop of Exeter 2, 4, 78–81, 89–91, 120
becomes bishop 80, 86
in Ussher's circle 87–8
Gibbons, Grinling 105, 108
Gloucester, Diocese of 8
Glover, Mary 46, 48
Godwin, Francis, Bishop of Worcester 25–8
Golser, Georg, Bishop of Innsbruck 51
Goodman, Godfrey, Bishop of Gloucester 39
Goodridge, Alice 48
Guest, Edmund, Archdeacon of Canterbury, Bishop of Salisbury 14
Gunter, Anne 46, 48–9
Grand Remonstrance (1641) 63
Graves, Michael 23
'Great Bible' 12

Great Fire of London 97, 106, 115
Green, I. M. 65
Grimston, Sir Harbottle 67
Grindal, Edmund, Archbishop of Canterbury 9, 33, 43, 45
discussed in *Abrahams Faith* 35–6, 40

Hacket, John, Bishop of Lichfield 97, 108
Hacket, William 47
Hall, Joseph, Bishop of Exeter 5, 40, 80
Hampton Court Conference 19, 21–2, 25, 37, 40, 47, 100
Harington, Sir John 2, 4, 19, 21, 37–8
anti-episcopal reputation 28–9
writes *Supplie or Addicion* 22, 25–32, 43
Harsnet, Samuel, Archbishop of York 2
investigates Anne Gunter case 46–48
investigates Darrel 46–8, 51–2, 54
investigates Mary Glover case 46–8
made Bancroft's chaplain 45, 50
as propagandist 50, 55–7
Hartwell, Abraham 50
Hascard, Gregory 82, 104
Heal, Felicity 3, 5
Hembry, Phyllis 29
Henry VIII, King of England 6, 9, 12, 15–16, 29, 51, 77, 118, 120
creates new bishoprics 8, 27
dissolves monasteries 30
Henry Frederick, Prince of Wales 22, 25–7, 29, 73
as 'Henry IX' 30
portraits of 29
reputation of for religious radicalism 30
Heton, Martin, Bishop of Ely 11
Heylyn, Peter 60, 64, 67, 73
A Briefe Answer 68–9, 73
High Commission 47, 50, 54–5, 94, 119
Hill, Christopher 23
Hodgkins, John, Suffragan Bishop of Bedford 14
Holbein, Hans 29, 101
Hooker, Richard 4, 83, 88
Hooper, Edward, Bishop of Bath and Wells 2–3, 94–5, 97–9, 102–4, 106, 109–15, 117, 121

Hooper, John, Bishop of Gloucester 5, 11, 31
Houlbrooke, Ralph 5, 11
House of Commons *see* Commons, House of
House of Lords *see* Lords, House of
Hutton, Matthew, Bishop of Durham, Archbishop of York 36, 104
Hyde, Sir Edward, Earl of Clarendon 86

Jackson, Elizabeth 48
Jackson, John 32
Jaffé, Michael 101
James I and VI, King of Great Britain 9, 16, 19, 24, 38–9, 43, 90, 100, 118
   Basilikon Doron 34
   at Hampton Court Conference 25
   and Witchcraft 48
James II, King of Great Britain 3, 121
James, Thomas 85
James, William, Bishop of Durham 36
Jewel, John, Bishop of Salisbury 4
Jonson, Ben 49
Juxon, William, Bishop of London, Archbishop of Canterbury 97

Kennedy, D. E. 3
King, Andrew 32
Knollys, Sir Francis 17, 24
Knox, John 90
Kramer, Heinrich 51

Lake, Peter 23, 25, 36, 41
Lambe, John 83
Lambeth Palace 14, 27, 48, 50, 55, 58–9, 75–6, 79
Lamplugh, Thomas, Archbishop of York 104
Latimer, Hugh, Bishop of Worcester 11–12, 31–2, 35, 101–2, 117
Laud, William, Archbishop of Canterbury 2, 4–5, 9, 17, 40, 42, 58, 83, 85, 93, 97–102, 118, 120
   as Bishop of London 36
   coat of arms 71
   Confession 70
   diary 64
   execution of 59, 63–4, 79, 81, 96
   and Laudianism 60, 64–6
   portrait of 101
   trial of 3–4, 58–9, 61–2, 64, 67–9, 72–8, 94
lectureships 18, 42
Lee, Maurice 41
Leighton, Alexander 102
Lichfield Cathedral 97, 106, 108
Lightfoot, John 5
Lincoln's Inn Chapel 65
Long Parliament 18, 63, 67, 72, 118, 121
   see also Commons, House of
Lords of the Congregation (Scottish) 8
Lords, House of 7, 9, 19, 93, 119

MacCulloch, Diarmaid 10
Magalotti, Count 100
Manning, R. B. 3
Marsh, Narcissus, Archbishop of Dublin 105
Marshal, William 35
Martin, Dr 65
'Martin Marprelate' 34, 47, 121
Mary I, Queen of England 10, 16, 31
Mary II, Queen of Great Britain 3
Matthew, Toby, Bishop of Durham, Archbishop of York 11, 36, 69, 104
Matthew, Sir Tobie 69
Melanchthon, Phillip 89
Melville, Andrew 100
'men of business' 23 *see also* Commons, House of
Miller, R. H. 29
Milton, John 6, 87, 101, 103
Monasteries, Dissolution of 8, 30
Montagu, Richard, Bishop of Norwich 39
Montaigne, George, Bishop of London 36
More, John 32
Morice, Ralph 28
Morrill, John 96
Morton, Cardinal Thomas, Archbishop of Canterbury 76
Moulin, Pierre du 87

Nag's Head Inn Fable *see* Parker, Matthew
Neile, Richard, Archbishop of York 120
Nichols, Josias 2, 4, 19, 21, 26, 38, 40–3, 45, 119–20

Abrahams Faith 22, 32–3, 35, 120
   definition of puritanism 34, 36
   deprived of living 32, 37
   Plea of the Innocent 22, 28, 32–3, 35, 120
Norway, Church of 88
Nowell, Alexander 99

Obry, Nicole 48
Oglethorpe, Owen, Bishop of Carlisle 14
Okines, A. W. R. E. 24
Ormerod, Oliver 38
Oxford, Diocese of 8, 27, 61
Oxford, University of 72

Parker, Henry 34
Parker, Matthew, Archbishop of Canterbury 6, 26, 30–2, 36, 119
   consecration of 7, 13–15, 18, 83
   Nag's Head Inn Fable 19
   writes history of Canterbury Archbishopric 26–8
Paul's Cross 47, 65, 89, 98
Peake, Sir Robert 29
Peckam, John, Archbishop of Canterbury 27
Peterborough, Diocese of 8
Pickering, Lewis 33
Pierce, Helen 94, 101
Pole, Reginald, Cardinal, Archbishop of Canterbury 10
Ponet, John, Bishop of Winchester 11, 40
Popish Plot 69, 95
Possession, Demonic 46–55, 57
Potter, Barnaby, Bishop of Carlisle 39
Prideaux, Humphrey 82
Privy Council 9, 16–17, 23, 38
Prophesyings 35
Prynne, William 2, 6, 42, 54, 103
   and Cosin 62–3
   and Laud 40, 62, 64–5, 67, 73, 75–6, 99–101
Puritans, Puritanism 4, 21, 23–5, 28, 30–43, 45, 47, 49–50, 52–3, 57, 65, 111, 117, 119

Reformation, English 2–3, 5, 13, 16, 19, 26–8, 30–2, 57, 61, 63, 71–2, 76–7, 82–5, 89, 95, 100, 109, 111–14, 117

Ridley, Nicholas, Bishop of London 12, 28, 31–2, 113, 117
Robinson, Henry, Bishop of Carlisle 36, 39
rochet 3, 40, 93–104, 111, 113, 115, 119, 121 *see also* vestments
Rogers, Thomas 38
'Rome's Masterpeece' 69–70
Root and Branch Petition 18, 110, 121
Roper, Margaret 51
Royal Supremacy 16–17, 80
Rudd, Anthony, Bishop of St David's 40

St Katherine Cree Church (London) 41, 65, 98–9
St Patrick's Cathedral (Dublin) 105
St Paul's Cathedral (London) 26, 65, 96–7, 106
Sancroft, William, Archbishop of Canterbury 3
Sanderson, Robert, Bishop of Lincoln 19
Sandys, Edwin, Archbishop of York 29
Scory, John, Bishop of Chichester 14
Scrots, Sir William 29
Sharpe, Kevin 64, 66, 99, 110
Sheils, William 3, 24
Sheldon, Gilbert, Bishop of London, Archbishop of Canterbury 37, 83, 97, 105
Sherlock, William 104
Short Parliament 63, 67 *see also* Commons, House of
Simon, Walter G. 4
Smart, Peter 62–3, 74
Smith, Lacey Baldwin 3
Solemn League and Covenant 87
Somers, Will 46, 48–9, 53–5
Sparrow, Anthony, Bishop of Exeter 100
Spottiswoode, John, Archbishop of St Andrews 90
Spurr, John 86
Star Chamber 41, 47–8, 67
Sterne, Richard, Archbishop of York 104
Still, John, Bishop of Bath and Wells 36
Stillingfleet, Edward, Bishop of Worcester 15, 89–90
Stow, John 96
Strong, Roy 29
Strype, John 28–9

Sweden, Church of   4, 88
Sykes, Norman   4–5

Tenison, Thomas, Archbishop of
    Canterbury   83, 104, 108, 118
Thomas, Keith   46
Thorndike, Herbert   89
Tillotson, John, Archbishop of
    Canterbury   3, 90, 96–7, 104
Trevor-Roper, Hugh   4, 64
Tuke, Hugh   32
Tunstal, Cuthbert, Bishop of Durham   12
    under house arrest   14
Turrell, James   66
Tyacke, Nicholas   41, 65–6, 75
Tyndale, William   12, 35, 82

Ussher, James, Archbishop of Armagh   40,
    67, 79–81, 85, 88, 91, 120

Vaughan, Richard, Bishop
    of London   27, 45
vestments   3, 36, 40, 60, 65, 75, 93–5,
    98–100, 103, 109, 111–12,
    115, 121

Walker, D. P.   52
Walker, Henry   69
Warboys, Witches of   47, 52

Warham, William, Archbishop of
    Canterbury   9, 12
    portrait of   101
Westminster Abbey   10, 67, 97
Westminster Assembly of Divines   68
Westminster, Diocese of   8
Whitaker, William   41
White, Peter   66
Whitehall Palace   1, 29
Whitgift, John, Archbishop of
    Canterbury   4, 9, 13, 17, 33,
    36, 38, 43, 45, 47, 50, 62, 89
    deprivation of clergy   32
    discussed in *Abrahams Faith*   35
    dispute with Thomas Cartwright   15,
    23, 98
    on imparity of ministers   51, 83
William III, King of Great Britain   3
Williams, John, Bishop of Lincoln,
    Archbishop of York   2, 40,
    42, 66–8, 72
Winchester, Diocese of   61
Witchcraft   3–4, 46–7, 50, 56–8
Wren, Christopher   108
Wren, Matthew, Bishop of Norwich,
    Bishop of Ely   18, 59–60,
    83, 97, 118
Wright, Katherine   51, 53, 55
Wycliffe, John   82, 85